CINEMA
AND SENTIMENT

CINEMA
AND SENTIMENT

CHARLES AFFRON

THE UNIVERSITY OF CHICAGO PRESS

Chicago and London

The University of Chicago Press, Chicago 60637
The University of Chicago Press, Ltd., London

©1982 by The University of Chicago
All rights reserved. Published 1982
Printed in the United States of America
89 88 87 86 85 84 83 82   5 4 3 2 1

Library of Congress Cataloging in Publication Data

Affron, Charles.
  Cinema and sentiment.

  Bibliography: p.
  Includes index.
  1. Moving-picture plays—History and criticism.
2. Moving—pictures—Aesthetics. I. Title.
PN1995.A265   791.43′01   82-2687
ISBN 0-226-00820-7   AACR2

Charles Affron, professor of French at New York
University, is the author of *Patterns of Failure in "La
Comédie humaine"; A Stage for Poets: Studies in the
Theatre of Hugo and Musset*; and *Star Acting: Gish,
Garbo, Davis.*

In memory of N. B.

Contents

Acknowledgments

I am delighted to be able to thank, in print, those viewers, friends, and colleagues who have shared their response to film with me, and others who have facilitated my research and writing.

My first debt of gratitude is to the members of the Seminar for College Teachers, supported by the National Endowment for the Humanities, that I directed during the summer of 1979. The extent of their collaboration, the high quality of their criticism, the generosity of their interest were of inestimable value to me. It is impossible to credit them individually for each of the insights they shared with me. Their names will have to suffice: Edward Benson, Barbara Bowman, Samuel Chell, David Fagan, James Gifford, Gerard Haggerty, Larry Klein, Steven Lipkin, Diane Menagh, Charlotte Schrader-Hooker, Mary Sullivan, Fred Wild. The participants in the seminar I gave in 1981 provided polish, modifications, and corrections, along with patience and good will: Stephen Baar, James Conlon, Judith Gustafson, James Hauser, Allan Hirsh, Donald Larsson, George Lellis, John Orlandello, Gerard Plecki, René Prieto, John Shout, Carole Weisz. Without the encouragement and good offices of Dorothy Wartenberg and her staff at the National Endowment for the Humanities, these seminars would not have been such positive and rewarding experiences for me.

The staff of the Motion Picture Section of the Library of Congress was helpful in countless ways. At the Museum of Modern Art, Charles Silver and Stephen Harvey were forthcoming with unstinting and friendly cooperation. Gloria Vilardell again provided her extraordinary skill as typist. Sara Levy and Matthew Affron gave valuable editorial and research assistance. Carol Jochnowitz's encyclopedic memory saved me from egregious error. Edward Forlie's computer program facilitated the indexing. My colleague at New York University, William K. Everson, once again proved generous with his advice and access to his collection of films.

Other colleagues and friends have read the manuscript in its various stages, and their remarks and suggestions have been most important to its development: Richard Barsam, Leo Braudy, Nick

Acknowledgments

Browne, Barbara Leaming, Gerald Mast, Michael Silverman, Linda Williams. Frank McConnell steered me to the University of Chicago Press.

Sections of chapter 6, in an altered form, appeared in *Cinema Journal*, vol. 12 (fall, 1980).

Finally, I wish to thank my wife, Mirella Jona Affron, for her precious judgment, intellectual rigor, clarity of mind, taste, and sense of rhetoric, and for the countless hours during which she generously gave of these talents and qualities.

Note on the Illustrations

With one exception, all the illustrations in this book are frame enlargements. These are copies of what appears on the film strip and therefore do not have the clarity of the publicity stills that are usually used in advertising and in most film books. Publicity stills are not shot contemporaneously with their respective films, and often bear only a superficial resemblance to what we see on the screen. I have chosen to sacrifice something of the clarity of the photographic still in an effort to provide an image text that sustains my analysis in as much detail as possible.

1   Identifications

Tearjerkers

"Bathetic" and "pathetic" are phonetic siblings and semantic twins. The first, a pejorative term, euphonically qualifies the second, the designation of a type of response. The sense of low artistic worth conveyed by "bathetic" all too easily appropriates both the initial bilabial stop of "pathetic" and its capacity to provoke strong emotions in teary-eyed spectators. This unfortunate lexical confusion has given "pathetic" a decidely negative connotation. Art works that create an overtly emotional reponse in a wide readership are rated inferior to those that engage and inspire the refined critical, intellectual activities of a selective readership. Much of narrative film falls into the first category, and indeed was designed to do so by its creators. The success of pathetic fiction has been continuous, ranging from the first decades of cinema and the one-reeled plights of childlike heroines to the triumph-over-adversity scenario of physically afflicted protagonists (a paraplegic, a sports hero hurt in an accident or dying of an incurable disease) of the late seventies. In the jargon of the daily press, the latter are three- and four-handkerchief films. And to many, freely flowing tears have about as much lasting value as the drenched tissues with which we wipe them away.

If we consider the movies to be a meaning-generating body of art, we cannot afford to dismiss proof that meaning has in fact been generated. Tears are that proof. Yet the affective power of narrative, responsible for so much of the cinema's popular appeal, has made textual and evaluative criticism loathe to examine some of the most *affective* film texts: the pejorative resonance of "sentimental" has deterred serious consideration of those films for which that adjective is an accurate characterization. It is argued that blatantly emotional films cheapen and banalize emotion *because* they are blatant. Their promptness to elicit feeling offends those who consider being easily moved equivalent to being manipulated, victimized, deprived of critical distance. Art works are judged *bad* when, in what are purportedly trivializing modes, they attempt to

1

convey deep feelings about the self, the family, love, commitment, ethics. Some directors identified by their affinity for sentimental fictions (Ford, Capra) have been rescued through political, sociological, and occasionally formal exegesis; others (Cukor, Sirk) have been canonized by auteurism. Critics are not uncomfortable in treating the mythic resonance of *How Green Was My Valley*,[1] the "America" of *Mr. Smith Goes to Washington*, the self-reflexivity of *A Star Is Born*, the irony of *Imitation of Life*. But most commentators, in ignoring the fact that viewers have a strong response to "tearjerkers," also overlook how and why that response is informed with both fiction and medium. Essential aspects of these films' narrative, visual, and aural strategies, and of the nature of the cinematic experience are reflected in those embarrassing tears.

Viewers are engaged and made to recognize their feelings in cinematic fictions, perhaps as they never recognize them in life, by the processes of representation that derive from the dynamics of films and from the specifics of their viewing. While "conventional" narrative films relish situations that seem to contain sure sentimental appeal—departure, doomed love, mother love, death—it is finally the degree to which these situations conspire with those specifics that ensures a given work's affectivity. The resulting *processes* of representation condition response perhaps more surreptitiously, but just as strongly and hypnotically as that which is represented.

Viewers respond to the medium when its conditions echo something of their feelings and their experience; viewers become involved in the image as image when that image engages them in its workings, when its constitution becomes a field as rich and inviting as those that effect involvement in life. Film provides a variety of accessibilities to its modes, beguiling viewers to enter into its processes and then using those processes to capture representations of emotional situations that are lifelike to a degree our eyes can scarcely believe.

Reading with Feeling

It is precisely the ease of such seductive beguilement that has caused some critics to be wary of affect. Affect extends the status of the work beyond what seems to be its integrity into an area that shifts with the vagaries of pluralistic readings. In a defense of textual integrity W. K. Wimsatt exposes what he calls "the Affective Fallacy . . . a confusion between the poem and its *results* (what it *is* and what it *does*)." A critical posture committed to affectivity "begins by trying to derive the standard of criticism from the psychological effects of the poem and ends in impressionism and relativism." Read as a function of the Affective Fallacy, "the poem itself, as an object of specifically critical judgement, tends to disappear."[2] I will leave it to other critics to debate Wimsatt's other, more renowned Fallacy, the Intentional. It is his dismissal of affectivity with the qualification "fallacious" that I question here. If his caution is useful in its insistence upon the reality of the text, its categorical nature prohibits the celebration of the very activity the text promotes (and in which he, of course, engages)—a sustained, concentrated, thoroughly committed reading. "Impressionism" and "relativism" are not the necessary outcomes of an analysis that considers, in addition to a text's rhetorical coherence, the mechanics of its effect upon the reader and the operations the reader performs upon the text.

With their often overlapping and mutually inspiring criteria, the methodologies of structuralism, linguistics, semiotics, psychocriticism, phenomenology, narrative theory, and reception theory hold reader and text in variable degrees of tension.[3] In doing so they release the text from the Pantheon of evaluation and from the ethical categorizations of high, middle, and low culture, and have helped authorize the examination of many of the texts that interest me, films that fail to satisfy either the canons of classical coherence or those of avant-garde subversion, but that elicit, in many viewers, passionate reading activity. It is that activity that then becomes something like a value in the critical enterprise. Stanley Fish's definition of "Affective Stylistics," a particularly polemical statement of readership theory, expresses the character of these recent critical approaches. Fish attempts to establish the critical relevance of texts that, "because of their alleged transparency, are declared to be uninteresting as objects of analysis." An examination of the dynamics of utterance in these texts "reveals that a great deal is going on in their production and comprehension (*every linguistic experience is affecting and pressuring*), although most of it is going on so close up, at such a basic, 'preconscious' level of experience, that we tend to overlook it."[4] As soon as the activities of "production and comprehension" become relevant to criticism, textual *evaluation* seems perilous, just as our taste seems vulnerable to time and culture. Yesterday we went to the marketplace and laughed at the *Farce of Maître Pathelin*, played by amateurs and itinerant actors on a hastily erected platform; today we consider it rhetorically, generically, semiotically, psychocritically in our graduate courses on medieval theater. A popular art by definition, the farce had to be immediately legible to naive readers. But a naive reader is not an unresponsive one, and a naive reading tells us that much about art is defined by its reading-generating elements. Narrative film is a popular art and has suffered from the stigma of its transparency, the ease with which it is read. Yet, as in the case of farce, our observation that a genre or mode is of easy access should not be taken to imply that this access is easily understood or that *easy* is synonymous with *facile*. Presumably, easy fictions contain a complexity of gears whose smooth meshing conceals how they come together and how, once they are engaged, the reader is also engaged in the functioning of the mechanism. As Stanley Cavell has suggested, popular films are not necessarily disqualified from serious viewing just because they are easily read. "If film is seriously to be thought of as art at all, then it needs to be explained how it can have avoided the fate of modernism, which in practice means how it can have maintained its continuities of audiences and genres, how it can have been taken seriously without having assumed the burden of seriousness."[5] Cavell then proceeds to demonstrate, through a catholicity of illustration, the "seriousness" of Olsen and Johnson's *Hellzapoppin* and Antonioni's *L'avventura*.

"Art" Films

Even a popular form such as narrative film has not escaped its hierarchies of taste. The word "art" itself has been used to designate movies marketed as high culture (in the silent period, the "film d'art," often the filming of a "serious" or "classic" play) or perceived as such by the public (almost all foreign films released in the United States after World War II were referred to as "art films" and played at "art houses"). This implies that other movies are not art at all, or have less art than those with the designation. Yet the works of the Italian neo-realist directors, for example, immediately recognized by intellectuals as challenging and by general audiences as "art," are awash with the same trappings of sentimentality—the child sorely tried by necessity (*Shoeshine, Open City, Bicycle Thief*), the faithful animal (*Umberto D.*), the pathetic death (*Shoeshine, Open City, Paisà, Bitter Rice*)—that are often considered negative in "commercial" narrative films. *Umberto D.*, one of the most stylistically austere of the neo-realist films, is the story of a dispossessed old man who spends the last hours before his attempted suicide trying to find a home for his dog. De Sica and his collaborator Zavattini may adopt a manner that creates an impression of objectivity, but they then apply it to the story of an old man and a dog! My exclamative punctuation is ironic to itself since I am not at all surprised that any narrative film, whether it be on a critic's All-Time Ten Best List or relegated to a collection of "guilty pleasures,"[6] is sustained by sentimental configurations.

No less exempt from these configurations are highly mediated cinematic fictions. Susan Sontag, in her essay on Robert Bresson, examines the function of mediation in the art work's emotional power:

> Some art aims directly at arousing the feelings; some art appeals to the feelings through the route of the intelligence. There is art that creates empathy. There is art that detaches, that provokes

reflection. Great reflective art is not frigid. It can exalt the spectator, it can present images that appall, it can make him weep. But
its emotional power is mediated. The pull toward emotional
involvement is counterbalanced by elements in the work that
promote distance, disinterestedness, impartiality. Emotional involvement is always, to a greater or lesser degree, postponed.[7]

Avoiding an overtly evaluative tone, Sontag opposes the direct,
empathetic response elicited by easily accessible, presumably popular art and the deferred one of "great reflective art." She then goes
on to describe how the spectator's awareness of form tends "to
elongate or to retard the emotions. . . . Awareness of form does two
things simultaneously: it gives a sensuous pleasure independent of
the 'content,' and it invites the use of the intelligence."[8] She seems
to be suggesting that the emotional response arrived at through
"distance," through "the use of our intelligence," through our
awareness of mediation (present of necessity in all art), is of quite a
different quality than reader involvement characterized by empathy
and immediacy. Yet, while Bresson's ellipses, both visual and
narrative, certainly require "intelligent" reading, his fictional configurations and iconography (the "content" referred to by Sontag)
are so blatantly pathetic (the country priest, victimized by his
village, dying of cancer; the Christ-like donkey Balthazar;[9] the
long-suffering adolescent Mouchette; the doomed lovers, Lancelot
and Guenièvre, etc.) provide immediate affective access. For the
reader who is then initiated to the mysteries of the director's style,
both the story and its manner of reading become moving, and do so
simultaneously. Bresson's stylistics is as familiar as Frank Capra's
to those viewers for whom reseeing, an activity invited by the nature
of the medium, further reduces whatever distance there may be
between reading a film and responding to it emotionally. Of course,
because of their unconventional editing and framing, it is tempting
to think of Bresson's films in terms of mediation, and of course,
Bresson's work has not had the wide-ranged popularity of Capra's
films. Yet clearly Bresson is drawn to the dramatic patterns of
sentimental art. The art film too, then, is subject to what Jean Mitry
has described as the priority of emotion in cinema. "In cinema . . .
we gain access to the idea through emotion and because of this
emotion, while in verbal language we gain access to emotion by
means of ideas and through them."[10] This is, in part, due to that
aspect of the cinematic image (and sound) that must remain un-
mediated, its *non*symbolic relationship to its reference—that which
was filmed—a characteristic of all cinema, from its art films to its
most popular, "bathetic," tearjerkers.

What follows is a dynamic model of affective response to cinema
that exploits various theories of viewer/spectator/reader identifica-

tion with the art object. At first, in the hope of accommodating the wide range of these approaches, I concentrate on identification as a function of the reader's situation vis-à-vis the text, and of the text's oscillations between verisimilitudinous representations and fictive artifices. It seems to me that the passage between the reader and the text's fluctuating status locates the energy and the affect of reading. The succeeding chapters will isolate, within this dynamics, specific elements of cinema as representational medium (framing, visual field, sound) and as fiction (display, self-reflexivity, closure).

Likeness, Sensation, and the Image of Absence

"I liked it because I identified with the characters" is a casual but insistent refrain heard in movie lobbies and classrooms. That such a remark is reductive of a complex experience in no way lessens its pertinance to the viewing of narrative film. It suggests the appeal of the surface of the fiction in its explicit semblance to the most familiar patterns and events of life, as they are conveyed by photographic images of human beings and their environments. Hugo Münsterberg describes this degree of identification in his early study of the psychological implications of silent film. "Our imitation of the emotions which we see expressed brings vividness and affective tone into our grasping of the play's action. We sympathize with the sufferer and that means that the pain which he expresses becomes our own pain."[11] This mode of identification is primarily generated by the movies' sensational aspects. Movies are able to convey sensational phenomena without recourse to codes. We perceive sensation as sensation, even though it is only a projected image on a screen. Cinematized sensation is often minimally qualified by what we call style, and therefore we distinguish its quality of presence from the deferrals of verbal and symbolic codes. In its figuring of sensation, film draws verbal and compositional articulation to a status of presence.

In Frank Capra's *It's a Wonderful Life* a complex fictional configuration is capped by an image of physical pain. The resulting dynamics transcends our sense of the image as representational, as a projection distinct from the moment and the circumstances of its creation. The young George Bailey, partially deafened as a result of saving his little brother from drowning, works at a drugstore. When he scoops up some ice cream for Mary (who becomes his wife later in the film), she whispers into his deaf ear (the locus of pain at the climax of this extended sequence) "George Bailey, I'll love you 'til the day I die." Mr. Gower, the pharmacist, drunk with liquor and grief after reading the telegram announcing his son's death, accidentally puts poison into a prescription. Aware of the error yet unable to confront the sorrowing man, George goes to his own father for advice. He interrupts a violent confrontation between

Mr. Bailey, the kindly banker, and Mr. Potter, the rich, meanhearted villain. (This part of the episode is prefigurative of George's adult conflict with Potter.) Finally, in a labyrinth of planes and shadows at the back of the pharmacy, Mr. Gower slaps George in the head, bloodying his ear, before the truth finally emerges and both the guilt-ridden man and the forgiving boy are united by an embrace and a sympathy of tears. The pain of the slap and the sight of blood qualify the whole episode, shade it, give it the coherence of a literary metaphor, without betraying the immediacy of the sensation it produces. It is a particularly efficient exploitation of the medium's expressivity as explicit surface and as a fiction of presence.

That fiction is indubitably a powerful link between viewer and screen. It is an extention of the world of experience that, in part, identifies the viewer as a perceptive, sentient being. Yet the mere record of that experience is only the point of departure for the models of identification proposed by psychocritical discourse, a point of departure that locates the self not only in the surface of the image, but in the rhetoric of imaging and in the specific modes in which the image is received. I do not mean to undertake here an exhaustive, systematic examination of this critical literature, but only to suggest its importance in detaching the viewing experience from the norms of photographic verisimilitude that have so often controlled identification theory. These approaches force us to consider the connections between who looks at the movies and how that looking occurs.

Mitry relates the dynamics of spectatorship to those of its prime factors:

> thanks to the mobility of the camera, to the multiplicity of shots, I am everywhere at once. . . . I *know* that I am in the movie theatre, but I *feel* that I am in the world offered to my gaze, a world that I experience "physically" while identifying myself with one or another of the characters in the drama—with all of them, alternatively. This finally means that at the movies I am both *in* this action and *outside* it, *in this space and outside of this space*. Having the gift of ubiquity, I am everywhere and nowhere.[12]

For Mitry, the viewer's rapport with the fictional character is equally ubiquitous. "It is not the situation lived by the hero that *I* suffer, it is a 'subjectivity' [*un subjectif*] that is actualized by *him*, a wish that I accomplish through his intermediary."[13] This "subjectivity," animated by the freedom of camera and of editing, affords the viewer a flux of spatial and fictional identification whose emotional appeal was already apparent to Münsterberg in 1916. "Not more than one sixteenth of a second is needed to carry us from one corner of the globe to the other, from a jubilant setting to a mourning scene. The whole keyboard of the imagination may be used to serve this emotionalizing of nature."[14] Identification is therefore liberated from the constraints of everyday experience and made part of a process suggestive of emotion itself—movement.

Movement has been located in the intersecting topologies of the work itself, the places of interchange between the work and the receiver, and in the receiver. And these topologies have been inflected by the ontological status of the screened image—its figuring of absence, its distance in time and space from what was photographed. Cinema, in its display of present (fleeting) images of an absent reality, makes the reading activity a pursuit, a desire for the fiction energized by a dialectic of possession and lack. Much of recent film theory in France and England, informed by Freudian and Lacanian thinking (to which I will return), posits the reading of cinema as a visual test of the tension between the self and intermittently mastered orders of image and symbol. For the moment I will rely on Christian Metz's work to summarize how the problematics of the viewing situation (and the viewer's identity) in front of a presence as unstable as that of cinema is made a property of the film's intelligibility. "In order to understand a film (at all), I must perceive the photographed object as absent, its photograph as present, and the presence of this absence as signifying."[15] Reading (and pleasure) are predicated on a rhythm of possession, loss, and restitution. Metz defines this rhythm in Lacanian terms, exploiting the implications of the mirror analogy:

> the durable mark of the mirror which alienates man in his own reflection and makes him the double of his double, the subterranean persistence of the exclusive relation to the mother, desire as a pure effect of lack and endless pursuit, the initial core of the unconscious (primal repression). All this is undoubtedly reactivated by the actions of that *other mirror*, the cinema screen, in this respect a veritable psychical substitute, a prosthesis for our primally dislocated limbs.[16]

Thus, the "endless pursuit" of the image is rooted in the child's initial effort at self-identification through (and in spite of) identification with the mother. Cinema's implicit mirrorness holds and withholds the promise of satisfying identifications in the activity of sight itself. Identification is therefore detached from the diegetic status of the fiction, from the pleasure of perceiving plot and circumstance, and effected by the viewer's most basic relationship to the image, a relationship made particularly crucial because of the mobility of the film image. We identify with cinema not only because of the likeness we find reflected there, but because the "reflection" forces us to acknowledge, somewhere in our apprehension of the screen image, that our looking is not predicated on the satisfaction of *finding*: what we look at is not *there*. (Thierry Kuntzel uses the Freudian analogy of the "mystic writing pad," with its disappearing inscriptions, to suggest the paradoxically dual status of the screen image.)[17] Metz is emphatic in his characterization of absence in a medium where "everything is *recorded*." Reading a film therefore requires the realization that "every film is a fiction film."[18]

Metz does not completely discard the notion that the viewer may derive satisfaction in finding semblance in the screen image, but he does characterize it as "a little miracle"[19] dependent on the unexpected and elusive correspondances between exterior and interior orders, the images we perceive as outside us on a cinema screen, and an experience of life composed of the constant play between sense impression and our inner beings. The fleeting, unstable nature of these inside-outside links is coherent both with the nature of the medium and with a model of identification that only intermittently calls for the recognition of lifelike representations. The realm of the lifelike is extended from identities with the world as we see it to the world of dreams, fantasies, emotions, beyond the purview of wide open eyes, ours and the camera's.[20] This requires a redefinition of reality that accommodates a lowering of our ability, our desire, and our need to test reality, a lowering of our vigilance that is allowed and invited by the comfort of art and the comfort of the situation in which we receive it—the darkened theater. Edgar Morin asserts that "the passivity of the spectator, his impotence, put him in a regressive situation. Being in the theater illustrates a general anthropological law: we all become sentimental, sensitive, tearful when we are deprived of our means of action."[21] Since watching a film requires that we sit still in a dark room and that we assume an attitude of physical inactivity, it indeed exempts us from the rigors of reality. "The novelistic film, a mill of images and sounds overfeeding our zones of shadow and irresponsibility, is a machine for grinding up affectivity and inhibiting action."[22] Protecting us against the dangers of circumstance, the demands of interactivity, the spectatorial situation renders us susceptible to the meaning of reality *as* fiction, since that fiction is the only *exterior* reality we perceive.

Dispensing with but the barest mediation of temporal and spatial contingency, both viewer and film enjoy their parallel privacies and the bliss of rhythms and decors that emanate from the self and from the work of art. Metz resists the temptation to fix these activities in the dream state, but chooses instead a flux of intensities, of passages between (1) reality, (2) daydream, (3) dream. The experience of the fiction film favors a new relationship, an "ongoing circulation among the three: authorizing, in sum, a sort of central and moving zone of intersection where all three can 'reencounter' each other on

9

a singular territory, a confused territory which is common to them and yet does not abolish their distinctness." Fiction, through its particular manners of identification, contributes to this dynamics and topography.

> the diegesis has something of the real since it imitates it, something of the daydream and the dream since they imitate the real. The *novelistic* as a whole, with its cinematographic extensions, enriched and complicated by auditory and visual perception (absent in the novel), is nothing other than the systematic exploitation of this region of reencounters and manifold passages.[23]

Working with Movies

These suggestive plays of oscillation between states of sleep and waking and between the mimetic elements of the fiction challenge a narrow application of the realist aesthetic of film. Decentered, delocated, rendered all-embracing, reality becomes a function of perception/imagination/fantasy. Identification is then found in flux between the *work* of the art and the *work* of the art perceiver, between surface and sense, between the work's motion and our emotion. This degree of identity links the real and the fictional through the patterns of their separate processes, and that linkage makes the reading of the fiction *as* fiction a reading of ourselves, of selves as free of material contingency as fiction can be.

Various exponents of readership theory have examined the dynamics of free passage between reader and text, and around reader and text, in a wide range of defining systems. This mobility requires that we reexamine those models of the film-reading situation that stress passivity, regression, and infantilism, models that need not be discarded, but rather understood as points of departure toward the specific *activities* of reading. For Wolfgang Iser, "the literary text activates our own faculties, enabling us to recreate the world it presents. The product of this creative activity is what we might call the creative dimension of the text, which endows it with its reality."[24] Iser reiterates this formulation in his more recent book, characterizing the text as event in its temporal activity:

> as we read, we react to what we ourselves have produced, and it is this mode of reaction that, in fact, enables us to experience the text as an actual event. We do not grasp it like an empirical object; nor do we comprehend it like a predicative fact; it owes its presence in our minds to our own reactions, and it is these that make us animate the meaning of the text as a reality.[25]

Iser's reader/text juncture is located in the kind of reading elicited by the written text (where images are symbolically coded), yet he has recourse to quasi-cinematic visual and spatial analogies to convey what he calls "the wandering viewpoint," the reader's shifting positions in the text:

The switch of viewpoints brings about a spot-lighting of textual perspectives, and these in turn become reciprocally influenced backgrounds which endow each new foreground with a specific shape and form. As the viewpoint changes again, this foreground merges into the background, which it has modified and which is now to exert its influence on yet another new foreground.

This mobile viewpoint is suggestive of the camera's freedom of vantage, the altered, reversed, widened, shortened, lengthened filmic field, and of Mitry's ubiquitous subjectivity, elements that contribute to the creation of the reality effect. Iser even finds something of the *presentness* of image viewing in the reality that emerges when a written text is read:

> Every articulate reading moment entails a switch of perspective, and this constitutes an inseparable combination of differentiated perspectives, foreshortened memories, present modifications, and future expectations. Thus, in the time-flow of the reading process, past and future continually converge in the present moment, and the synthetizing operations of the wandering viewpoint enable the text to pass through the reader's mind as an ever-expanding network of connections. This also adds the dimension of space to that of time, for the accumulation of views and combinations gives us the illusion of depth and breadth, so that we have the impression that we are actually present in a real world.[26]

Claudine Eizykman provides strong counterargument to the notion of passive spectatorship at the cinema in her elaboration of an "energetics" (*énergétique*) of response. She evokes the violent effect made by film on the viewer who, after leaving the movie house, feels "extremely undone, perforated, shaken by a thousand intensities much stronger than those of television, by a thousand light beams more refractive than those of any pictorial, musical, or theatrical space." A desire for such violence runs counter to a desire for repose and passivity:

> What force moves us to shut ourselves up for two hours (minimum) in a black room where we will be inundated, invaded, bombarded, in a situation of surrender and profound discomposure without contact with the actors, the audience, that we find at the theater or a museum? No, it is not passivity that compels us. Or then, if passivity compels us, it is because it suggests something other than banal servitude, submission; it is a passivity that dilutes, that dilutes our selves, our resistances, our puny shows. Passivity, but also passion.[27]

Passion, but also dynamics, energetics. Using Freud's model of Economy, and Marx's of Circulation, Eizykman asserts that viewer reponse is provoked more strongly by the various functional processes of cinema than by its "references, contents, motivations, meanings."[28]

11

Belief

Because they consider process prior to surface, the various psychocritical and material modalities, whether they emanate from the apparatus, the screen, the story, the image, the viewer's psyche, memory, intelligence, or body, share a common redefinition of the status of fiction and our belief in it. It is no longer quite necessary to suspend disbelief if we assume that belief is engaged in the reality of the fiction's fictivity (as opposed to the reality of the fiction's illusion) and if *that* reality is to a large degree inflected by the complexity of *our* reality. When we use music as a paradigm for the art enterprise, we can see the extent of our capacity to believe in a work of art thoroughly detached from the lifelike, exempt from the need to reflect action, character, the world of things. Referring only to its own order without recourse to the registers of symbol and image, music produces such strong emotional responses and identifications that we often overtly manifest them by tapping and humming. Melodies "haunt us night and day," as do fictions when we share and enjoy their fictivity.[29] Our complicity gives a different emphasis to the factors that have often been described as the *work of art* and its *content*. Do we respond primarily to the work or the content, to the activity or the schema of a fiction that urges us to hum along, as it were, tuning ourselves to its various tensions? Robert Scholes argues strenuously that the spectator's consciousness of the fictional is a rich source of reading satisfaction. "I should like to suggest that the proper way for narrative artists to provide for their audiences an experience richer than submissive stupefaction is not to deny them the satisfactions of story, but to generate for them stories which reward the most energetic and rigorous kinds of narrativity."[30] A fluctuating shape, an undulating texture, a mobile face caught between the medium and fiction, elements of cinematic narrativity, call attention to the art as object and invite our continued efforts at possession, activities that ultimately determine our experience of the work.

These activities force us to transcend our ideologies and our most cherished censuring mechanisms. Legions of viewers and critics proclaim their abhorrence of the politics of Ford and Capra films, to say nothing of Leni Riefenstahl's *The Triumph of the Will*, yet willingly submit, and repeatedly resubmit, to these films' emotional resonance. We reject the "cavalry" ethic, the pie-in-the-sky populism, the nazi mythology; we respond to the modes of their conveyance. These modes do not necessarily force viewers to subscribe to the values of the fictive worlds they depict. What happens is often quite the contrary precisely because films invite us to perceive them in the purity of their fictional status, and often therefore to respond to an emotional dynamics whose pressure far exceeds that of uniforms, emblems, speeches, mere signs.

Many of the meanings relevant to this emotional dynamics, this system of affect, resist thoroughly explicit articulation and thrive only in the sublimations, projections, metaphors, and allegories of fantasy and fiction. Here belief survives the menace of evidence, experience, logic; it sustains the presence of patently unreal agents and blatantly artificial formal devices. Belief can be achieved by fiction even when fictivity denies us the comfort of "real" illusions. O. Mannoni, in his analysis of theatrical illusion, *Clefs pour l'imaginaire ou l'autre scène*, traces this property of art to the Freudian notion of disavowal and the fetishist's belief in the maternal penis. The mechanics of simultaneous belief and disbelief becomes a model for other kinds of "beliefs that survive the denial of experience."[31] One of these is the viewer's belief in the baldest manifestations of theatrical (cinematic) illusionism. Mannoni locates the properties of such (dis)belief in a fluctuating movement through dream and varieties of consciousness (thereby anticipating Metz). His remarks on the mediation of belief by masks, spirits, actors are particularly helpful in explaining some of the most troublesome conventions of sentimental fiction: "If we ourselves are not victims of an illusion at the theater or in front of masks, it seems, however, that we need someone else who, for our satisfaction, is prey to this illusion. Everything seems contrived to produce it, but in someone else, as if we were in collusion with the actors."[32]

Soon after the credits of *It's a Wonderful Life*, we see a Hollywood sky, replete with what seem like moving, talking light bulbs; we hear a conversation of angels, one of whom will materialize (not unlike movie stars) and conjure a fiction of the hero's absence within the fiction itself (George is made to see what life would have been like had he not been born). Capra elicits the utter incredulity of the audience through the transparency of the angelic configuration to elicit later a much deeper belief in the whole of the fiction. We witness a film mediated by an angel, and a hero who through the angel's power is made to see his life as a movielike fiction of presence and absence. So frequent is the oscillation between the levels of credence (ours, George's) that by the end of the film Capra has reminded us of the essential pertinence, in this visual medium, of the proverb "Seeing is believing." It is indeed enough to see a movie fiction, no matter how fantastic, to believe it.

Melodrama and Reality

Peter Brooks suggest that the reality principle functions as a boundary through whose traversal the melodramatic mode releases meanings that wither in less emphatic registers. "The melodramatic utterance breaks through everything that constitutes the 'reality principle,' all its censorships, accommodations, tonings-down. . . . Desire triumphs over the world of substitute-formations and detours, it achieves plenitude of meaning.''[33] This extent of meaning is often masked by complex linguistic and stylistic mediations of art and the highly conventionalized discourse we use in life to avoid the pain of confrontations with others and revelation to ourselves. Brooks hears something of the speech of the psyche in melodramatic utterance as it drives toward the clearest articulation of what we prefer not to say:

> The desire to express all seems a fundamental characteristic of the melodramatic mode. Nothing is spare because nothing is left unsaid; the characters stand on stage and utter the unspeakable, give voice to their deepest feelings, dramatize through their heightened and polarized words and gestures the whole lesson of their relationship. They assume primary psychic roles, father, mother, child, and express basic psychic conditions. Life tends, in this fiction, towards ever more concentrated and totally expressive gestures and statements.[34]

It is melodrama's fullness, intolerant of the strategies of conventional expression, that is considered excessive by standard critical canons.

Brooks's psychodramatic analogy challenges the widely held prejudice against melodrama's simplicity of articulation and access. He has taken on the major task of rehabilitating what has long been considered a minor genre.[35] Many of his arguments are obviously applicable to narrative films of sentiment, works that have their sources in the melodramatic literary traditions of the nineteenth century. The affinities between narrative, cinema, and the pathetic are exemplified in the films of D. W. Griffith, whose prolific output and whose commercial success prove the viability of the melodramatic register in cinema. Griffith acted in and wrote stage melodramas before working at Biograph. Peril-rescue and evil-good scenarios (although not Griffith's *only* fictional types, as is sometimes believed) are pervasive, from his first one-reeler, *The Adventures of Dollie* (1908), through the grandiose *The Birth of a Nation* (1915) and *Intolerance* (1916), to his loving adaptation of the already "old fashioned" melodrama *Way Down East* (1920), and beyond. The pathos of these films had a formative effect on many directors, an effect evidenced in Eisenstein's theory and practice,[36] and in the work of artists less well remembered, right to the present day. Yet, despite its obvious applicability to narrative in film, Brooks's formulation of melodrama as it is manifested in the novel and the theater is insufficient when we consider that cinema, in its modes of production and perception, is like neither written nor "live" acted texts. Cinematic melodrama must therefore be examined in the specifics of the specular activity it elicits. Its discourse must be distinguished from the incessant symbolic codes of prose, its enactments from the presence of performers in theater's real space and time.

A more nuanced analogy for film is perhaps the Italian *melo-dramma*, the opera, because of its amplificatory, hyperbolic regis-ters—the utterance of singers and orchestra. I think it useful to draw a parallel between the massed effects of ensemble in the music theater and cinema's synthetic simultaneities, conveyed by long shots and montage, of decors and multitudes that would not fit on any stage. The solo/choral (emphasis on individual/emphasis on group) and the linear/harmonic (depiction of progressive action/ spectacular mise-en-scène) juxtapositions of the film epic from *Intolerance* to *Close Encounters of the Third Kind* demonstrate cinema's expansion of fictional space through such syntheses. And for the sake of argument I will extend the operatic analogy of hyperbolic performance (vocal projection, extremes of range) to the close-up, a uniquely cinematic mode of theatrical presentation.

Yet, with its insistence on the uniqueness of the performer, the close-up does not belong to a melodramaturgy that, for good reason, Brooks bases upon the audience's perception of type rather than individuality. A victimized, unwed mother who baptizes her dying baby is a melodramatic configuration, but it ceases to be that when she is Lillian Gish in close-up performing that act in *Way Down East*. While the close-up sustains Brooks's notion of melo-dramatic plenitude, it subverts melodramatic moral typage. And further, distinct from the modalities of both spoken and musical theater, the photographic naturalism of cinema proves to be parti-cularly intolerant of melodrama. A stage version of *Way Down East*'s spectacular catastrophe on an icy river would undoubtedly seem both melodramatic and ludicrous; Lillian Gish's hand and hair floating in real, frigid water are not. (The sequence was shot, at peril to life and limb, at White River Junction.) When melodrama

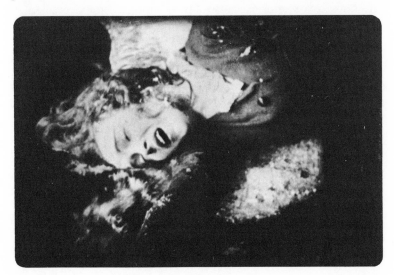

ceases to be schematic, through the cinematic particularizations of enactment and photography, it transcends that which is reductive in its mode (other aspects of performance often counteract the reductive in melodramatic live theater), pushing the specific work and the perceiver beyond type to the status of unique experience. Nor can we respond to the image as "simple" when it is read as part of a series of images whose very essence of flux violates the categorical nature of melodrama. Films cease to engage us not when they exhibit their melodramatic inflections, but when they cease to exert the lure of cinematic movement, whether that movement be defined by images of stasis or furious action. The medium has the power to rescue the surface of the fiction through its processes of movement, its illusionistic and fantastic projections, and its stagings. That surface is invested with psychological, spatial, and temporal depths into which we are invited to plunge, depths that are both distinct and inextricably mixed in their successive and renewed promises of satisfaction and fulfillment.

Genres

If melodrama is a term insufficient to cinema, and therefore to an understanding of its types of fiction, are there other generic designations more appropriate to cinematic affectivity? "Tearjerker," "weepy," and "sentimental" are negative and implicitly judgmental of the films to which they are applied.[37] The "woman's film" is ambiguous and inaccurate. It suggests that such a film is only about women or that it appeals only to women. Neither is true. The word "family" in family film is more indicative of the kind of audience for which the fiction is intended than it is of its type, although almost all family films have elements of sentiment. This is also true of "romantic" films, love stories. Because of their imprecise, impoverished, or evaluative semantic resonance, these terms do not accommodate the affective range of film narrative. What is the genre of *Potemkin*? *The Last Laugh*? *Mr. Smith Goes to Washington*? Tears are elicited by films about well-heeled lovers, indigent mothers, little boys, dogs, proud cavalrymen, and glamour girls, in modes that range from light comedy to the "serious." Strong emotions are often displayed in drawing-room comedies, thrillers, and action-westerns. Genre distinctions are excessively limiting even when applied to those texts that seem to define the genre. Is it not fruitful to read (as has in fact been done) Hitchcock's thrillers as love stories? The temptation is great with *Notorious* and *Rear Window*, to name two of the most obvious examples. Raymond Bellour has done a meticulous psychocritical reading of *North by Northwest* in which sexual identities and conflicts are no less perilous to the hero than a crop-dusting plane and a narrow ledge of Mount Rushmore.[38]

Yet, faced with the omnipresence of affectivity in cinema, generic categories have helped me to identify some texts as peripheral to my argument. In mysteries, thrillers, most westerns, and *very* light comedies, affect may be pervasive, but it is only intermittently perceived on the surface of the text. The love scenes of *Notorious* and *Rear Window* punctuate what appear to be suspense films. This is not true of David Lean's *Brief Encounter* or of Frank Borzage's *History Is Made at Night*. For the purpose of examining the affective response, I have chosen a corpus of film in which, for the most part, the rendition of emotional states involving the expression of sentiment constitutes the superficial and primary fictional mode. The medium clearly displays its affectivity in films that dramatize affect itself, films in which the expression of sentiment is at the center of the narrative, films that, even after the most casual viewing, can be recognized as having as their project the dramatization of relationships of sentiment. It is precisely these films that have been judged negatively because of their sentimentality and their ability to draw strong, yet uncritical, responses from viewers. They usually image the flow of tears, and they succeed in making audiences' tears flow in sympathy. They employ and enjoy strategies that sustain significant durations of feeling; they insistently manifest how and why emotion is manifested.

Audiences have affective responses to many films. Those treated in this book obviously reflect both the generalities and the particularities of *my* affective response. I have tried to remain consistent, however, in choosing films that force us to consider the workings of affect itself—in the fiction, in the medium, and in us. By doing that I do not wish to imply that a film will automatically trigger an affective response if it foregrounds affect. Some readers may be disconnected from a text because they have insufficient knowledge to read it. Others have expert knowledge of a given subject and will therefore be intolerant of distortion and fictionalization. The specifics of an individual's personal experience and situation may force the rejection of the text. A nine-year-old boy will most probably remain unmoved by the plight of the consumptive, love-struck courtesan; the historian will find ludicrous the inaccurate, falsifying "version" of Marie Antoinette's life and death; the committed feminist is likely to have a negative response to a film that idealizes a woman's sacrifice of her career to wifely subservience.

There are yet other films for which it would be difficult to identify what Stanley Fish has called an "informed reader" or an "interpretive community."[39] These are texts that fail through their own confusion, their clumsy use of conventions, their involuntary betrayal of readers' expectations. (As I will attempt to explain in chapter 6, voluntary betrayals are often a rich source of affect.) A mother-love film will certainly not draw forth tears if its rendition is perfunctory, awkward, inappropriate, if its structure is inadvertently illogical. The death of a child and a mother's grief are affectless, fleeting episodes in *Call Her Savage*, whose plot is as hyperkinetic as the familiar gestures of the star, the post-"It" Clara Bow. Even performers and directors renowned for their work in fictions of sentiment succumb to textual incoherence. In 1938 Frank Borzage directed *Three Comrades* and *The Shining Hour*. In the first, the death scene of Pat, the character played by Margaret Sullavan, is the emotional peak of a narrative that forms a dense and consistent pattern of situations of friendship, love, and idealism. Pat sums up our feelings about these feelings in her suicide. She has just undergone surgery for tuberculosis. Warned that the slightest movement will prove fatal, she laboriously rises from her bed, goes to the terrace, and stretches out her arms to her husband in the courtyard below. Unwilling to be a burden to those who are dear to her, she sacrifices herself in a gesture that acknowledges the coherence of the fiction. Acting and direction satisfy us in their completion of an

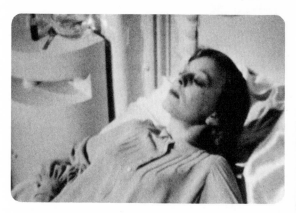

emotional trajectory, drawing us up along with performer and camera. This trajectory is denied the "interpretive community" for which *The Shining Hour* was intended. A "major studio classic narrative" film, *The Shining Hour* is meant to provide a reading perceived as coherent by a wide range of audiences. The plot itself does not prevent such a reading. A nightclub performer, Joan Crawford, unfulfilled by big-city success and sophistication, marries a rich Wisconsin farmer, Melvyn Douglas. Her arrival at the family estate provokes her husband's sister, Fay Bainter, to jealous rage, and her husband's brother, Robert Young, to adulterous desire. Bainter burns down Crawford's new house; unloved Margaret Sullavan seizes the occasion to attempt to immolate herself, thereby authorizing the love of her husband, Young, for Crawford. The audience expects a resolution whose intensity, in complementing the logic of the fiction, is a prime source of affect. The conclusion offers instead a shot whose eccentricity reflects the kind of reading that the text repeatedly generates. Margaret Sullavan, playing yet another self-sacrificing woman in love, lies in yet another bed. This time, though, she has been rescued from her suicide attempt. All we see of her face are her eyes, isolated in a cosmetically glamorous, perfect opening in the bandages around her head. A touch of the absurd, with odd echoes of *The Invisible Man* and *The Mummy*, might have been avoided if a traceable design had been established. We are even denied the satisfying outcome of the conventional "bandaged face" scene—the removal of the bandages. Emotional response to this image is short-circuited by the reading that the text's disorienting ingredients have imposed. Among the troubling configurations: the opening sequence in which Crawford, "the toast of New York," does her nightclub act, a series of "modern" turns to Chopin, partnered by MGM's resident adagio dancer, Tony De Marco; the "humorous" use of the black maid, Hattie MacDaniel, who at one point is compared to a farm tractor; the strenuous shifts in tone Fay Bainter is made to display, from sarcasm to pyromania-cal fury (she has barely a hair out of place during her lunatic incendiary activities) to morning-after repentance and good sense; the shot of Crawford carrying Sullavan out of the burning house in her strong arms (one asks why Young and Douglas were not more alert); the very premise that Young prefers Crawford to Sullavan, given the personas and abilities of these particular performers. This curiously heterogeneous mixture of textual constituents is conveyed by a publicity still of the stars, grouped as they never are in the film, their smiles and frowns in discordant array against an ominously shadowy background. The photograph thwarts the most energetic attempt to supply it with narrative meaning. In this, as well as in style and composition, it resembles stills for films that are paragons of narrative coherence. What is remarkable, however, is how pre-

cisely it emblemizes the nearly impermeable narrative pattern of
The Shining Hour.

There are undoubtedly viewers so attracted to some aspect of *The
Shining Hour* that they are able to ignore its elisions and inconsist-
encies. Most of us are forced to read the film as a function of an
eccentric combination of incompatible elements. How else are we
to make sense of those bandage-framed eyes that stare out, perhaps
in wonder at what has preceded? We stare as well and wonder, not
at the film's improbability, but at the absence of the web of gestures,
words, and images that sustains improbability where it belongs—
within a fiction.

Angels

In his study on time and fictional coherence Frank Kermode
evokes the status of angels as defined by St. Thomas. His angels are
"neither matter, with its potentiality, nor pure act, but immaterial
with potentiality. . . . They are therefore neither eternal nor of
time."[40] So it is for the material immateriality and the eternally
repeatable durations of movies and their stars, who effect the
transformations once reserved for angels. The ideal medium for
angels has often the properties of the fictivity of sentimental cinema, with its constellation of idealizing conceits. This ethos of
fictivity is exemplified in the films of Frank Borzage, a director
whose long career is marked by an obsessive pattern of sentimental
configurations. The title of Borzage's *History Is Made at Night* is
suggestive of cinema's penchant for artifice, improbability, idealiza-
tion. The very notion that history, in this case a fiction film, can be
"made" at night, therefore in the absence of light, suggests a
distance between the medium and its requisite light. Making history
at night asserts the cinema's trickery, its seductive search for what
seem to be lightless photographic contexts, and its subsequent
creation of purely cinematic light. This gesture is defiant of the
patently documentary quality of each film frame. It posits the
fictivity of a medium that for Edgar Morin projects "the world of
spirits or phantoms, such as it is manifested in a great number of
archaic mythologies: an aerian world in which omnipresent spirits
navigate."[41]

The narrative premise of *History Is Made at Night* proclaims the
force of fiction through its profusion of unlikelihoods and
coinicidences.[42] Paul, "the greatest headwaiter in all Europe"
(Charles Boyer), saves Irene (Jean Arthur) from her estranged
husband's plot to prevent their divorce. The husband (Colin Clive),
frames Paul for murder and then blackmails Irene into renouncing
her gallant lover. Unaware of the murder and of why Irene gives
him up, Paul goes to America and transforms a dreary restaurant
into the most fashionable dining place in New York in the hope that

21

his beloved "Miss America" will appear. Meanwhile, Irene has fled from her vicious husband, but agrees to return with him to Paris when an innocent man she believes to be Paul has been apprehended. On the night of the couple's departure they just happen to dine at Paul's restaurant. Irene's joy at finding Paul out of danger is short-lived; Paul will not let the innocent man stand trial. The lovers sail for Paris on the liner owned by Irene's husband, who in a fit of mad jealousy urges the captain to reckless speed and certain disaster amid the ice fields of the North Atlantic. Paul, Irene, and the others are saved from death when the last bulkheads of the "Princess Irene" hold against the surging water.

The style of the film's narration does nothing to mitigate improbabilities that it in fact relishes. At the beginning Paul rescues Irene by masquerading as a jewel thief; they fall in love about two minutes later, in a taxicab; alone in Paul's restaurant, they dance the tango the night through, Irene barefoot, in a fur coat. They speak of love in fictions: the menu for a perfect dinner, a pair of puppets drawn on their hands. Their feelings, freed by these fictions, are replayed when Irene returns to Paul in another restaurant, in another city, and yet again, when they order that perfect meal aboard ship and dance the tango in their stateroom. They achieve a state of transcendence in the context of the final disaster, the end-of-the-world configuration of the sinking ship, the life and death enactments of couples being separated, the de rigueur, in extremis rendition of "Nearer My God to Thee" by the brave little orchestra. Awaiting what seems like certain death, enveloped in fog, the faces of Paul and Irene are suffused with the complexities of fiction and of cinematic light. The nick-of-time rescue shifts the film to yet a higher register of joy and miracle, offering the satisfaction of fiction at its purest.

This is the satisfaction too of Borzage's *Seventh Heaven*, where Diane (Janet Gaynor) and Chico (Charles Farrell) transcend harsh necessity in their Parisian garret, and transcend space, death, and blindness through their telepathic relationship, fully conveyed by the simplest of shot juxtapositions—Diane in Paris, Chico in the trenches at the front. Chico's reappearance is a miracle of faith, light, and cinema.[43] Such is the miracle of communication between the living and the dead in *Smilin' Through*, the miracle of variable photographic density in the last images of *Three Comrades*, where the survivors link arms with the dead. Myra (Catherine McLeod) and Goranoff (Philip Dorn), the protagonists of *I've Always Loved You*, "speak" through art, live as if life were the Rachmaninoff Piano Concerto no. 2, appear in sets decorated to such a high degree that they can be nothing *but* decor, and in colors so vivid that they cannot for a moment be mistaken for those we perceive in nature. At the climax of *I've Always Loved You* we perceive the extent to which cinema itself is emotion for Borzage. The last shot is not of the protagonists but *of* the means through which their feelings are conveyed—piano and surrounding decor (the source of the aural/visual image) and the camera (the recording apparatus). The invisible camera becomes the principal actor as it tracks back up the center aisle of the auditorium, away from the piano that Myra has just abandoned. The concerto thunders to its conclusion despite her absence. As music mirrors, transmits, and subsumes the emotional power of the medium, it demonstrates how for Borzage, and for so many others, there is almost no distinction between art *for* feeling and art *as* feeling.

Many sentimental narratives tend to generate improbabilities in proportion to the strength of the feelings they express. In such narratives the very activity of fiction making becomes so expressive that it reflects a measure of incompatibility between feeling and necessity, between emotion and logic. Experience tells us to reject Chico and Diane's "seventh heaven," Myra and Goranoff's audiovisual harmonies, Irene and Paul's historic night. But we succumb to these idealizations, the glamorous close-ups, the molding of faces and bodies in images whose artifices are compounded by plot, light, and the "magic" of cinema. Feeling is located in this ambiguous field of probable improbability, where real yet absent performers play out situations that both happen and do not happen. Emotional engagement is powered by the deployment of cinematic strategies that liberate actors from flesh, objects from matter, emotion from necessity.

2   Thresholds of Feeling

The edges of a frame are a threshold to the visual field of data and to whatever meaning is conveyed by the experience of cinema. The impending activity of the off-screen world, not less present for its being beyond periphery, inflects the field when it impinges on its borders. Passage over these sharp edges constitutes a dynamics of inclusion and extrusion that delimits a spatial model for presence and absence. What appears on the screen is enclosed within a frame that immediately identifies it as image. There it is. To leave the screen and step out of the frame is to abandon the place of being.

The stage proscenium insistently calls upon the activities of entrance and exit, and is therefore an obvious analogy for film as dramatic frame. Yet the sense of frame as an essential element of visual limits is perhaps more clearly expressed as it functions in painting, and particularly in those works whose compositions take into account the integrity of their edges. Jean-Louis Baudry argues that the movie camera, "fabricated on the model of the camera obscura," produces an image "analogous to the perspective projections developed during the Italian Renaissance." He goes on to distinguish Western easel painting from Chinese and Japanese painting in its capacity to present "a motionless and continuous whole."[1] While the motion picture image is neither motionless nor a continuous whole, its frame, according to Stephen Heath (who refers to Marx's discussion of the camera obscura), "is the reconstitution of the scene of the signifier, of the symbolic, into that of the signified; the passage through the image from other scene into seen; it ensures distance as correct position, the summit of the eye, *representation*."[2] Heath reaffirms the frame's priority in establishing the ideological relationship between the perceiver and the representation of reality. The centrality of the perceiver, the viewing subject, is guaranteed by the painting's version of plenitude, the sense of fullness produced by its containing edges. That figure of wholeness is one of the most urgent reasons for looking at a painting; it problematizes the perceiver's identity, his/her own distinctiveness as an entity.

An Annunciation of Lorenzo Lotto

In one of the most favored configurations of Renaissance art, the Annunciation, an event of transcendent knowing is invariably captured in the frame of a window, a door, a portal. The frame becomes the hinge of an extended or a double universe, focusing the plenitude of heaven on the capturable wholeness of Mary's room. The frame gives access to an angel, the image of a miraculous presence apprehended only through the painter's framed vision. The Annunciation draws the edge of a painting within its field. It suggests transcendence through its depiction of imminence at that edge; it holds a model for the value of a circumscribed visual field.

25

When we cannot see beyond the frames of doors, windows, and horizons, we transform them into coordinates of the beyond, proofs that they visibly connect to the invisible, or even contain the invisible. The frame is comforting evidence that we can bring knowledge into purview, and grasp it with a strength that tests and validates our own powers of perception and imagination. It *holds* the perceiver's attention.

Let me pursue very briefly the notion of the frame's holding power in painting. With few exceptions, the outside limits of a painting set it off from the wall on which it hangs, a wall that, whatever intrinsic beauty it may have, is distinct from the painting. The set of limits we find within the painting—the doors, windows, and other apertures—are part of a manneristic vocabulary that also asserts the work's artifice. The pietà configuration, an essentially pathetic category of Western painting, supplements its emotional iconography of grieving mother and dead son with manneristic framing devices. Many of the Renaissance masters include backgrounds of heart-stopping serenity whose verdure is in ironic counterpoint to the foreground figures of Mary and Jesus. The fore-

A Pietà of Giovanni Bellini

26

ground space sustains the content's mythic-religious resonance through attitude and gesture; the painting's affect is inflected by the contrast between the mother/son configuration of grief and the beautiful *paesaggio*, a sign of a world unaware of loss. It is an affect as much a part of the medium's framing processes as of the particular thrust of the content.

The self-reflexivity of blatantly mannerist art seems to close in upon its fields, engaging artist and viewer in a complicity of viewpoint through the various interior framings, as if to dispel, by the complexity of its strategies, the absence implicit in any gesture of representation. In Velásquez's *Las meninas* the hermetic play of surfaces and energetic manipulation of planes express some of the affective limits of art—what happens when some people put others in frames and other people watch them do it.[3] The painting's ostensible subjects, the King and Queen, are posing for a portrait whose surface is turned away from us. We see, in midground, the painter near his easel looking toward the subjects and toward us; in

the foreground, the Infanta and her *meninas* (servants); in the background, a mirror in which are reflected the faces observed by Velásquez and the Infanta—those of the "real" subjects, the King and Queen. This vibrant set of interior-exterior tensions animates our viewing of a collection of views reflecting upon each other.

For Vermeer, enclosure is essential to a painting's organization. An overwhelming majority of his canvases are structured by interior frames—windows, doors, curtains, edges of tables, and images of other pictures. Vermeer draws our eyes to a *Lady Reading a Letter*, her face reflected in the panes of an open window. This configuration locates near the center of the canvas the image as it is seized by reflection and further qualified by the implied framings of

the window casement, the carpet-covered table, and the curtains, one drawn, hanging the full length of the right foreground, the other draped over the window panes. These characteristic motifs of Vermeer provide a dynamics of visual activity that forces us to match the letter reader's intentness.

Vermeer, obsessed by framing gestures and confident of their visual appeal, makes us sensitive to art as a passionate seizure of reality.[4] To see the "lady," a function of these frames, becomes the activity of the artist and the pleasure of the viewer. The scenes of daily life, the subjects of genre painting, are Vermeer's pretexts, but whether it be a maidservant pouring milk, a girl drinking from a glass, interrupted at music or with a water jug, he is showing us the price of sight and the value of its intricate seizure.[5] Vermeer's enclosures promote as well the value of the *inside* that is seized, a topos worked out dialectically by Gaston Bachelard in terms of inside/outside, positive/negative spatial limits, of "a *yes* and a *no*."[6] The various modes of identification of the self and the art object I outlined in the previous chapter seem to be generated by the desire to fix and to hold the artwork, the *inside*, a desire that is intermittently satisfied by the nature of our perception, our belief, our attention, and by the fluctuations of medium and fiction. Much of our affect is therefore a function of seizure and possession as we are caught in the teasing identificatory plays of our eyes, our imagination, and art.

The frame further guarantees that what we are looking at is being seen by our eyes since it places us in a verifiable, chartable relationship to the perceived. The art making that satisfies the artist's need to appropriate reality through representation, or to create reality in the work itself, is transmitted to us as a finished, bordered object, that can be grasped if we respond to the frames that lead to Velásquez at his easel or Vermeer's "lady" poring over her letter. These depictions suggest how some of the ways in which we identify ourselves, how in fact we *locate* ourselves in the world, are sources of affect in art. Our attempts to grasp experience through perception and creation are not tranquil ones. The particular feelings of Velásquez and Vermeer are exposed in the tensions connecting painter, object, and frame(s), tensions expressive of the artist's effort to possess, in the reality of the created work, the elusive reality of life. The work provides the viewer with a set of acquisitive frames, borders both apparent and implied, that create a model of possession through the affirmation of form and the imposition of limits.

Inside and Outside

In film theory the frame has, of course, been given a privileged position among the elements that constitute the image's intelligibility and its affectivity. Jean Mitry states that the frame is "the *absolute referential* of any cinematographic representation" and that it enters into a "formal unity" with what it contains.[7] Noël Burch devotes a whole chapter to this "dialectical relationship between off-screen space and screen space."[8] For Pascal Bonitzer, the space beyond the frame is "a place of uncertainty, of anguish that endows it with great dramatic power."[9] Before proceeding to examine the specific functions of the frame in this activity, I will outline, with a broadness that does no justice to the nuances of its articulations, the critical discourse that has concerned itself with the representational status of the framed image, with the way it is perceived, with the notion that it in fact creates the perceiver.

For Lacan and Lacanian-derived criticism, the authoritative delineation of the viewing subject is found in Freud's *Beyond the Pleasure Principle*, and in the evocation of the child's game in which a toy is made to disappear and reappear.[10] Pleasure is the result of mastering and playing out a situation that in *non*play experience would cause pain rather than pleasure. This game, accompanied by sounds prefigurative of the German words *fort* (gone) and *da* (here), is interpreted by Lacan as the birth of desire and language in the child. "There is consequently no further need to have recourse to the outworn notion of primordial masochism in order to understand the reason for the repetitive utterances in which subjectivity brings together mastery over its abandonment and the birth of the symbol."[11] O. Mannoni characterizes this game of mastery in theatrical terms, the child being both impresario and spectator in a rudimentary marionette theater.[12] Freud himself locates mastery at the root of adult satisfaction in viewing theatrical fictions (in "Psychopathic Characters on the Stage"). "Being present as an interested spectator at a spectacle or play does for adults what play does for children, whose hesitant hopes of being able to do what grown-up people do are in that way gratified."[13]

It is from the position of the spectator vis-à-vis the spectacle that the principle of "suture" has evolved. "Suture names the relation of the subject to the chain of its discourse."[14] The principal architect of the suture concept, Jean-Pierre Oudart, using as paradigm the shot/countershot pattern of film rhetoric, states: "Every filmic field is echoed by an absent field, the place of a character who is put there by the viewer's imaginary, and which we should call the Absent One. At a certain moment of the reading all the objects of the filmic field combine together to form the signifier of its absence."[15] Oudart considers the frame essential to this place of Lacan's Absent One, the field of the imaginary. The viewed is punctuated, is shaped, is replaced by, and replaces the nonviewed; here and there, in-frame and out-of-frame define each other as they alternately pass from the seen on the screen to the field of the imaginary hovering beyond the frame. Oudart's formulation has provoked much discussion and polemical response,[16] a debate summarized by Stephen Heath, who asserts that "the realization of cinema as discourse is the production at every moment through the film of a subject address, the specification of the play of incompleteness-completion."[17] Whether we call it a play of *fort* and *da*, of absence/presence or of incompleteness/completion, we recognize the status of film in a flux that threatens our ability to locate it and to locate ourselves in relation to it.

Interior framing tests those abilities in a medium, the cinema, that is emphatically framed by its magnifying projections. The comprehensive frame of the screen implies the cinema's automatic gesture of framing.[18] When a director frames within that frame, he is recognizing the medium's intrinsic power of possession and the formlike capacity of its limits. This power is often summoned in situations of emotional and dramatic intensity that coincide with passage and transition in the strictly narrative sense. The beginnings and endings, the arrivals and departures integral to time and duration in fiction find their natural placement in the framing structures in which they are played. When that natural placement is made to bear the emotional qualities of the film, either in anticipation or retrospect, its form becomes emotionally reverberant. The window that ushers us into Hew's memories at the beginning of *How Green Was My Valley* and the open doorway that expels the figure of Ethan Edwards (John Wayne) at the end of *The Searchers* are memorable examples of John Ford's significant framings at the boundaries of a given fiction. We cannot avoid being struck by the phenomenon of interior framing when it is coincidental with the shape of the fiction and its thematic cotent. The introduction of threshold at a film's opening and its recollection at the final fade-out are ways of making a viewer sensitive to how borders punctuate a work's duration.

But the boundaries of story, duration, and image also delimit the blankness from which art emerges. A sense of inevitable loss is written on the cinema's fleeting frames, on boundaries that are made of darkness as well as light. The possession generated by such negating shadows, that in fact proclaims imminent loss through the boldness of its delineation and the repercussive formality of its interior framing, endows the image with the depth of an implied shadow. It is from this depth, illusory in its molding, created by the encompassing blackness at the edge of the frame, that the image derives value. We acquire it from its own absence, on loan, as it were, from invisibility, and we hold on to it, in some films, in the fullest awareness of the frame's implicit power to refuse the very field its containment creates.

Frames for Fictions

When the cinematic frame imposes stasis on the human body, it suggests the possessive capacity of photographic portraiture. In still photography this sense of acquisition was especially strong when slow film and the desire for fine detail required stasis of both camera and subject. The concentrated time of sitting and exposure enhanced the frame's ability to capture the subject in a strictly delimited image, and through the capture endow it with value.[19] In silent films the close-up vignette and the masking of areas of the field used interior framing to put the faces of performers in high relief. These vignettes exemplify the grip of the framing process, counteracting to some extent the fiction's flow. Henrik Sartov's halated, backlighted epiphanic shots of Lillian Gish in Griffith's *Broken Blossoms* establish a standard for radically stylized portraiture in films. The filters, the gauzes, and the eccentric lighting procedures that qualify the face of Marlene Dietrich in the films of Josef Von Sternberg, and the vaseline-coated lenses that soften hardening features of aging actresses are part of the cinematic portrait's idealistic bent, its power to grasp an image, to hold it in distinction from existential reality and abstracted from the flux of a film's unfolding.

It seems to me that the eerie perfection of these portraits suggests the ways we are meant to perceive many of the most improbable conventions of sentimental films. In their emphatic dissimilarity to existential reality they assert the artifice and make-believe of cinematic images. They call upon the modes of mechanical transformation that bring us those images and the frames that insulate them against the presence of our viewing and the blemishes of our everyday lives. In John Cromwell's *The Enchanted Cottage*, through the magic of the cottage's charm and the characters' love-filled eyes, the homely Laura (Dorothy McGuire) becomes beautiful and Oliver (Robert Young) loses his battle-inflicted scars. But

the true enchantment is in the magic intrinsic to all films—the discretion of frames that can show an actor made up to seem horrible one moment, handsome the next, and an actress, first unflatteringly lighted and stringy-haired, then softly glamorous. The frame of *The Enchanted Cottage* is to the love of Laura and Oliver what the movie frame is to our eyes. It holds their pristine aspects against the force of contingency. Images like these are essentially absent from us, splendid in their makeup, their flattering shadows, and their primrose paths of coincidence.

Viewers with "cool" and "good" tastes will not tolerate, let alone be moved, by *Maytime*, the warbling of Jeanette MacDonald and Nelson Eddy, MGM's slick production, and the ethos of operetta. Yet it is precisely such a film that fully tests the mechanics of the sentimental response.[20] In *Maytime*'s final sequence a dowager Jeanette (made up to appear more glamorous than her supposed advanced age would allow) gently dies under a rain of blossoms and then materializes, young and radiant, to sing along with the ghost of her murdered lover. Here, the conventions of operetta and melodrama, and the particular rhetoric of the movies conspire to create affect through a complicated series of frames of context and register, as well as the more familiar physical and filmic ones—the enclosed garden so profuse with flowers that it all seems to be painted, the code of musical utterance in a narrative situation, the ghostly visitation, the juxtaposition of contrastive photographic densities that I evoked in my remarks on Borzage.[21] The logical outcome of these elements is the rebirth of the young heroine from the body of the old lady, and the reprise of "Sweetheart, sweetheart, sweetheart, will you love me ever?" as two happy ghosts stroll down the garden lane.[22] Films like *Maytime* court a viewer's disbelief by liberating art from the fiction of experience, and succeed in conveying their program of transport because their cinematic frames so openly acknowledge the medium's stylistics of absence. They exploit the manifest fictivity of these sentimental fictions.

The frame, as affective element of that fictivity, is repeatedly dramatized in Frank Capra's *Lost Horizon*. Threshold is offered and denied in access both miraculously easy and perilously brief, and in the baldest conventions of cinematic narrative. The conventions of the adventure film shape the frantic escape of the airplane from revolution-torn China, the mysterious journey, the individuation of the passengers, the storm, the crash, and the sudden passage from the frozen wastes to the temperate Shangri-La. In some way, Conway (Ronald Colman) and his party cross the magic threshold because they are in a movie and subject to its transformational clichés. They are brought to a utopia through peripeties that recall voyages to Conan Doyle's Lost World, the center of Jules Verne's Earth, King Kong's Skull Island, and Dorothy's Land of Oz.

33

Whether these never-never lands have a novelistic provenance or not, they belong to and are refashioned by the framed world of film. Passing into their domain is suggestive of enclosing a fiction in framed, moving images through the cinema's familiar photographic techniques and artifices. The initial entry to *Lost Horizon* is just such a paradigm for access to these illusions of movie-making. We are whisked away to Shangri-La in the movie's particular modes of melodrama, vehicle and decor.

In the last sequences it seems that Conway, after being tricked into leaving Shangri-La, finally regains its threshold, but his spiritual victory and the fiction's utopianism are finally engulfed in the mode suggested by the title, *Lost Horizon*. The threshold to Shangri-La is important to us because it is so vulnerable. What we gain by crossing it and its enclosed fiction is lost when we experience it as sign of inaccessibility, when we see it as a reverberation, locked in cinema's permanent retrospection. Cinema need not resort to special effects to "show" actors as ghosts. The dark image of Conway struggling through the snow toward his lost horizon is just as transparent as Jeanette MacDonald's in *Maytime*'s melodious garden. Both of them expose through their fictive transparencies the unstable criterion of the reality effect in an illusionistic medium.

Sentimental rhetoric, whether abundant or intermittent, is bothersome to viewers unprepared or unwilling to read it as a function of cinema's fictional modes and the conditions of its apparatus. Even *How Green Was My Valley* and William Wyler's *Mrs. Miniver*, films that have achieved greater critical esteem than *Maytime*, and whose fabrics seem to be more true to life than those of *Lost Horizon*, have sequences in which the "inspirational" iconography is undeniably hackneyed. In the first, the paralyzed young Hew (Roddy McDowall) regains the use of his limbs and walks toward the open arms of the minister, Mr. Gruffydd (Walter Pidgeon), on a flower-covered hilltop. In the final sequence of the second the parishioners are united in the bombed church, and both pastor and camera memorialize the dead to prove the power of faith. The sermon and the empty spaces in the pews are blatantly pathetic, and designed to wring tears from the audience in sympathetic response to those glistening in the eyes of Mrs. Miniver (Greer Garson). The film's success is some proof that the tears were indeed wrung (and are still wrung at present-day showings, when the bravery of the English middle class in face of the Nazi hordes is no longer a factor in the response). These tear-producing scenes are shaped by Hollywood's most dependable sentimental conventions, culled from preceding traditions in the theater and the novel. We may snicker at their excessive familiarity; we may object to their manipulatory power, the way they are designed to produce almost automatic reactions in viewers. Yet we cannot deny that power's existence or afford to overlook its sources in the medium's capacity for infusing us with the anguish of loss and the joy of fulfillment.

The Frame as Vessel

The notion of capacity implies filling and emptying, and the frame within a frame is a clear model for these processes. The frame's iconographic content may trigger an emotional response through associations, both artistic and experiential, but it is also perceived as a set of visual functions, transmitted to us in images of varying degrees of density from filled to emptied. These functions have an emotional value distinct from what they represent.

In *How Green Was My Valley* the configurations of the family group united at the dinner table are first posited in their fullness so that the subsequent departures and deaths can be expressed as an emptying of that fullness. This is the dynamics too of one of the most subversively poignant passages in Ford. It comes near the end of *The Sun Shines Bright* (1954). The reelection of Judge Priest (Charles Winninger) is an affirmation of the values of the past, specifically those of an antebellum chivalry expressed in the film's extraordinary set piece—a funeral procession for a "loose woman." But the morally and politically triumphant hero, after receiving the greetings of the townspeople as he stands on his porch, is engulfed in darkness as we, from the vantage point of the front fence, see him turn away, enter the house, walk through two open doors, and finally disappear out of those receding frames. The very reason for Judge Priest's heroism, his anachronistic code of honor, expels him from the film's *present*; the frame filled with his victory finally holds nothing but the place where he *was*.[23]

The empty frame achieves monumental scale at the end of Sam Wood's *The Pride of the Yankees* where the dying Lou Gehrig (Gary Cooper) makes a farewell speech to a packed Yankee Stadium and then, in isolation, walks away from the camera into the shadows at the depth of the dugout. A more ambiguous but no less affecting disappearance from the frame supplies the sense of the end of Fred Zinnemann's *The Nun's Story*. There the patterns of claustration are made explicit by the subject matter. Sister Luke (Audrey Hepburn), about to leave the religious order, dresses for the world. A door clicks open revealing an alley down which she slowly walks away from the stationary lens. In the depth of the image, framed by the alley's walls, she hesitates and finally exits from the film. The hard-won tranquility represented throughout *The Nun's Story* by the symmetrical patterns of nuns filling chapels and corridors is dissipated in the void of the last frame. Whatever liberation the character finds beyond the film's borders is subverted by the emptiness sketched by her passage out of that frame.

These voids are redolent of the fullness promised by framing, a fullness implied by the integrity of the cinematic field and the defined continuity of viewing time. Our impression (quite real when we view a film in a dark theater) that nothing takes place outside the unfolding work is sustained by images of spatial completion and emotional satisfaction. The hilltop miracle of *How Green Was My Valley* resounds with the sonority of a chord composed of the separate elements of its literary and religious iconography, and distinct from the music on the sound track. Some viewers may consider this image, as well as *Maytime*'s tuneful garden of flowers, filled to excess, straining at the edges with an abundance of sentimental data, aural and visual. The obsessively repeated madonna/bambino configurations of "mother love" films such as George Stevens's *Penny Serenade*, Mitchell Leisen's *To Each His Own*, Jean Negulesco's *Johnny Belinda*, and Curtis Bernhardt's *The Blue Veil* bear what to others may seem to be overwhelming affective weight. A perceived threat to the critical enterprise itself, inherent in these films, explains for Peter Brooks the strong negative reactions of many:

> The critical resistance and embarrassment that melodrama may elicit could derive from its refusal of censorship and repression—the accommodations to the reality principle that the critical witness himself then supplies, from his discomfort before a drama in which people confront him with identifications judged too extravagant, too stark, too unmediated to be allowed utterance.[24]

To accuse Stevens, Leisen, et al. of excess may therefore be a reflection of excessive censoring in the face of a fiction menacing in its directness or an inability to read the fiction in the fullness of the essential properties of the conveying medium. The conventions of sentiment, the accoutrements of joy and sorrow, greeting and farewell borrowed from the traditions of visual and theatrical art do not perforce violate the extent of the frame. The medium repeatedly proves that its magnifying and unfolding nature thrives on what our fluctuating cultural criteria define as excessive. From the length of Eisenstein's Odessa steps (*Potemkin*, 1925) to the breadth of Lawrence's desert (Lean, *Lawrence of Arabia*, 1962), from the snowy infinity of humanistic internationalism (Renoir, *La grande illusion*, 1937) to the starry site of interplanetary friendship (Spielberg, *Close Encounters of the Third Kind*, 1977), the expanse of the screen easily accommodates itself to emotional hyperbole.

Homes and Horizons

Genre films are contextual "homes" for the viewer. Their familiarity is preserved by the interreferentiality of scenarios, situations, visual motifs, performers. Both Ford and Ozu use the intellectual and conventional fixity of genre—the western, the family drama—

to establish frames whose borders are exceptionally clear.[25] The styles of their films are suggestive of acts of patient witnessing, Ford's through the sharp assertions of his porches, doors, and windows, Ozu's through low camera placement, fixed vantage point, and extended shot duration. Non-Japanese viewers of an Ozu film are made sensitive to the complexities of essentially alien cultural patterns because the camera's patience and possessiveness make their visual fields so familiar. The fields seem to extend to us eternally accessible information whose slightest alteration leaves us as truly bereft as they do the characters, members of families whose constitution is menaced by even a hint of change.

We think we know all the rules that govern the stylistic, narrative, and thematic characteristics of genre films, but our knowing those rules, and the holding power of their frames, both physical and conventional, are repeatedly challenged by shifts of key, register, or tone. Farce and sentiment become intimate in Capra's *It Happened One Night* in the famous "Walls of Jericho" sequence where a blanket strung between two beds, Ellie's (Claudette Colbert's) oversized pajamas, and Peter's (Clark Gable's) striptease somehow lead to romantic backlighting, rain on a window, and a night of painful separation. The fixed form, whether it be the sonnet, the screwball comedy, the western, or the soap opera, offers us at one and the same time the comfort of the known and a field liable to breaches in the intimacy of that comfort, and therefore to meaningful disarrangement.

Disarrangement is forcefully conveyed after the frame first asserts the integrity of the human body, thereby positing its aspect as something like a fixed form. Through its grace and tension the dance duet figure then tests the delimiting function of the frame. Fred Astaire insisted on having the dancers' bodies photographed in their wholeness to show in simultaneity their articulations, from arms raised over the head to pointed feet. This visual insistence on connections operates in two-shots that seem to draw the dancers together, creating something like a single being, an intimacy of partnership woven into many of the Astaire-Rogers numbers. In the structure of "Never Gonna' Dance" (George Stevens, *Swing Time*), coming together and separating are worked out in the distances traversed by camera and dancers, in the patterns that first unite the dancers' images (Ginger on the staircase, Fred pleading down below), only to divide them at the conclusion. Ginger spins out of the frame, leaving Fred slumped dejectedly against a pillar. The frame, respectful of the wholeness of the dancers' bodies, their selves, and their relationship, becomes the locus for affect when life is shown as a dance. And the frame that displays Ginger's body in all its degrees of tension and urgent response to Fred's despairs at her absence.[26]

The human figure's place in the frame is heroically demonstrated by dancers who seem to be endowed with superhuman energy and grace, and whose natural abodes, the grandiose "big white sets," the nightclubs with their curving staircases and art deco spaciousness, locate experience in spectacular sets that are made to be looked at through the movable proscenium of the cinematic frame. Much of narrative cinema recounts the search for simpler environments, for contexts that echo the narrowness of borders rather than their expanse, for spatial integrities that draw their edges from the cinema's own bent for enclosure.

In films like Frank Borzage's *A Man's Castle*, George Cukor's *Little Women*, George Stevens's *Alice Adams*, *I Remember Mama*, and *The Diary of Anne Frank* the frame is the home, the hearth, the context necessary to the fiction's existence and congenial to the human identity at its center.[27] The narrative pretext of *A Man's Castle*, Bill's (Spencer Tracy's) intermittent urge to free himself from Trina's (Lorretta Young's) warm affections and their shantytown nest, is resolved in the film's final image—the couple embraced on a bed of straw in a moving boxcar. The "nested" family is recalled throughout *Little Women* in the tight little rooms, in the figures huddled together, forever embracing in joy and sor-

row—Beth thanking Mr. Laurence for the piano, the "little women" saying goodbye to Marmee, Beth's death. At the end, Jo (Katharine Hepburn) adds her body and her happiness to the frame that reconstitutes the family. Stevens's affinity for enclosed configurations is reflected in his "family" subjects, and situations whose staging and editing pull toward a clearly defined emotional center—*Alice Adams*, finding true love on the porch of her genteel but shabby house, the camera's perusal of the homely domesticity that ensures we all remember Mama, the hiding place that is Anne Frank's diary, her decor, and her film. Even the proportions of *Giant* accommodate Stevens's sense of hearth in the image of a house isolated in the disproportionately wide horizon lines of prairie and CinemaScope. The "expanse" of feeling is endlessly variable.

Tight borders are sufficient to our vision when we are meant to draw within the fiction, a process coherent with familial transport, the selective focus of sentimental art and of the easy accessibility of its images. In *Little Women* Beth regains the use of her legs when her father returns home after the Civil War. The film has the allure of an old album, and the therapy of love that cures Beth belongs in the modest living room of the March family. The film's power is collected within its modest enclosures, and the miraculous cure implodes toward its center. Grand horizons suit romantic myth and religious, historical, and social configurations of epic loss.[28] They quicken our desire to see beyond the frame. The cure scene of *How Green Was My Valley*, although framed by trees and branches, opens out toward an infinite background. Its implied horizon befits a miracle of faith and community as opposed to a miracle of the hearth. The centrifugality of a frame is called upon when our feelings radiate toward surrounding contexts, to standards that stretch character beyond personality. Attempting to escape from Nazi tyranny, Freya (Margaret Sullavan) and Martin (James Stewart), the lovers of Borzage's *The Mortal Storm*, carry the weight of Western Civilization with them as they ski down a mountain toward freedom, a setting reminiscent of the snowscape that engulfs Rosenthal (Marcel Dalio) and Maréchal (Jean Gabin) at the end of *La grande illusion*. When Gil (Henry Fonda), in *Drums along the Mohawk*, marches off to fight, John Ford gives Lana (Claudette Colbert) a hilltop and an endless vista for her sadness. Civilization

makes heroic demands on feelings, and only the most open frames will properly test them. In *The Grapes of Wrath* Henry Fonda, an essential figure for Ford, earns perhaps the noblest horizon line. Tom Joad's farewell to his mother (Jane Darwell) is suffused with such idealism that his hilltop seems to be the gate of heaven, a horizon that stretches the tight dark frame of mother and son in the previous shots to beyond the ends of the earth. The departure of Tom Joad toward anonymous immortality in *The Grapes of Wrath* and the departure of the hero (Richard Dreyfuss) of *Close Encounters of the Third Kind* from the earth itself (subsumed in the frame of a hollow mountain) to the movie-made infinity of space are designed to evoke an amplitude of absence.[29]

Whether they draw us in to their enclosed figures or urge us to transcend their boundaries, the clear delineations of interior framing make us conscious of placement. That consciousness is exploited in films that make us care about where their characters are. However much John Ford's political conservatism may have detached him from John Steinbeck's populist ideology, his feeling for home made him an ideal director for *The Grapes of Wrath*, a film about people pulling up roots and searching for a new place to live. The sense of settlement pervades Ford's work, from the pre-Revolutionary fort in *Drums along the Mohawk* to the encampments and wagon trains of *Wagonmaster* stretching the frontier ever westward. The hearths at the core of life are protected against the menace from without in configurations that express intimacy and communal respect. In *Drums along the Mohawk*, Widow McKlennar (Edna May Oliver), fearless of the Indian attack and fire, refuses to leave the bed she once shared with her husband; Wyatt Earp (Henry Fonda) dances for civilization on the square platform of Tombstone's yet-to-be-built church and destroys the uncivilized Clantons in the chaotically rendered space of the O. K. Corral in *My Darling Clementine*. Ford repeatedly shows us that people belong in homes, and his films move us because the threshold of these homes, emblemized by the framed home of the cinematic image, are in constant threat of disaggregation.

Windows and Doorways

Among the correlatives for the movie frame the window captures, with particular force, the medium's specular nature. A mode of presentation as well as a presentation itself, we both see it and see through it. In *Broken Blossoms* the window through which the Yellow Man (Richard Barthelmess) gazes at Lucy (Lillian Gish) offers him an image he can grasp fully, in spite of its softened contours. The window holds that image in close analogy to the movie frame, and confers on it precious separateness for the Yellow Man, whom we see looking through it in rapt attention, and for ourselves, in another shot, looking through it from his point of view. In these consecutive framings of the viewing and the viewed, affect is achieved through the identification of perception with the means of access to the perceived. The Yellow Man falls in love with Lucy when he sees her through his window and thereby acquires her image.

Such acquisition is made parallel to fiction itself in Renoir's *Le crime de M. Lange*, where a pattern of windows, of shooting through windows, of opening windows relates complementary functions of the protagonist: as storyteller (he writes pulp fictions), as the prime source of affect in the emphatically inscribed courtyard-community (it is his spirit that involves everyone in a collective enterprise of fiction making), as the champion of the community's bonds (he shoots the adversary, the menace to the community.)[30] Closed, barred windows are negative values. The camera's freedom that in so many of Renoir's films represents both joy and deep feeling, here, through optical effects, pierces a billboard placed over a window, an "opening" that Lange will accomplish later in the film when he tears down that barrier. The openness of the framed courtyard is finally dramatized through the camera's activity, when it follows Lange's pursuit of the villain through the building, past the open windows, before the shooting in the courtyard. The camera in *seeing through* the windows posits the double resonance of specular freedom and of framing limitations in a fiction whose likable protagonist "sees" the American West in his Parisian courtyard, then possesses the vision through his writing.

But in the flux of cinema the assertion that sight is acquisition implies that in nonsight there is loss. The window that *does not* contain the image is also a sign of longing. In Vincente Minnelli's *Meet Me in St. Louis* a window links a snow-filled garden and Esther (Judy Garland) singing "Have Yourself a Merry Little Christmas" to console her little sister Tootie (Margaret O'Brien), who is about to suffer the loss of home (a home whose frameness is announced in four painterly "seasonal" inserts that punctuate the film). In William Wyler's *Wuthering Heights* windows consistently yearn for images—Heathcliff (Laurence Olivier) calling for the ghost of Cathy (Merle Oberon) through the broken window of the room where Lockwood slept; the young Heathcliff breaking a window when he feels Cathy has betrayed their love for the fripperies of Edgar Linton; Heathcliff holding the dead Cathy before the bedroom window that overlooks the scene of their love—the wide

expanse of moors and Peniston Crag. The grandly romantic conclusion of Borzage's *A Farewell to Arms* finds loss in a similar configuration—Frederic (Gary Cooper) holding Catherine's (Helen Hayes's) sheet-draped body in the window of her hospital room. A man's arms and the double enclosure of window and film frame pathetically display their inadequacy to contain presence. They show us that sight is not enough. The window frames through which we are meant to see thwart our desire to hold an image of emotional significance.

When these windows are taken from us, they signify a denial of access to their fictions. They remind us that fiction is vulnerable to the distancing effect of narration, to the removal that is part of any act of retelling.[31] From a vantage point outside the house, the last shot of *I Remember Mama* shows Mama's (Irene Dunne's) shadowy face in the window, her family seated behind her at the dinner table. The camera pulls away over a representation of the street and the

city. The narrative locus, the family, and its emotional agent, Mama, are engulfed in the sorrow of relating what is no more. A window passes from our view, carrying with it the affect it contained. The present is lost in the framing of film itself.

The doorway and its variant portals, gates, and French windows are the cinema's most insistent configurations of affect. A threshold that invites crossing, the doorway is both vibrant with the dynamics of entrance and exit, and informed with the tread of our own experience. The range of that experience, from the habitual departures and arrivals through the front doors of our workaday lives to the rites of passage, initiations, and ceremonies enacted under ornamental canopies and aisles of crossed swords, is captured on the sills of cottages and cathedrals. Whether routine or mysterious, these traversals resonate with our sensorimotor responses and our memories. The modes of access to where we live, work, and worship are privileged within the decorum of cinema. Their privilege is not unrelated to that crucial point of contact between the viewer and the fiction, the opening of any film, a nexus figured by the projection of a rectangle on a screen during a theatrical occasion. Theatrical, religious, humdrum, and cinematic, these various accessions are mutually reflecting paradigms for the notion of pos-

session upon which is predicated our affect as loss. They ritualize
the occupancy that precedes abandon.

John Ford finds transformative rituals at the core of all experience, from the repentance of Gypo/Judas during Mass (*The Infor-
mer*) to the obligatory square dances of his westerns, the funeral
procession of *The Sun Shines Bright*, and the dress parade of *The
Long Gray Line*. But less theatrical rituals are just as apt for Ford in
marking the thresholds that convey the integrity of character and
place.[32] Soon after the beginning of *How Green Was My Valley* that
integrity is established on a threshold consecrated by the humblest
sort of dramatic action and its modes of cinematization. After the
day's work in the mine the men are returning home down the street
bordered on one side by a descending row of houses and on the
other by a low wall. A shot of Mrs. Morgan waiting at the gate of the
house links her nurturing, mediating presence to the threshold. A
double entry, front gate and front door, extends the area of transition as if to linger on the movement of traversal by drawing out the
breadth of its enactment. The presiding figure of the mother will be
recalled throughout this film, whose script explicitly designates her
"the heart" of the family. Here, each singing Morgan drops his pay
into her lap before he enters the house. The visual and dramatic
statement of the mother figure at the threshold and the verbal one
offered by the script (in the film's first image the hero, leaving the
valley, is tying his belongings in his mother's shawl) charge access
with affect. The commonsensical, warmhearted woman portrayed
by Sara Allgood and the conventional echoes of the "good" mother
exploited by the fiction are fixed at the sill in a readily identifiable
image of satisfaction generously bestowed. Crossing that sill toward
her welcoming hearth means finding one's home. The sill will bear
an ever-increasing burden of affect—the mother kissing her returning sons and then grieving at their departure, a young widow
holding her infant, hellos and goodbyes that demonstrate how the
door that is filled with presence is just as easily emptied of it. The

loss of home, the relinquishment of its comfort, is signaled when the sill is traversed for the last time and abandoned for darkness beyond mother, affect, frame, and film.

In *I Remember Mama* the mother, situated at the locus of exit, is specifically designated as the mediator of loss. After the death of Uncle Chris (Oscar Homolka), a screen door frames Mama, who looks over "our shoulder" toward a field in which Chris's widow is walking. Inside the house, barely visible, Katrin (Barbara Bel Geddes) calls, "Will you come with me?" Mama turns and enters. A shot from the side shows the screen door closing, followed by a pan left to the field and the figure of the widow off in the distance. This postlude to the death of Uncle Chris (inexplicably cut from some of the release prints of the film) contains both mortality and Katrin's coming-of-age in a screen door, in the depths behind it, in the expanse before it, in the ministering figure of Mama who looks without and within, who holds their knowledge in the fullness of paradox, and who is held, the source of knowledge, in the known shape of the frame. Her benevolent possession of life and death is passed on to us through the intrinsically cinematic process of framing in a frame, catching us in a tension of borders expressive of limitless vision. We see Mama with something like Mama's acuity until she is engulfed in shadows, momentarily lost in death; we are then all lost in a field fit for a widow.

The domestic doorways in which mother love perches are equally apt for the yearnings of romantic love. Max Ophuls, whose roving eye usually supplies its own dynamics as an outline for spatiality,[33] lingers over the glass-paned front door of a small apartment house, the frame for the love-filled eyes of Lisel (Joan Fontaine), the heroine of *Letter from an Unknown Woman*. Near the film's beginning she opens the door for the object of her infatuation, pianist Stefan Brand (Louis Jourdan), and foolishly tries to hide her blushing adoration behind its transparency. Stefan pauses, looks at the girl, continues walking, pauses again to see her clutching the open door, her body outlined in its solid frame and the reflection of its panes behind her back. For Lisel, the door signifies access to Stefan's love and music. It establishes a labyrinthine pattern of entry that extends through the whole film. The transparent frame of this door defines the access of Lisel's eyes and the camera's lens, transforming the heroine's desire and her specular activity into a form of filmic apprehension that is passed on to us. Looking at the framed glance of Lisel, we are filled with our own desperate urge to see. Our curiosity about Lisel's curiosity and about the fiction created by her desire are tested in the doorway, a trope for sight and passage. Its power is validated at the film's end. Stefan has finished reading a letter from Lisel, a woman unknown to him but whom he has encountered repeatedly during the course of his life. As demonstrated by Lisel's narrative, knowing is loving, and this is finally transmitted to Stefan as he leaves to fight a duel with Lisel's husband, an appointment he had not intended to keep before reading the letter. The callous Stefan has never *known*; his eyes have never seized the images so precious to Lisel. He again hesitates at the entry, turns and sees a ghostlike version of the earlier shot, the girl caught between the door and its shadow, between frames of access and depth, with the look of Ophuls's loving camera in her eyes.

Framed in Retrospect

The recapitulated doorway in *Letter from an Unknown Woman* is a motif of interior framing that, in creating a visual echo, accentuates the effect of cinema's perpetual backward glance on phenomena, and on the unbreachable gulf between the present of a film as it is being created and the present during which it is projected for an audience. Visual echoes allow us to assess the distance between seeing and the seen. Ford's empty doorways and faded young Lisel bear the heavy weight of cinematic memory. They convey something of our permanent alienation from the images we so cherish.

The pastness of all films is implicit in the retrospection of their frames, a property of the medium demonstrated by polished "Hollywood" features and by our out-of-focus, badly lighted, uncentered home movies. The embarrassed and graceless movements of dead relatives and friends overwhelm us with a poignancy that most still photographs of the same faces and bodies do not produce. The cinematic frame, by dint of its serial projections, has a precarious grasp on the presence and activities of life. Whether in the artfully composed 35 millimeter close-up of a movie star or in the super-8 grimacing countenances of once young parents, the frame makes us pay dearly in affect for beholding its vacillating modes of present and past.

When films acknowledge the pastness of their fiction, they in-

volve us in an affect of loss that pervades other acts of retelling and reminiscence. It is not simply the thrust of an ongoing tradition that links the nineteenth-century novel to twentieth-century film. The cinema's affinity for retrospection accounts for its easy appropriation of so many conventions of prose narrative. Near the beginning of Cukor's *Little Women* Marmee and her four daughters are shown in a pyramidal grouping that evokes the stasis of old tintypes, holding the characters in an affective, familial, and pictorial relationship. Then each of the girls is vignetted in close-up, creating a figuration of inwardness within the framework of the previously established group portrait. In this sequence, where framing devices peculiar to still photography are repatterned by cinematic cutting, the flux of frames controls the relatioship between the viewer and a visualization of what is manifestly past. *Little Women*, from its credits projected on the exaggerated rectangularity of a primitively drawn frame house to its repeated images of figures embracing each other literally and verbally, uses iconography emphatically disconnected from the time of its making and even more emphatically disconnected from the present of our viewing, to enhance our awareness of life that is no more. Cukor's success with "period" subjects (*David Copperfield*, 1935; *Camille*, 1936; *Gaslight*, 1944; *Heller in Pink Tights*, 1960) comes in part from his conviction that what is past is indeed past, a belief that emerges in the fervor of these films' enactments and the care of their decorative reconstructions. Films whose epochs predate the creation of the movies play on this aspect of temporality. Not photographed in a contemporaneous present, their images cherish the intrinsic style of anachronism in the medium's perpetual backward glance.

In many of Ford's films, the first statement of a visual "theme" already seems to be its own recapitulation. The opening image of *How Green Was My Valley* shows the narrator's hands tying his belongings in his mother's shawl. His voice, issuing from a mouth we will never see, announces his imminent departure from his once green valley. The camera pans slightly to the left, catching through the window a view of old women in dismal surroundings; the next shot reveals the slag-covered valley. The narrative voice and the window provide a double frame for pastness. We perceive the echo before the sounds and images that produced it—the voice of the narrator as a boy singing out over the green valley in response to his sister who calls from behind a wall. The frames of this film foreshadow and aftershadow each other. The doors and windows of the Morgan house, the threshold of the church, and the elevator of the mine shaft are variants on the unforgettable fixed form of the film's principle set, the street descending from the mine past a row of houses, their front doors, and their defining front gates. The corrupted, slag-laded image of this set, a prefiguration of loss, contains the frames that control all the essential aspects of the narrative: the front door and the disruption of the family; the threshold of the church and the thwarted love of Angharad (Maureen O'Hara) and Mr. Gruffydd (this threshold ironically filled and emptied by Angharad's wedding veil after her marriage to the mineowner's son); the framework of the mine elevator holding two pietà

variants—the first, Mr. Morgan (Donald Crisp), cradling his dead son Ivor (Patric Knowles), the second, Hew, cradling his dead father.

All these echoes belie the strength of the frame. The sense of reiteration, rather than affirming acquisition, suggests cinema's intermittent hold on phenomena, for *showing again* implies that what we see is not always there and may indeed not be there for much longer. Pictures on walls have frames whose hold is firm enough for our needs. Frames are meant to hold; moving pictures, with their illusion of fixity, fluctuating syntax, and finite duration, show us that they do not. When the frame becomes its own echo, it demonstrates the imperfection of its fixity; our relationship to its shifting standard, repeatedly tested by the medium, makes us vulnerable precisely to standards that shift.[34] The movable frame of cinema is one of the clearest signs that the experience so perfectly reproduced on film is only fleetingly accessible to us.

Framing the Fiction of Presence

Cinematic framing that asserts the absence of the viewed accounts for the sentimental impact of the memory film, where recollection, often represented as a narrative voice-over, envelops the frame of fiction in its own frame. Whether it be the open window at the start of *How Green Was My Valley*, the mirror in *I Remember Mama* in which the face of the narrator is replaced by the images of her past, or the world-weary face of the man who receives a letter from an unknown woman, the bias of cinematic retrospection offers evidence of how the seen separates us from what we long to see. These devices and referents are indeed mirrors, catching images in surfaces that both invite and refuse our entry. The frame of memory, so appealingly softened by the voice of the various narrators (the uncredited one in *How Green Was My Valley* has an aural presence no less nostalgically sonorous than those of Barbara Bel Geddes and Joan Fontaine), may be captured in equally appealing configurations, but the softness of both voice and configuration is held within the hard set of edges that border the image.

This pathos of absence in apparent presence is demonstrated even more forcefully in films that are not suffused with nostalgia's patina, but in which the intrinsic sense of cinematic past subverts the present of the dramatic action. In Billy Wilder's *Sunset Boulevard* Norma Desmond (Gloria Swanson), during the showing of one of her silent films (made more than twenty years previously by Gloria Swanson herself, of course), announces, "There just aren't faces like that any more," then stands in the projection beam to prove her point. The cinema, once it has shown a face on film, shows us what is not "any more." Its frames are apt boundaries for absence, often inflecting empty fields with the implied image of what should be there or with the memory of what once was there. The doorways and unbroken horizon lines in Ford's films hold the reverberation of all that seemed to inhabit them. They are a test of our ability to fill them, just as the borders of a work of art, between its edges, its first and last pages, its first and last images, test our reading and viewing. The affective value of the cinema frame wells from our passion for completion and our need for forms whose complexity and accessibility account for our presence. The frame, filled and emptied, catches our pulse in its fluctuation. Each time a character passes in or out of a significantly posited frame configuration we are involved in a mode that proclaims our exclusion.

That exclusion is most unsettling when the frame's promise seems fullest. In *How Green Was My Valley* the convalescent Mrs. Morgan laboriously makes her way toward the bed of her paralyzed little boy. As she extends her arms toward Hew she shows us what it means to reach into a frame. Her ability to then grasp what she finds there is a sign of completion that corresponds to the most elementary experience of fulfillment in the viewer's life; as a sign within its own frame, it holds the pattern of our exclusion as well. Our eyes permit us to reach in, but only just so far. Should we attempt to invade the frame by approaching the screen or standing in the beam of projected light, we would obliterate the image. Metz states that "the 'perceiving drive' . . . *concretely represents the absence of its object* in the distance at which it maintains it and which is part of its very definition: distance of the look, distance of listening."[35] This distance denies us the tangible grasp demonstrated by Mrs. Morgan, and the embrace of countless couples framed by the doors and windows of Morocco and Main Street.

But as the frame prohibits the viewer's physical intrusion it displays its most comforting function. It identifies us as we watch from outside its borders, enveloped in a darkness that holds our integrity, even as we lose ourselves in the illusion projected on the screen. The sentimental film effects a paradox of identification. Its apparatus of highly controlled decor and mise-en-scène, its reliance on thickening codes of music and familiar iconography, and the conventions of its genres all conspire to involve the viewer in its illusion and its affect. Yet, as the viewer is drawn to merge with the work of art, the rigor of its frames prevents that from happening. Embedded in the empathetic response that film is designed to elicit through its magnification of our own likeness is the sense that we are *not* there on the screen and are excluded from its field. We must be far enough away from the image to see it. We must respect its frame and accept it as a mark of presence that is forever denied, as a privileged view that taunts us with its nearness.

To refuse the frame's call is to render its space superficial, deprived of its motility and dynamics of composition. Our experience shows us the contrary. The illusion of depth and the multidimensionality supplied by the physiology of our perception and the camera's shifting point of view prove the medium's power over the objects it photographs. At the movies our eyes are not less powerful, particularly if we grant the camera its processes and use the frame of its lens as a model for an aperture that endows the world's revelations with the semblance of life. Although we never penetrate the frame, we do become conscious of its acquisitive strength. It urges us to fill the voids, the inviting space within its boundaries that are too true to the ones that torment us in life. It quickens the rhythm of our desire with its gestures of possession. And that desire, satisfied by the allure of cinematic images, is acted out in the surge of our affect, in the joy of perceiving and recognizing that we perceive, and in the sorrow of having to relinquish those promise-filled frames, separate from our darkness, receding from us in time and space.

3 Private Demonstrations

At the climax of *Oedipus Rex* the hero plucks out his own eyes, metaphors for knowledge, witnesses to his acts of parricide and incest. By learning to recognize himself, he has seen too much and is filled with horror at sight itself. The Oedipal scenario, so familiar from the Freudian model, is capped with a gesture that reflects back upon us, the spectators of tragedy, and our position as witnesses to the visualized, enacted fiction. Our eyes behold a display of sight's power and of the moral implications of that power. The lesson of the play is that eyes should not behold the fatal consequences of the primal bedroom scene.

Oedipus Rex represents a crisis of sight at the core of classical dramatic aesthetics, where the degree to which we see and the quality of gestural, dramatic discourse polemicize word and spectacle. In the plays of Corneille and Racine, examples of classical tragedy in its last flowering, in seventeenth-century France, physical movement and stage action are reduced to their essentials. Seeing these plays consists largely of seeing actors speak and respond to each other's speaking. The issues of tragedy, as Freud and Jung have indicated through their own style and rhetoric, cry out for language, metaphors, myths, and sublimations, for the very modes of performance that nourish the theater. Racine's Phèdre is desperate for invisibility. She wants to hide the shame of her incestuous passion from the light of day itself. Yet this desperation, when verbalized, is a dramatic event that she can enact and that we are called upon to watch as well as hear. We are moved by the sight of a woman who reveals through her speech what she is unable to hide. The poetic style of Racine so sonorously magnifies Phèdre's utterance that we are shaken by the force of its disclosure. We blush with embarrassment at catching her so defenseless, so at the mercy of our eyes and ears. Much of tragic affect (and melodramatic affect as well)[1] stems from a sense of witnessing that which we feel we should never see. It resounds with our own need for privacy, for the clothes that cover our nudity, for the words that hide our desire beneath strategies of social behavior. The tension of disclosure and concealment that animates our inner and social lives is incorporated into the processes of art and into our response to art. Oedipus's curiosity leads him to blindness; we submit to tragic art because of its intermittent revelations, the glimpses it offers of that which in life we fear most and are yet compelled to see—the fully disclosed self.

Cinema has elicited considerable psychocritical/semiotic discourse because its intermittent modes of disclosure seem also to reveal fundamental aspects of spectatorship, those that identify the viewer as a psychological subject. The desire to see that which in *on* view, as well as that which is hidden *from* view, is central to the constructs of voyeurism and the scopic drive (*Schaulust*) developed by Freud and redefined by Lacan in his problematic of the gaze.[2] The movies satisfy the appetite for the visual, gripping us with frames that hold all the seen within their borders. Cinema draws the viewer's sight to its state of display; it also transmits representations as a function of shadows and near-invisibility. Intimacies, confidences, and solitary secrets, radically transformed by the magnified displays of the cinema, belong to the medium's most efficient registers of affect. Spurred by a fundamental desire to see, enticed by the relentless demonstrations of the cinematic field, the viewer gains access to the concealed, to the privileged moments and places where merely *seeing* is an emphatic gesture.

The erotic, voyeuristic privacy of the viewing situation at the movies has been evoked by Barthes ("In the darkness of the movie theatre . . . lies the very fascination of the film [whatever film]").[3] Metz declares that "cinema practice is only possible through the perceptual passions," one of which is "the desire to see (= scopic drive, scopophilia, voyeurism)."[4] Exploiting the familiar model, the child's unauthorized witnessing of the parental couple's sexual embrace, Metz focuses on the voyeurism of spectatorship ("In this respect the cinematic signifier is Oedipal in type")[5] and on cinema's fetishistic nature. The fetish impedes, masks, precedes the gaze of the child who has seen too much; cinematic representation becomes fetishized through the energy of its altering visualizations, stimulating our incessant visual curiosity through the maskings and unmaskings of its framing. If these processes are indeed fetishized, we come to care as much about *how* we see as about *what* we see.

The ability of a film to move its audience is to some degree lodged in the medium's acknowledgment of our anxiety about seeing too much or too little. The implicitly whole image is modified in patterns that call attention to a dynamics of disclosure and concealment, and make the viewer part of that dynamics. Our response is controlled by the variable density of visual data and the changing rhythm of its presentation. We are caught in the inflections of the promise of sight and in the fluctuating degrees of display so precisely held by the screen's exterior frame. Barthes finds that "the pleasure of the text" is generated by precisely these provocations:

> it is intermittence, as psychoanalysis has so rightly stated, which is erotic; the intermittence of skin flashing between two articles of clothing (trousers and sweater), between two edges (the open-necked shirt, the glove and the sleeve); it is this flash itself which seduces, or rather: the staging of an appearance-as-disappearance.[6]

For yet another Frenchman, Méliès, at the dawn of cinema history, the movies were just such an erotic, disquieting, spectacular disappearing act.[7]

The image is the lure, the goal, the boon for our eyes in this play of vision. It has a meaning all its own, one often masked by whatever coded, symbolic, expressionistic meaning it may also have. These latter blind us to the value of sheer imageness, something akin to Barthes's third, obtuse meaning. "I believe that the obtuse meaning carries a certain *emotion*. . . . it is an emotion which simply *designates* what one loves, what one wants to defend: an emotion-value, an evaluation."[8] The emotion produced by such vision belongs to that part of our private beings impermeable to articulation, to subsequent rendering. It simply is. This is the meaning of pure display, proffered as surface to sensation. "The obtuse meaning is a signifier without a signified, hence the difficulty in naming it. My reading remains suspended between the image and its description, between definition and approximation."[9] For Barthes, the image of "emotion-value" was a still of *Ivan the Terrible*; for us, it may be a landscape, a costume, a face, anything that is on display. We are finally moved because we see at all.

In the pages that follow I will examine how sight and display are engaged in an affective game of hide and seek by various states and processes of the movies: (1) the virtuality of disclosure in a field whose elements can be seen from different points of view and can turn in our field of vision; (2) the dynamics of scrutiny created among in-frame perceivers, out-of-frame perceivers, and ourselves; (3) the degree of disclosure as a function of scale (altered through magnification and distancing of the objects) and texture (qualified by lighting); (4) the iconic familiarity of the face of the screen performer and the affectivity of its potential for alteration; (5) the eyes of the screen performer as a model of affective response within the fiction; (6) the disclosive value of dissimulating and sublimating codes of manner and dress.

The Dark Side of the Image

One of the ways that cinema overcomes the manifest superficiality of its all too accessible field is through its own mobility and the mobility of the elements, animate and inanimate, within the field. To enable us to see behind the surface of what is photographed requires a conscious retrieval of the hidden side through cutting or tracking around the object, or, as so many directors have discovered, through the inclusion of a mirror that reflects the part of the image that is not frontal to the camera. This aspect of the image's reverse is not unrelated to the virtuality of off-screen absence that is at the core of the suturing effect. Oudart writes of the necessity of exchange between on- and off-screen space to articulate "the ideal chain of a sutured discourse."[10] In this articulation the surface of the screen image becomes a virtual screen for that which we are about to see, will perhaps see, are desperate to see, are desperate to avoid seeing, have seen, and wish or wish not to see again. Oudart uses "tragic," an affective qualification, to describe the oscillatory characteristics of the sutured reading. He speaks of "the tragic and unstable nature of the image, a totality synchronically elusive, made of structurally opposite and mutually eclipsing elements. The cinema is characterized by an antinomy of reading and *jouissance*, because the space in fact always abolishes the object, and the depth of field makes the bodies inscribed within it vanish."[11] In this eclipsing play the aura of "the other side" of the image gives a pulse to the viewing experience precisely because it is denied us. By calling it into play through staging or cutting, the filmmaker amplifies the pulse, connecting the "beat" of seeing to the intermittent disclosure of the camera and involving us in the possibilities of the doubled field.

The visual rhythmics of this doubling is emblemized by the turning figure of a waltzing couple, in which each partner's face is alternately disclosed to the camera. In Anatole Litvak's *Mayerling*, during a grand ball, Rudolph (Charles Boyer) suggests to Marie (Danielle Darrieux) that their only freedom is in death. The audience is engaged in the dance and the revelation of the characters' private truth through the rhythm of two sets of eyes that see more and more with each revolution. The waltz that ostensibly unites the dancing couple is a sexual/social embrace sanctioned by the very protocol of the Imperial Court that prohibits their love. The waltz executed for the camera unveils the secret of love-death in a design of magnified and sequential disclosure. *Mayerling*, a "romantic" film that enjoyed enormous success at its release, is distinguished less for its thematic conflict of private and public life than for the way that familiar conflict is rendered in the surface of images. The waltz demonstrates that to "see it all" means to see death. This fatality of surface is visualized in a previous scene where Rudolph, frantically attempting to forget Marie, swirls at the center of an orgy only to confront his own image in a mirror. His passion for Marie cannot be hidden from his own eyes, and, in a prefiguration of the

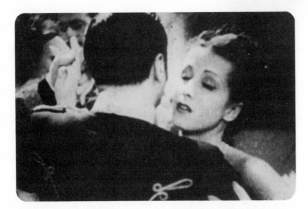

film's climax, he shoots his reflection. Images can indeed show too much.

Under Painful Scrutiny

The privacy of Rudolph and Marie, exhibited by the camera and hidden from the other dancers at the ball, is a model for the ironic pathos produced by futile efforts of concealment within cinema's ineluctable demonstrativeness. When such concealments are opposed to figures who represent authority and society—mothers, fathers, priests—the pathos strikes deeply at our own sense of identity. We squirm with the protagonists who fear being seen and judged incorrectly, who are desperate to hide from uninformed scrutiny. For fiction's sake, what they reveal to the camera cannot be revealed to the critical presence within the frame. Again, it is the alternation of concealment and disclosure that gives such circumstances their affective force.

These opposing standards of visual knowledge painfully stretch the heroine's sense of self in Mervyn Le Roy's *Waterloo Bridge*. Myra (Vivien Leigh), attempting to keep the news of the death of her fiancé, Roy (Robert Taylor), from her prospective mother-in-law (Lucile Watson), faints from the exertions of her subterfuge. Myra submits to polar vantage points—that of the all-knowing camera and that of Roy's prejudiced and uninformed mother. The viewer is caught in this simultaneity of revelation and dissimulation. The dramatic irony basic to theatrical processes is transformed by the amplificatory display of cinema where knowledge often is drawn from aspects of the visible accessible only through the camera's mediation. Myra can be seen better by the camera and the viewer because of their privileged point of view and mobility than she can by any eyes enclosed with her in the fiction. Embarrassment is added to this pattern of visual discrepancy when Myra, having turned to prostitution, shows herself to the the arriving servicemen at Waterloo Station. All but one of them see her as clearly as we do. Roy, mistakenly reported dead, unexpectedly appears and, blinded by love, is unable to read the signs that Myra has not the courage to

interpret for him. She is trapped between our eyes and Roy's, simultaneously revealed and hidden and therefore able to transmit the fullness of anxiety about her subterfuge while she is fully on view. This quality of viewing is distinct from that afforded the audience of live theater. The stage places coactors in a realm in which their perception of each other is superior to that of any spectator. The movie camera challenges that superiority. Through its mobility and its magnifications, objects can be perceived in greater detail and more clearly on the screen than in a nonphotographic reality or through the stylistics of stage representation. The pathos of Myra's situation is compounded by its medium of presentation; her concealment trembles inside of frames that repeatedly show that showing is all.

This figuration is as pervasive in cinematic fictions of sentiment as it is specifically in the films of Mervyn Le Roy. Eclectic to what might seem a fault, Le Roy's work ranged from Warner's *Gold Diggers of 1933* to MGM's martyred Christians in *Quo Vadis?* (1951) via the adventures of *Anthony Adverse* (1939), to the steadfastness of *Madame Curie* (1943) and a bland, technicolored version of *Little Women* (1949). His most memorable films are marked by images of pathetic display—Paula (Greer Garson) gallantly playing the role of secretary to her amnesiac husband Charles (Ronald Colman) in *Random Harvest* (1941); the schizophrenic (Jean Simmons) thinking herself beautiful in vulgar makeup and a grotesquely oversized evening gown in *Home before Dark* (1958); the mother (Rosalind Russell) of *Gypsy* (1962), body splayed, voice raucous, stripping to her unsightly ambition. And even if the blackout climax of *I Am a Fugitive from a Chain Gang* (1932) was caused by a providential power failure during shooting, it remains a fitting climax to a film whose hero (Paul Muni) must avoid recognition. As demonstrated by the last shot, the only way to do that on film is to recede into blackness at the depth of the frame. For the chain gang fugitive, for Myra in *Waterloo Bridge*, for countless characters whose identities are inflected and jeopardized by the glare of exposure, to be seen is the cause of intolerable pain. And the dark safety of our spectatorship is an ironic and critical vantage point for seeing what it means to be seen. Our invisibility vis-à-vis the fiction's revelation is made sensitive as cinema probes the implications of display in each of its concealments. Shadows are there to be banished, corners to be turned, reverse angle shots to be seen straight on. As surely as mastershot is followed by medium shot and close-up, we will bore in upon the cinematic object as relentlessly as the camera does, plumbing the surfaces it offers us as its essential nature.

The Scope of Feeling
In the fluctuating scale of presentation within the fixed screen ratio of a given film, the close-up is often the final element in a series of magnifications leading toward intimacy.[12] Dominant in the affective style of George Stevens's *A Place in the Sun*, the close-up is posited as a sign of observation so penetrating that the characters themselves seem to be aware of its power. No sooner does Angela (Elizabeth Taylor) confess her love to George (Montgomery Clift)

59

than she exclaims in panic that people are looking at them. The only observer who, in fact, has taken notice is the camera, but it has done so through emphatic close-ups that explicitly clash with the implied and occasionally glimpsed presence of other couples on the dance floor. *A Place in the Sun* draws the viewer to the fiction's affect of display, where the hero's ambitions and his feelings coincide in the "sun" of the film's title, and where he is undone by a squalid, loveless affair consummated on a rainy night and by a drowning on a dark lake. The spectacular exhibition of George and Angela's love is accommodated by increasingly large close-ups of the face of Elizabeth Taylor, in tension between adolescence and young womanhood, and Montgomery Clift's introspective glamour. When the declarations of love are resumed on the veranda, just after Angela cries out her fear of being seen, the stars' faces literally become too big for the frame. Stevens is here suggesting that the scope of the camera's grasp of surface, through these magnifying close-ups, is equivalent to the sentiments of the characters.[13] Film appropriates their privacy, making viewers their accomplices. We share their feelings because we see more of them than does anyone else in the fiction, sometimes more than they themselves do.

Other kinds of magnification tune an audience to a more public pathos, where the expanse of field seems to yield a proportionately expansive affect. This is the ratio operant in John Ford's films, in which the horizon lines challenge our eyes to encompass their breadth and in doing so relate the magnitude of display to the emotional resonance of the displayed—the wagon train, perilously stretching itself through the wilderness, the heroic cavalry line, a horseman matching the valor of his solitude to the monumentality of the director's preferred valley. In *Gone with the Wind* the death of the Old South is shown in dimensions and modes apt for a sense of mythic rather than personal loss. Spectacular feelings are made part of the film's epic scope. While Scarlett (Vivien Leigh) walks through the Atlanta railroad yard, on which lie the bodies of wounded and dying soldiers, the camera pulls up and away in a celebrated crane shot (a shot so long that a construction crane had to be used). The effect of the increasing distance from the figures is an amplitude suggestive of the epic, an accumulation of anguish within the framed field that demonstrates how we can be moved by the more we see. The figure of Scarlett is a surrogate for us in this ever-expanding locus of pain. While we remain attached to the familiar character, we actually see more anguish the further we get from it. Here, the cinema's capacity to show is calibrated to move us through the motion of sight, a strictly timed revelation that builds from what we see to what we can scarcely believe we see.

Chiaroscuro lighting qualifies cinematic magnification through its denial of areas within the cinematic field; it supplies a sense of modeling, depth, and mood lacking in films that are too flatly lighted (in Leo McCarey's *An Affair to Remember*, 1957, technicolor and wide screen wash out and dissipate the affect so abundant in the shadows of his first version of that film, *Love Affair*, 1939, in black and white and conventional ratio); it accentuates the shadows within the frame that image our repressions and our anxiety about not wanting to see all that the frame can show us. The play of light and darkness is obviously apt for the concealments so much a part of emotional display. In John Ford's *Arrowsmith*, just after the death of the young doctor's first patient, Martin (Ronald Colman) and Leora (Helen Hayes) huddle in the darkness, avoiding the spare shaft of light in the frame, a scheme that prefigures the staging of Leora's own death later in the film. In *The Grapes of Wrath* Ma Joad sacrifices her keepsakes in the dark stillness of the home she is about to abandon. Tom Joad's farewell to his mother is shrouded by night. Hew and his dying father embrace in the almost total blackness of the mine in *How Green Was My Valley*. William Wyler captures Heathcliff's anguished flight after overhearing Cathy's description of his boorishness in the obscurity of a vestibule intermittently illuminated by flashes of lightning. Even MGM, celebrated in the thirties for its "well-lighted" sets, exploits "shades" of feeling in one of the most memorable sequences of Rouben Mamoulian's *Queen Christina*, where Christina (Greta Garbo), trying to fondle the shape of her sentiments, explores the shadows and the surfaces of her love nest.

The night's special light and even more special shadows serve lovers as grand as Marie Walewska (Greta Garbo) and Napoleon (Charles Boyer) on a wintry terrace in Clarence Brown's *Conquest* and middle-class Laura (Celia Johnson) and Alec (Trevor Howard) in the gloomy railroad depot of David Lean's *Brief Encounter*. All that is impermanent and intangible in feeling is respected by light in jeopardy of darkness, light that trembles at the menace of darkness just as feeling trembles at the threat of blatant articulation. One of our anxieties about revelation is our sense that in its apparent completeness it is false to the complexities it seeks to articulate. The double standard of chiaroscuro accommodates feelings in the same way that words and silence do—in flux between virtuality and imperfect, incomplete expression. Not only are we afraid to see/hear all—we know that to do so is to risk denaturing the very experience that moves us.

Examples of expressive, affective chiaroscuro can be found in all film genres, all periods of film history, and are as much a function of the medium itself as of the medium's stylistics. As long as films were "black and white" their very existence hinged on our perception of shades on the gray scale. Since color films have become the rule rather than the exception, some filmmakers have explored monochromatics to achieve the control possible with black and white cinematography. The deep shadows of Francis Ford Coppola's *The Godfather* (1972) and *The Godfather, Part II* (1974) suggest the thirties matrix for the gangster film, with its nocturnal cityscapes and claustrophobic interiors for hiding and "holing up." The extraordinary candelit scenes of Stanley Kubrick's *Barry Lyndon* (1975) enhance the film's period cachet and make us aware of the virtuosity of its photography and its new technology. *The Godfather*, *Barry Lyndon*, and other important films of our becolored era hark back to a cinema whose screen held as much darkness as it did light, if not more, and whose light-streaked fields engaged us in processes of search and discovery.

The Mask and the Breach
The cinema's most familiar locus for emotional expression is the performer's face, a surface whose expressivity seems to echo that of the medium itself. The shadows of chiaroscuro mold the face, diminish its imperfections, bring out its formal elements and therefore its memorability. The magnifications of cinematic display of

faces join our being too close for comfort to our sense of seeing too clearly, and consequently compel us to interpret what we see. In William Wyler's *Dead End* Francey (Claire Trevor) turns her face to the light, a gesture of disclosure that far surpasses the scope of confession allowed the actress by the character's limited verbal competence and a script bound by the prudish standards of the

Production Code. That slight turn of the face shows Babyface Martin (Humphrey Bogart) what he has been loathe to see—that Francey is a prostitute. The blatancy of exposure makes him see what we already know. It is the blatancy that moves us. Light is not meant to show Claire Trevor's face with such cruelty, but because it does, it itself is read as a specifically coded sign. I do not mean to suggest that the acting is inadequate to the situation. (Here, as in Ford's *Stagecoach*, Claire Trevor proves her aptness at playing the embarrassed prostitute.)[14] Yet in *Dead End* the revelations made by words and gestures gain their affective power from the strategies of modulated visual display that involve us first in knowledge (*we* always know that she is a prostitute), then in feelings about that knowledge (we respond to the response of both Babyface and Francey that is a function of light).

A similar pattern of light-projected truth was used by Elia Kazan in the stage version of *A Streetcar Named Desire* and in the film when Mitch (Karl Malden) examines Blanche's (Vivien Leigh's) face with the light of a naked bulb to verify allegations about her "shady" past. Previous to this shattering exposure Blanche struggles to maintain a glamorous image of herself through those movie star conventions meant to display to advantage—costumes, make-up, a soft, flattering light. She reminds us of the legendary search for the good angle, the good profile, we frequently see dramatized in films about Hollywood. And it is so often in the refusal of the "good" angle and the most flattering display that films move us.

Whatever the angle or pattern of its display, the face is the field in

which most of cinema's significant emotional activity takes place.
The strategies of this activity need not be as brutally exposing as
Streetcar's naked light bulb to achieve their harrowing effect. In Leo
McCarey's *Make Way for Tomorrow* merely a succession of conventionally framed shots, first of an old woman's back and then of
her face, is sufficient to involve us in an affect compounded of guilt
and embarrassment at seeing that face, the face of the mother we
can never love enough. A phone call between Lucy (Beulah Bondi)
and Bart (Victor Moore) an old couple forced to live in separate
cities when they lose their own home, interrupts their daughter-in-
law's bridge class. During the first part of the conversation, her back
turned to the camera and the uncomforable bridge players, Lucy
voices her love, her loneliness, and her anxiety about her husband's
health. Then we see her face, and the guilt on the faces of our
in-frame surrogates. The back/front order of shots, first submitting
us to the sound of the actress's voice and the decorum and pride so
painfully borne on the slope of her shoulders, then "facing" us with
face, engages the dramatic pretext in a mode of display. We pay
dearly in affect for our spectatorship, for seeing even more than
those squirming bridge players.

The display of face has a different resonance when the face is that
of a star, a face not only magnified through projection and shaped
by the force of light and frame, but seen and reseen in a succession
of roles, at the center of a series of fictional contexts. And while
such a face is cherished for its pristine aspect and iconic familiarity,
it is forever liable to alteration through the exterior imposition of
light and the more shocking changes wrought by the performer him-
or herself. We identify a film star through a mask of persona that
weds physical presence and personality. When that persona is inflected, it is as if the mask were loosened, showing us what it has
previously hidden. The persona as display is an appearance whose
power, eternalized by the processes of film and institutionalized by
its aesthetics, its marketing, and its history, is ripe for challenge by
the performer who projects it. This is one of the cinema's richest
paradoxes. The face that identifies the movie star shows us less the
more we see it. Acquiring familiarity through a succession of films,
it becomes an increasingly coherent and readable visual sign, the
image of the star's unchanging persona.

Some of the cinema's "symbolic" faces have, of course, specific
emotional value. Sylvia Sidney's tear-filled eyes, high cheekbones,
and pointed chin *mean* proletarian misery in the thirites; the faces of
Jean Gabin and Humphrey Bogart are Gallic and American versions of existential despair. When Greer Garson plays Mrs. Miniver, she emblemizes the features of the courageous, human, sensible, sensitive middle-class woman. A prototypical emotional icon,

65

the face of Lillian Gish is significantly isolated in vignettes that are keepsakes of suffering, cinematic mementos, ever-ready triggers of sentimental response.

But even Sylvia Sidney can smile. The cinema adds mobility to the mask it creates. Lillian Gish, so often terrorized, can turn aggressive, as she so splendidly demonstrates in Griffith's *Orphans of the Storm*. The tears of Jean Gabin in *Le jour se lève* and Bogart's tenderness in *The African Queen* are precious because they violate the actors' masks and call forth unexpected aspects of display. We are moved by the vulnerability of the performer's persona. The star's mask is no less liable to slippage than are comic or tragic masks. And it is not less masklike for its human aspects and its individuality. We come to know Garbo's face because it has been so frequently exhibited to us. We possess it as we do a painting we remember, and we become aware of that possession in the reseeing. The medium captures the surface of the face in serial familiarity, in versions distinct from each other in distinct times, dramatic contexts, decors, costumes, and hairdos, yet so alike as to be affirmations of the singleness of the face that seems to defy expression. Yet it is precisely the expression, qualifying the matrix, that shocks us and moves us through its revelations. Elsewhere I referred to a shot in Cukor's *Camille* representative of the impact of expression on the Garbo persona, where the slightest alteration of her well-known features is a sign of affect.[15] This degree of revelation is possible only because the camera is able to magnify the variation of the face/form it has previously fixed through its relentless scrutiny. After deciding she must give up her lover, Marguerite assumes a false gaiety, pretending boredom with her country idyll. Armand (Robert Taylor) is dismayed and confused by her ironic manner. She continues to tease him but then, with unnerving suddenness, pulls her lover to her while showing her grief to the lens. The face that is familiar to us in its near-expressionless harmony briefly opens itself to display what even tragic masks hide—utter vulnerability. This vulnerability becomes momentarily accessible in a field whose mere exhibition is usually sufficient to our specular needs. It is because Garbo's mask seems perpetually on view that this variant becomes privileged.

Garbo's mask slips throughout her films, intermittently showing us intimacies we thought we were never meant to see. The altered mask is perceived not because we relate it to other familiar altered masks but because it is a breach of the familiar. Cinema, an art that initiates us into its rites of presentation and makes us expert at assimilating its codes, challenges that expertise when it disarranges its artfully composed surfaces. The altered mask and the unveiling demonstrate how the usual modes of cinematic display are unable to account for certain phenomena. The emphatic conventions and

techniques of the movies move us when they admit the inadequacy
of their norms. The breaches are ironic to the surfaces they rend.
Gabin's tears and Bogart's yielding, little-boy glances are finally the
exceptions that justify the rules, signs in a process of detachment
from their codes and whose dynamics engage us in similar detach-
ments—from the comfort of our assumptions about normative behavior and from the visual mediocrity of everyday experience. On
such occasions it is as if we accidentally came upon a half-open door
and, in spite of ourselves, saw with terrible clarity what the door
should have hidden. The unguarded expression of our parents'
sexuality, their mortality, their hatred, or merely their separateness
from us are models for the unintentional revelations made by our

husbands, wives, friends, lovers, and children. Overheard and overseen, they tempt us with a knowledge that moves us closer to self-knowledge—too close for comfort. Drawn to the peepholes of experience by our voyeuristic curiousity, we strain back from their uncensored, half-glimpsed, fugitive revelations.

The Eyes of the Beholder

Film takes account of these revelations when it displays, in addition to the object seen, the process of sight itself. This is, of course, captured in the eyes of the performer, a reliable locus for expressivity and affect. Photographed in response, the eyes engage us in a specular activity that invites us to attain their standard of acuity, a "deep" sight that measures depth of feeling. The eyes on screen that register an emotional response are cues for the emotional response of the viewer. Other visual/dramatic media, deprived of the magnifying and kinetic power of close-ups, cannot capture the urgent processes of a performer's sight. The enormous eyes on the screen intimate that even their surfaces can be penetrated as they, mirrors of the character's feelings, penetrate the dramatic and emotional fiction they scrutinize.

In situations and configurations of furtiveness the very eyes that attempt to see all are also the surfaces that hide all. Double mirrors that face inward and outward, they catch the concealed and the displayed in simultaneity. I know of no richer example of this pattern than in David Lean's *Brief Encounter*, where Celia Johnson's face, distinguished by her enormous eyes, is featured in almost every shot. The framing device for Laura's remembrance of her affair with Alec is a close-up of the actress, her eyes wide open as if she were staring at memory. During the course of this re-

trospective narrative there is an episode during which she fantasizes scenes from a romantic life with Alec (in a box at the opera, on a tropical beach, etc.) by literally projecting them from her eyes onto her own reflection in the window of her train compartment. Laura's eyes and her obsessively displayed face are ironic yet pathetic signs in a film about a clandestine love affair.

The characteristic patness of Noel Coward's dramatic strategies favors this pathos of sight. The lovers, seen clearly only by each other, meet when Alec extracts a bit of cinder from Laura's eye. This intimacy of strangers is more than a ploy to bring the protagonists together. It establishes the relationship between pain and sight in a series of contexts whose tension is provided by the repression of visual data. Alec and Laura must not be seen "in love." In fact, anguished by the sight of their love, they look at each other with compassion. Near the end of the film Alec, ever the good doctor, says to Laura that "a sudden break now, however brave and admirable, would be too cruel. We can't do such violence to our hearts and minds." And a moment later he asks her forgiveness "for everything—for having met you in the first place—for taking the piece of grit out of your eye—for loving you—for bringing you such misery."[16] The solicitude and decorum suggested by his first statement allow him and us to perceive the logic of the second, expressive of the connections between the whole of their situation, the figurative force of its initial circumstances, and its sentimental and moral implications. If Laura had not been so wide-eyed perhaps that piece of grit would not have found its way to torment her. Her eyes opened by love, and shown to us repeatedly through the film, mock her need to hide.

Indiscretions

In *Brief Encounter* every concealment becomes an act of display. Furtively meeting in a borrowed apartment, the lovers hear the unexpected arrival of Alec's friend, and Laura, in her hasty retreat down the backstairs, leaves behind her scarf. The leer and the insinuations of the "friend" do not, of course, correspond to our attitude toward Laura and Alec, but they do account for why they hide. Laura runs from her fear of disclosure and then, seated on a bench, diminished in the depth of the frame by the size of a war memorial that looms in the foreground, finds comfort in distance from the lens in an image that releases her from its threatening grip. But there is no true safety in cinematic distance. During a previous sequence, in the underground passage that connects their separate platforms, a medium close-up of Laura and Alec's kiss is interrupted by a prudish cut to a long shot. Prompted by the sound of footsteps, the sudden long shot is a gesture of embarrassment that accentuates the lovers' display. Such gestures connect the explicit

69

dramatic pretext of *Brief Encounter* to the film's visual structure. It is from this sort of connection, rather than from the familiar context of adultery, that the film derives its capacity to move us. Devices designed to dissimulate emotional states heighten cinema's demonstrations. Han Suyin (Jennifer Jones), seen in extreme long shot on her "high and windy hill" (Henry King, *Love Is a Many Splendored Thing*), turns her grief away from the lens and thereby fills all the intervening space with her concealed/revealed emotion. In Lean's *This Happy Breed* the emptiness of a lower middle-class back parlor is sufficient to the grief of a silent couple. The camera, through its obliquity and measured movement, becomes an accomplice of characters who *express* their emotions by seeming to *repress* them. The mechanics of display—the empty room, observed and slanted by the camera, the pulling back, the cut to a medium close-up of the couple followed by a rapid backtracking away from them—involve us in a dynamics of sight that decorum cannot hide. The camera's movements penetrate sorrow by charting its presence through a shifting pattern of approach and retreat. In this way, the camera, through its privilege of access and its observing presence, can assert the emotion of our sight even when the style demanded by the fiction's content is ostensibly one of "understatement." Mise-en-scène and acting style conspire with the camera to transmute the conventions of concealment into schemes of emotional display.

Transparent Uniforms

The modes of restraint and concealing rituals of the religious life are themselves designs of display; their tense decorum becomes an analogy for emotional revelation. In Fred Zinnemann's *The Nun's Story* everything from the humdrum activities of daily life to complex moral and spiritual states are sublimated by the decorum of a strict religious order. Near the end of the film the absolute stillness of Sister Luke's figure conveys what it means to her to renounce her vows. The scene begins as a conversation between Sister Luke and

her beloved Mother Superior (Edith Evans). They are seated on a bench in front of long, framing panes of glass. The older nun, finally convinced that Sister Luke cannot be dissuaded from her decision, rises, crosses in front of the camera, and walks out of the frame while the camera slowly tracks back. Sister Luke's motionless figure recedes. The strength of the affective link between the nuns cannot be made overt through a physical gesture, nor can the sense of renunciation be fully manifested by a character who has spent years learning how to hide her feelings. Both of these sentiments are, however, fully accounted for by a frame that first links and then separates the figures and a camera slowly moving away from a nun whose style prevents her from showing what it means to stay where she is and what it costs to leave.

Similar sublimatory concealments supply a different register of affect in a very popular sentimental film, Leo McCarey's *The Bells of St. Mary's*. Every viewer knew that there *had to be* a love interest in a film co-starring Bing Crosby (as Father O'Malley) and Ingrid Bergman (as Sister Benedict), and this expectation was adequate to satisfy many of the audience's emotional needs. Although there is no overt suggestion of romantic yearnings in either performance, the good Catholic wife (Bea Arthur) in *Lovers and Other Strangers* declares the Crosby-Bergman relationship to be the ideal romance. How wonderful it is to express love by never referring to it! *The Bells of St. Mary's* exposes the stars' personas through the repression (in fact the omission) of the rhetoric appropriate to love stories. Yet director, stars, and audience are aware of the subversive conventions of religious uniforms and hierarchies, and affirm that awareness when, in the film's final scene, Father O'Malley tells Sister Benedict that she is being sent away to recover from tuberculosis rather than as punishment for some imagined insubordination. Ingrid Bergman's cowl does not begin to conceal the full smile of sexual/romantic gratification familiar to the audiences of *Intermezzo*, *For Whom the Bell Tolls*, and *Casablanca*, proving that in films, if you wear the right uniform, you can show anything.

This lesson is taught consistently by John Ford in whose cavalry films the sense of a character's rank and duty, shown by the uniform he wears, often provides both the context and the tension for the expression of feelings—toward wife, children, peers, or "men." The audience watching a Ford film knows "the place" of the characters within the film just as well as the characters do themselves, and that place, while often implying a decorum that inhibits certain kinds of emotional manifestation, also *places* feeling within the frame, securely exhibiting it in the virtuality of its concealment. Big hearts, throbbing with love and filled with responsibility, beat beneath those cavalry uniforms.

For Appearance's Sake

In King Vidor's *Stella Dallas* (1937) modes of display constitute the film's dramatic pretext. Its script explicitly calls for situations in which identity is judged and acquires moral value through outward appearances. The codes of dress and manners establish a rigid standard of suitability and fitness that is worked out according to the logical expectations of the bourgeois ethic that shapes the codes. Yet the processes of film are not completely hospitable to those expectations. The display/concealment pattern of *Stella Dallas* undermines the fiction's ostensible values. The film finally demonstrates how feeling transcends appearance through images critical of conventional standards of appearance. The visual energy of Vidor's films is often expressed through signs of excess that challenge "normal" modes of behavior: *The Big Parade* (1925), where John Gilbert madly gesticulates his passion to Renée Adorée, who is hanging onto a chain dangling from his departing truck; the musical abandon of *Hallelujah* (1929); Dolores Del Rio and Joel McCrea kissing while hanging in wooden frames before they are to be sacrificed, in *Bird of Paradise* (1932); Bette Davis's fatal attempt to escape from small-town goody-goodness in *Beyond the Forest* (1949); Charlton Heston and Jennifer Jones driving a convertible into the waves in *Ruby Gentry* (1952). In Vidor's work conventional patterns and conventional ways of perceiving beauty are there for the disrupting.

Throughout *Stella Dallas* both the characters and the audience are forced to acknowledge Stella in spite of her appearance. The strategies of display that are intrinsic to the medium's theatricality and its demonstrativeness are signs of transparency, veils that invite us to peer through them. Vidor draws us to the Stella who is perceived only through love and the camera.

Stella's transformation allows us to gauge the power of appearance in the film. First seen as a young girl on the make, Stella passes through stages of display meant to signify vulgarity in a system of upper middle-class refinement. Since she is the standard of true feeling in the film, her appearance has an ironic effect on "good taste," on what appearance is indeed supposed to mean. Vidor's challenge to "face value" is illustrated in two scenes near the end of the film. In the first, by using a mode of display that we have learned to interpret, Stella (Barbara Stanwyck) succeeds in forcing her daughter Laurel (Anne Shirley) to reject her for a life of money and opportunity. Laurel witnesses a full staging of vulgarity—Stella reading a lurid magazine, puffing on a cigarette, a phonograph blaring "Some of These Days." We suffer acute embarrassment at seeing the good mother having to play the bad mother. Stella's feigned raunchiness is a fundamental display of what she is concealing. Her mode of rejection, in the pain we know it costs her, is a measure of how much she loves her daughter.[17]

Of course, all that love is shown to the camera. At the film's climax, Stella, a spectator to the drama of her maternity, is released from the need to keep up any kind of appearance. On a rainy night, standing in a street in front of a large window, wearing a floppy hat and a shapeless coat (after a film full of flounces and fur pieces), she watches her daughter's wedding to a rich young man, an event that is taking place because she is absent from it. The spatial separation between the mother and the object of her love is enhanced by the intervening window and fence, and dramatized by a policeman who urges the onlookers to move on. Stella is a mediating presence in the spectacle of the wedding, a ritual that demonstrates the affective power of appearance and decorum (people are supposed to cry at weddings). She is also a spectacle in her own right when, shorn of her habitual appearance, she *shows* her feelings. And although this showing is indicated through emotional clichés—tears and a handkerchief literally held in the actress's teeth—its placement in the film guarantees our belief in its inwardness. As Stella smiles and

jauntily walks away from the window on which was projected her daughter's wedding (a surrogate screen), she becomes a model for our emotion in watching a motion picture. We have been brought to a sensitivity of sight as an analogy for a sensitivity of feeling as we follow Stella's appearance—first the primping girl trying to attract a man's attention, on display in front of a fence; then the woman whose vulgarity is an accusation against "good" taste; finally, at another fence, the mother who, invisible within the fiction, collects all our vision at her concealment.

4 Depth of Feeling

Here and *there* are necessary elements in the gauging of the depth implied by our spatial relationship to phenomena, the space between audience and spectacle, between conversants, between the reader and the pages of the book. In the specific case of cinema the magnitude of the spectacle is provided for by the medium's mechanics, the distance between screen and viewer, and the greater distance (in most cases) between screen and projector. These various distances are charged with our need to see and with the energy producing the images, forces that are deployed and that are amplified by the traversals: the image magnified in direct proportion to its distance from its source of projection, the viewer's sight caught somewhere between projector and screen, bridging the distance to the screen, obliterating that distance as illusion succumbs to the reality effect. Viewer identification with the screen image is in part a function of the distances through which such an effect occurs. These distances are depths, spaces that are filled and that resonate in front of and behind the illusory screen, invested with the sight of viewer and the light of projector, holding in its flatness the fiction of three-dimensionality produced by distance, projector, and eyes.

Jean-Louis Baudry likens the projector/screen viewer relationship to the topography of Plato's cave, a *dispositif* that Frank McConnell calls a "phenomenology of cinema."[1] Yet Platonic idealism does not seem especially applicable to the viewing of cinema, where the image (reproduction/reflection) on the screen is the ideal, not that which the screened image presumably reproduces or reflects. And paradoxically, that "ideal" image is more accessible to us than the strip of film that is the matrix for the projection. It also has more permanence than the reality surrounding us in life. Fleeting and distant from us, the image on the screen is also repeatable and therefore reaccessible to a degree that life is not.

Cinema's specific editing procedures have a further effect on our claim to its projections and our ability to grasp them. The duration of our access to images and the rapidity with which they are replaced by other images catch us in clearly definable rhythms that hold and withhold what the screen has to offer. The photographic realism of cinema seems to promise the comfort of what we recognize, and that very recognition becomes a source of affect when it is challenged by the displacements and alterations of cinematic editing. The wholeness of the image displayed in the frame is jeopardized by the fracturing of spatial and temporal continuity that is such a pervasive element of the film experience. This fracturing was dictated by the apparatus itself as soon as the duration of a film surpassed the capacity of the camera to hold enough film to record that duration. Material necessity, along with the selectivity of the camera's framings, required and invited filmmakers to cut up the world into bits of film, and then link those bits in fictions.

The emphatic intervention of editing in the continuity of the image distinguishes Griffith's earliest films. In Griffith's narrative the very manner of conveying information is charged with energy and emotion through the crosscutting of time and space; in his colossal, fugally structured *Intolerance* the narratives themselves are intercut, their stories, characters, and locales qualifying each other in a temporal, spatial, and emotional crescendo. Soviet theoreticians and filmmakers codified many of these editing practices in a theory of montage whose modes of spectator manipulation are rooted in psychological and linguistic models of affectivity. Boris Eikenbaum relates the viewer to montage through the concept of internal speech. He describes the connections between shots in terms of verbal articulations, the "construction of film-phrases and film periods."[2] And for Eisenstein, "the secret of the structure of montage was gradually revealed as a secret of *the structure of emotional speech*. For the very principle of montage, as is the entire individuality of its formation, is the substance of *an exact copy of the language of excited emotional speech.*"[3] More recently, Norman Holland has asserted that there are close analogies between filmic punctuation and the most familiar elements of Freudian vocabulary. "The formal devices of cinema act out for us ways of dealing with the unconscious content. Cutting acts like displacement, flashback like regression, superimposition or a dissolve like condensation, and so on."[4] This extends indentification beyond the viewer's conscious recognition of context and characters to include properties of rhetoric as well as those of content.

The processes of Eisensteinian montage force the viewer to create the film and, in doing so, to reach a state of ecstatically charged pathos. Eisenstein's ecstatic prose is similarly charged with the urgency of the transformations he finds at the epiphanic core of a medium so highly reflective of the emotions of its perceivers. This kind of montage creates its effects through the energy of its juxtapositions, through the sense of process conveyed by editing, a system of organization and puctuation that is as much, if not more, apparent to the viewer than that which is punctuated—the faces, bodies, places within the shots. Eisenstein is explicit in his preference for process over image:

> We understand a *moment* of culmination to mean those points in a process, those *instants* in which water becomes a new substance—steam, or ice-water, or pig-iron—steel. And if we could register psychologically the perceptions of water, steam, ice and steel at these critical *moments*—moments of *culmination* in the leap, this would tell us of something of pathos, of ecstasy![5]

Eisenstein establishes an analogy between the affectivity of film and our *temporal* apprehensions of solidity and three-dimensionality. When the rooms we occupy, our fellow occupants, and even the eternal mountains on the horizon yield to the unseizable moment, we know that our experience of the world is in perpetual evanescence.

Eisenstein stresses process in his description of the external manifestations of the pathetic response:

> Pathos shows its affect—when the spectator is compelled to jump from his seat. When he is compelled to collapse where he stands. When he is compelled to applaud, to cry out. When his eyes are compelled to shine with delight, before gushing tears of delight. . . . In brief—when the spectator is forced "to go out of himself."[6]

This activity reverberates inside the screened fiction and the viewer, is expressed by the fiction, is expressed between screen and viewer, and finally is *e*xpressed by the viewer. Precisely because of its violent iconography and editing, the Odessa Steps sequence from Eisenstein's *Potemkin* is exemplary of the pathetic process on film and, undoubtedly, of that process in the viewer. The cutting edges of swords and the cuts between the shots establish contact between the representation of sensational action and the way it is perceived. Here, and elsewhere in Eisenstein, editing fractures space, time, and objects only to reconstitute them through its own dynamics. We often see more of what things are *doing* than of what they *are*. This is true also of the crosscutting in Griffith's films. Although space is more "whole" in Griffith than in Eisenstein, it tends to gallop along with Klansmen as it does with Cossacks.

The Griffith-Eisenstein modes of analytic montage did not disappear from cinema with the coming of sound, but their use was greatly diminished, even in the films of Eisenstein. In American cinema the word "montage" was reserved for sequences whose pronounced editing procedures made audiences aware of frescoes of activity, of thematic configurations, of time passing, of journeys, of hallucinations and other states of altered consciousness. Montage was relegated to the category of special effects, along with matte shots and miniatures. In the decade of the thirties cinema developed its narrative voice and its narrative eye, through both practice and theory, in unfragmented space and in compositions whose durations on the screen allowed the viewer to establish connections and to peruse the visual field. The primary spokesperson for this "human-eye" aesthetic, André Bazin, found an ethical system in the presumably democratic realism of cinematic compositions that respected the integrity of space, thus anchoring film to its mimetic, reproductive nature. From films that bore the most pedestrian "studio" look to those stamped with the individuality of directors we now call auteurs (Renoir, Welles, and Wyler), this positing of film space, in its graspable coordinates, became the rule rather than the exception.[7]

What I now propose to examine is the affect generated by the "deep space" of cinema, a space less whole and democratic than Bazin suggests, a space that in its illusionistic power manipulates viewers' feelings with an insistence equal in force to the last-minute rescues of Griffith's spine-chilling juxtapositions and the smashed eyeglasses–rolling baby carriage of Eisenstein's logic of pathos.

Illusions of Depth

Pascal Bonitzer declares that the cinematic effect and the reality effect are connected in the deployments of deep-field stagings, and that reality is obtained through the viewer's disavowal of surface. This echoes both Mitry's notion of the ubiquitous viewer and Metz's situation of the cinema-viewing phenomenon somewhere between the dream state and the waking state, oscillating through daydream and partaking of various intensities of alertness. Bonitzer uses terminology familiar from Mannoni ("Je sais bien . . . mais quand même"), the "as if" of narrative that locates fiction and reality in a complementarity of viewer engagement and disavowal, "a problematic of reality," a reality inflected by the artifice of art and the art perceiver's intermittent awareness of that artifice.[8] These various accounts of a viewer's position vis-à-vis the screened fiction are linked by modes of passage that occur in depth. The oscillations between fiction and reality, between dream and wakefulness, reverberate in the distance between differing intensities of our viewing status and distinct gradations of consciousness. The spatial model of depth-of-field staging on film suggests a potential for such oscillation in purely visual terms, offering, through the medium of sight, a dynamics that sustains and perhaps even fosters both the processes of fiction and our attention to the fiction. Our varying degrees of awareness vary with the knowledge imparted by the fiction. Our sense of fiction's fictivity echoes within a depth that accommodates shifts and inflections of that awareness. We go in and out of the illusory depth on the screen with a dexterity not dissimilar from that demonstrated by the human figures who set and reset planes within the screen's flatness.

The juxtaposition of distinct foreground, midground, and background planes, a feature of deep-focus staging, is an optical phenomenon created by camera lenses and the projection of an image on a two-dimensional screen. In life, our eyes must compensate for the distance between near and far, a compensation that takes time. Although we cannot focus on everything in our field of vision at once, the impression that we actually do so is favored by the eyes' ability to make rapid focal adjustments. The deep field presented to us on the screen, despite its lifelike aspects, is accessible to us with an immediacy the same field does not possess in life. The screen can relate the near and the far to such a high degree of visual coherence that it generates fictions of clarity, completeness, and depth. Artfully contrived depth-of-field stagings acknowledge the authorial point of view, not the witnessing perspective. In fact, the refusal of the human eye-level point of view shot is a commonplace in most depth staging configurations. When the depth is stated in clearly defined enclosures, the low camera angle gives an impression of access to yet more information than would eye-level position because of the sharper inscription of a base upon which are posed full figures of objects and people.

William Wyler's *Dead End* is a useful illustration of the privileged camera eye whose point of view is often established in a gutter or hovering over the edge of a pier or perched on a crane specifically constructed for movie vision. This same system of camera privilege is apparent in those films of Wyler upon which Bazin comments—*The Little Foxes* and *The Best Years of Our Lives*.[9] The very multiplicity of angles employed in these films seems to deny the relative fixity of the human witness. It is a multiplicity whose power is increased by the closure of the "sets" in which it is generated. The depth created by these strategies of radical vantage often gives the impression that there is nothing beyond the *closed* set, whose integrity so favors depth, and whose depth becomes a model for all-seeing and for penetration. There is even some comfort in the knowledge that a sequence will *not* open out. If the space is limited, it can be wholly known, much as a fiction can be known. Limitation is a mode of knowing; the enclosure is all there to be explored. It is neither menaced by extrafictional space nor measured against space intolerant of the fiction's closure. It promotes our awareness of the emergence of data within the frame, data that belong to the frame at the inception of the shot and during the course of its viewing. That which the frame frames may indeed shift, but at the core of the

79

deep-field configuration is information that is, in effect, *known* by the frame (it was and is there during most of the shot), and therefore should be known by the viewer.

Our possession of this knowledge is inflected by the disposition of the elements resonating forward and back in the illusion of depth. This movement is minimized by analytic montage, where the traversals are made, either for us by the filmmaker through the juxtaposition of shots, or inside our heads as we connect shot A and shot B. We compose, as it were, through processes of association and analogy, separate bits of visual information. Pushed to the extreme, editing constitutes a near denial of vision. Indeed, one of Bazin's principal objections to analytic montage is that it forces viewers to internalize sight; deep-field staging, on the other hand, provides a fiction of penetration. The most important traversal of the deep field is that of our eyes. They tend to want to go into an image that apparently recedes toward its own boundaries.

These boundaries constitute a high degree of artifice in *The Best Years of Our Lives*. The lenses and the lights required to make the hallway in the Stephenson apartment look real in depth make Wyler and cinematographer Gregg Toland submit to limits that charge the space with a tension not dissimilar to the tension that sustains any fixed form. The search for realism through depth in Wyler's films becomes a search for a distinct style whose increasing focus catches us in a clarity ever more distant from what we recognize as reality. In *Best Years* the size of the sets demands a new code of lighting procedures and a virtuosic mise-en-scène. What results is a new shape for the fiction.

If the view of the deep-focus lens and its requisite stagings convey apparent reality through just as apparent contrivances and artifices (even in so touted an improvisational flow as Renoir's deployments in *The Rules of the Game*), what are we then to make of this reality? What is *our* take on it when that take is so distinct from that of the lens? What kind of possession does it imply for us, the final witnesses, the ultimate viewers of the illusions of depth? The lens, in fact, challenges the conventional ways through which we "take" or hold on to reality. We gain a heightened sense of possession of the filmic field when its processes appropriate reality through the patently false focus of depth-of-field staging.

The mechanics of these processes are manifest in a scene that occurs near the end of *Best Years*, the *plan-séquence* (a term used to describe a shot that has the complexity of a sequence) cited by Bazin to prove the "democracy" and "truth" of his cinematic ethic.[10] In the right foreground the amputee Homer (Harold Russell), using his hooks, is playing a piano duet with his uncle Butch (Hoagy Carmichael). At the upper far left segment of the frame, Fred

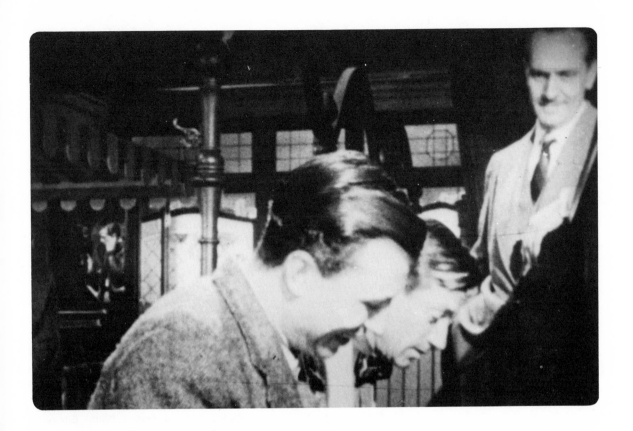

(Dana Andrews), in a phone conversation, is breaking off his relationship with Peggy (Teresa Wright). Al (Fredric March) stands near the piano, trying to divide his glance and his attention between the phone booth and the piano. Here, an analogy for the conventional shot/countershot pattern of editing is inscribed at midspace in Al, the viewing agent. The linear relationship between the observed and the observer is radically altered, catching oscillation in a model for simultaneity. That simultaneity, the full capture of the viewing field, is a function of depth. It implies that viewing can take in the "whole" of a set of data. In what he calls the "motionless and continuous whole" of easel painting, Jean-Louis Baudry locates cinema in the Western tradition of representational art, in the desire for "a total vision which corresponds to the idealist conception of the fullness and homogeneity of 'being.'"[11] It seems to me that the images of this totality in Wyler (and in the films of other directors characterized by their affinity for such configurations), precisely because of the density of the information they convey, limit our option of choosing between elements, of focusing on a dominant element, as Bazin would have it. We focus on focus, on

81

the art of focus, and on the image of the whole that is the staging per se. The juxtaposition of foreground and background, the piano lesson of an amputee, and a phone call of rupture break down our expectations of theatrical focus and involve us in the challenge of the whole image. We see an "all" that is in our purview only because the lens chooses that it be so by creating a fiction of depth. We are made to possess that depth through the camera's eye. It places us squarely in front of the cinematic illusion of a totally comprehensible, deep world.

The Fiction of Body

The enactments effected by whole human bodies in space favor the figuration of movement in depth, even in fields whose clarity is intermittent. The Astaire-Rogers dance duets, without relying on sharp focus to delineate the depth of the field, allow the virtuality of deep space to define the characters' movements. It is a space whose depth provides an *adequate* field for these performers, adequate to the scope of their dance figure, to their feelings for each other, and to the full deployment of their bodies. The integrity of so many of their numbers, filmed in very long takes, depends upon that integrity of space. It is that integrity, rather than the sharp detail in all planes of the field, that Bazin signals in his appraisal of the shot in Wyler's *The Little Foxes* during which Horace (Herbert Marshall) proceeds agonizingly from foreground to background in search of his heart medicine, while Regina (Bette Davis) remains murderously rooted to her seat.[12] The death to which Horace recedes is NOT in sharp focus, but it is there in the depth. As in so many films of the thirties that predate the Wyler-Welles-Toland systematic use of depth-of-field staging, the depth implicit in the frame is a controlling factor of the staging, one that endows action and character with a sense of fullness, a place of origin, a goal. When we become aware of the whole of the space of performance, it is not the sharpness of the background that is at stake, but, rather, the mere presence of the background. This illusion of wholeness endows the walking, the dancing, the glancing with what we identify as a depth of feeling, a charge of affect concordant with depth of enactment. Its planes and its suggestion of roundness allow us to account fully for performers, objects, space.

That accounting is not unrelated to mirror effects, effects understood in their most literal sense of optical reflection and ranging to the primary definition of the self in Lacan's formulation of the "mirror stage."[13] The mirror is a privileged analogy for the screen image just as it is a privileged item within screen images. Both surface and depth, it captures the eye as it captures an image. On screen, mirrors prolong the images that are reflected/projected by the cinematic apparatus; they catch our vision in a play of surface that transcends depth. As Metz asserts in "The Imaginary Signifier," the source of the cinematographic signifier is a chain effect of mirrors formed by the conditions of the apparatus—camera, projector, film, screen.[14] *Best Years* contains a shot that clearly expresses the dynamics of this linkage. Al, the morning after his return home from the war, compares his beard-stubbled face to a photograph of Fredric March's matinee-idol countenance, a comparison that is stepped up when it is caught in the bedroom mirror, a mirror that also catches the specular activity of Al, the lens, and the

audience.[15] When we add to this set of visual reverberations the extratextual echo of Fredric March, past and present, the shot becomes an especially emphatic figuration of roundness. This mirror play scores the value of the image's point of generation in the confusion of planes, as it posits one of the representations as genuine. But it also provides for an enactment of imperfect capture. (Various inflections of the suture principle account for this sense of imperfect capture, characterized by Stephen Heath as "the play of incompleteness-completion.")[16] The reality recorded on film is forever lost in the series of reflections that constitute the cinematic process. It is passed through time, through the recording procedures of the camera, and through the amplificatory/reproductory procedures of the projector to be received by our eyes in an irony of presence, permanently displaced from its origin, caught in mirrors whose very fidelity to that point of origin display their distance from it. In what plane is our sight situated when we acknowledge our distance from that origin? It is a plane uncomfortably distant from Bazin's eye-level, human point of view vision. The illusion of depth, reflected through cinema's filmed mirrors, and implicit in cinema's own mirror-like status, confounds our notion of planar locus, and shakes our faith that sight can "seize" phenomena at all.

One of the emotional peaks in the long homecoming sequence of *Best Years* places the mirror effect in just such a crisis of vision. The crisis is compounded by the mirror's attempt to capture fully the particular human body at the center of the configuration. The three servicemen, repeatedly framed in the window and the rearview

mirror of the taxicab conveying them to their respective homes, are made to see their own arrivals as problematic and incomplete. The first to descend from the cab, to arrive home, is Homer, the amputee. The depth of vision inscribed in the reflected gazes inside and finally outside the cab is lengthened by the deep space posed just beyond the window frame. Homer stands forlornly, separate from the comfort of the taxi and the true sight of his comrades, trapped in the depth of the lawn before his own front door, from whence his pitying and uncomprehending parents emerge, and the porch of the house of his sweetheart, Wilma (Cathy O'Donnell). Wilma runs through the intervening space, throws her arms around Homer, but will be unable to capture him until the fiction itself provides its own emotional resonance through the depth of its duration and its staging strategies. Homer, the image of the incom-

plete body, is unseizable until that image is detached from its status as surface, as a "flat" representation of the returning serviceman. Flatness, posited from the point of view of Homer himself, and from that of Fred and Al during their plane ride over the surface of the land and past stereotypical views of their hometown, will be transcended by the spatial and theatrical models for depth that are the sum of the film. Here, near the film's beginning, the depth of the mirror is the real point of departure for the homecoming that will take place at the film's end, when the eyes of the on-screen perceivers as well as our own have become so finely tuned to depth that they are intolerant of flatness.

Depth and Narrativity

Through its characteristically long shot durations and the resulting imaging of simultaneity and of protracted time, depth-of-field staging often has a countereffect on the linearity of conventional narrative progression. While much narrative information is conveyed through the deep-focus *plan-séquence*, both extended depth and extended duration often lessen a viewer's sense of succession in cinematic storytelling. The expectations created by the editing patterns characteristic of classic narrative film, the rhythms of shot/countershot, or long shot/medium shot/close-up, or even those produced by analytic montage, are more consonant with the sequential nature of the film strip and the movement through images from beginning to end. The deep *plan-séquence* seems to settle into a pool of space and time that modifies sequentiality and movement. Thus, in *Best Years* the viewer is not propelled forward by the thrust of the narrative, and the even more heavily plotted, "storied" films of Wyler such as *The Letter* and *The Little Foxes* are characterized by mood and stasis rather than bold dramatic thrust. I think it possible to argue that even Welles, whose theatrical instinct is never absent from *Citizen Kane*, is working toward a pictorial theater, arrested in the vivid clarity of the shots. Its deepest images tug against the narrative's rapid pace, prefiguring their function in the elegiac *The Magnificent Ambersons*.

The moments of crisis and transition that punctuate the narrative of *Best Years* submit to the depth and duration of shots, to the stasis of the film's ultimate homecomings. The dramatization of these homecomings—Homer's acceptance of Wilma's love, Fred's detachment from his wartime identity and marriage, Al's affirmation of humanistic values in the materialistic postwar society—is a pretext for our attention rather than its focus. We become more concerned with where the performers are and how they inhabit the surrounding, defining space than with what is about to unfold. I have chosen to concentrate on *Best Years* precisely because it so consistently subdues dramatic effect within its deeply engraved patterns of simultaneity. The narrative's 167 minute duration is shaped by a series of temporal and spatial depths plumbed by the patient mode of its initial sequences. There, a common dramatic/cinematic configuration of homecoming is so protracted in time and concentrated in space that it transcends conventional viewing expectations and creates a model for attention to time that barely passes and space that reverberates in consonance to that small degree of passage.

The temporality of prose fiction offers a strong analogy to the stasis of depth configurations. In the often cited opening of *Le père Goriot* Balzac concescrates spatial locus (the neighborhood, the exterior and interior of the Pension Vauquer) and physical portraiture (the descriptions of the *pensionnaires*) as the business of the novel. These are fictions of stasis discordant with the inexorable linearity of words strung together in unfolding patterns. In the novels of Balzac, as in the many nineteenth- and twentieth-century narratives of which they are exemplary, we are forced to *stop* and look more often than we are asked to witness the staging of action.

Through the cinema's deep-focus time/space appearance of fixity something like the nearly stopped time of description in novels, and the nearly stopped time of our station in front of paintings and statues and panoramas, is accommodated in the medium's inexorable flux.[17] This fixity serves a degree of linear narrativity inferior to that borne by the dialogue and action reported in prose or enacted on film. When such fixity becomes dominant in a film text, I think it is possible to speak of its strong pull against narrative. It is almost as if the ongoing story were on the verge of being engulfed in the inviting depth of prose or in visual stasis. Bazin prizes depth of field for its narrative efficiency, but the utterly manifest strategies of that efficiency tend to subsume what they convey. When the narrative information seems to be stuck in a deep field, we are made to possess placement rather than that which is placed. This depth is both a functional imaging of spatiality and a value unto itself. Its time offers us what appears to be the comfort of eternal access; we appropriate it as the camera appropriates it. Thus, deep space intermittently overpowers the narrative flow until the image is snatched away by the durational scheme of shot and film. The eventual loss of that depth often subjects us to an almost palpable deprivation.

The positing of the deep field in its integrity allows for the generation of meaning through merely the slightest inflection of the visual "known" within that field, an inflection that is a factor in all durational art. We reach out to a staging figure of simultaneity with full knowledge that the field must and will change. Its static depth is finally dependent on the *unfolding* of narrative and the *unreeling* of the filmstrip. Our expectations of any narrative are informed by patterns of change and alteration. The longer that alteration is withheld, the greater the viewer's anxiety about change. Protracted shots seems to be of intolerable length precisely because, in both its narrativity and its filmicity, cinema leads us to expect change. Films in which deep-focus, uninterrupted shots are the rule (Dryer's *Gertrud*, Jancso's *Red Psalm*, Duras's *India Song*, for example) skillfully force viewing to undulate with the adagio of action and camera. One comes to care how things are going to arrange and rearrange themselves in the patiently posited field. Viewing becomes a series of questions: how long will this camera position be held? when will the cut come? when will the character move? Our sense of possession is rendered excruciating by the denial of cinema's characteristic movements and its conventional rhetorical patterns of editing. Depth then supplies us with many things that fall into the category of information; it also supplies us with a space adequate and conducive to feeling. It is impossible to reject the facile figure of speech, "depth of feeling," in light of the cinematic experience in which spatial depth so often sustains feeling by pro-

87

viding it with a fit area for reverberation, in which emotional reverberations are produced by the inflections of depth.

Virtual Depth

Complementary to the denial of time's inexorable unfolding in the narrative is the denial of areas within the posited depth, the exclusions and omissions that draw the viewer's attention to *unutil-ized* depth. In Stevens's *A Place in the Sun* there occurs a long *plan-séquence* that plays upon the virtuality of foreground (occu-pied by a table inside George's room) and background (a tele-phone, far off in the hall outside). George first leaves the table to call Alice. He recedes in the depth, diminished, anxious about Alice's suspected pregnancy and dejected when his suspicions prove to be correct. After returning to the foreground table, he is again summoned by the ringing of the phone, this time to hear Angela's voice inviting him to a party. The foreground and back-ground oscillate with George's oscillating presence in them, and with the voices, unheard by us, of Alice, the agent of his degrada-tion, and Angela, that of his transcendence. The space and time, posited in their integrity by the uninterrupted shot and unmoving camera, permit us to grasp the emotional echoes that connect George's presence and voice as he passes from the near-mute acceptance of Alice's information to his exultant acceptance of Angela's invitation (and love). It is through the simultaneously seen and alternately occupied foreground and background that Stevens inflects space, charging it with George's values. We linger in that patiently established space, cherish it, apply the rules governing its dimensions to that which it contains, and apply, as well, the shape and aspect of the contained (George) to the container.

A further inflection of virtual depth is derived from the tight frames that squeeze the field between foreground and background. The elements within that field are then thrust into a spatial intimacy creating configurations that are claustrophobic for both the in-frame enactors and, despite the expansive space that accommo-dates their viewing, the film viewers. Wyler makes this squeezing effect serve comfort and discomfort in *Best Years*. Homer, in his living room, is caught in the circle of parents, little sister, sweetheart, and prospective in-laws, witnesses whose presence cre-ates a pattern for depth that focuses our gaze upon his hooks, witnesses who painfully try to demonstrate that they are NOT look-ing at those hooks. The hooks, a figuring of lack, a figuring of the *partial body* that Metz and others have described as generative of our fetishistic love for the screen image,[18] inflect our desire for the deep space and the depth of the fiction at the film's end. There, Homer's dexterous pseudohands that in the early scene dropped a glass of lemonade will draw everyone's attention as he expertly puts

a wedding ring on his bride's finger. Mutually defining, the fulcrum, Homer's hooks, and the surrounding field, the living room, transfer to each other their meanings and their imageness. Our vision is organized by the fulcrum and made sensitive to the forces in the deep field that locate it. But in order to function, the fulcrum need not be as dramatic or extraordinary as artificial hands. On the night of Al's homecoming, Milly (Myrna Loy) spends what seem like long minutes in a wing chair while her nervous husband roams through foreground, midground, and background. She is indeed "home," the home of deeply reverberant living rooms that favor the roundness of the human body and that are at the center of *Best Years*. Al, not yet ready to be home, disrupts the order of the space, an order preserved by Milly's position as fulcrum.

The modest living room, so often an equivalence of entrapment, seems to compress all the narrative and spatial depth of this film into its severely limited dimensions. It succeeds in doing so because the director has persistently demonstrated how the informed gaze finds unsuspected depths within these limits. Why look for depth in the patently shallow if not to exercise the depth of the onlookers' eyes and to prove their ability to find depth in that which seems to be manifestly deprived of it? In Wyler's stagings, middle-class living rooms appear deep; they rarely do so in life. The cinematic illusion creates depth in shallowness, endowing it with its photographic and dramatic values.

This paradox of depth in shallowness is illustrated in the scene of Al's return, the peak moment in the crescendo of homecoming that constitutes the first section of the film, a peak arrived at through the "depths" of ever-shortening distances. Al enters a rather long downstairs hallway, starts toward the elevator, but is interrupted by the unfriendly receptionist who does not recognize him as Mr. Al Stephenson. Upstairs, he proceeds down the corridor from elevator to front door and pauses there before ringing. The traversals are fully spatialized and temporalized. Once inside, greeted by son and daughter, he pauses again, in the foreground of a short interior hall. Milly appears in the depth of the hall, and the couple embrace somewhere near the center of what has finally turned into an exceptionally deep area that takes into account the time and space of separation, the emotion of reunion, in the affirmation of the whole body that is the embrace. This depth, generated optically through low-angle camera placement, narrowness, and the receding pattern formed by doorway, window, and shafts of light, and generated narratively from that which precedes in the film, makes a virtue of shallowness. The space acquires length and resonance through filmic and narrative activity. This miracle of the hearth is a singularly cinematic one. Indeed, how many angels can dance on the head of a pin? As many as can squeeze into a flat bit of film, a bombadier's bay, a taxicab, under the low ceilings of a Welsh miner's house (*How Green Was My Valley*), or cavort in a French chateau.

90

The staging deployments of *The Rules of the Game* transform the chateau and park into a labyrinth (prefiguring Resnais's *Last Year at Marienbad*), and seem to call for the deep vision exercised by the Marquise, who, in looking at a squirrel close up through a monocular (a lens), sees an adjacent "close-up" of her husband kissing his mistress.[19] Even these depth-defying optical devices are questionable. At the film's end Renoir collapses the film's depth structures, thereby expressing his feelings about this fiction and the movies in general, in homage to a dying class and to his apparatus. The characters of the film become nothing more nor less than their own shadows, played/projected on the appropriate screen, the facade of the chateau.[20]

Excess and Depth

The illusion of depth, so often created through limits, planes, and other defining features, takes on a different resonance when it is made to figure an abyss, a limitlessly extended space. Such depth may appear to be on the verge of engulfing that which is on view at its threshhold. Then, the depth of shadows behind the foreground figures, through its undifferentiated mass, provides the resonating factor in the field. There are shadows that we never need penetrate, that in fact we perhaps should not penetrate, since they are usually suggestive of a quasi-metaphysical space, an obscure background (and occasionally a foreground) that hovers beyond the reach of physical/theatrical action. This abyss effect is put to several uses in *Best Years*. At the beginning, when Al, Fred, and Homer fly over the United States, the land surface spread out beneath them, seen in daylight and darkness, is not a completely unmitigated promise of opportunity and a happy future. America's depth and breadth, so thoroughly questioned by the film, are presented ambiguously here at the outset when, at dawn, Homer, the film's most persistent sign of incompleteness, wakens. His doubting face is twice intercut, in medium close-up and then close-up, with an infinite expanse of

fleecy clouds. The close-up of a handless man is the ultimate measure of this conventional vista. A more menacing deep-field engulfs Fred's figure near the film's climax when he wanders through a graveyard of planes that stretches further than his eye, or ours, can see. Such grandeur of vision breaks beyond the boundaries of deep-field staging that the cinema conspires to stretch from foreground to disappearing background—the awe-inspiring string of trucks in King Vidor's *The Big Parade*, the railroad yard strewn with wounded men in *Gone with the Wind*, John Ford's wagon trains, cavalry columns, and in *Cheyenne Autumn*, a whole Indian nation. These images of magnitude are visual and emotional tests, calling the viewer to measure the fiction of measureless depth against the measurable screen, to measure the specifics of the moviegoing experience against the illusions that most radically challenge those conditions as they attempt to *move* viewing as far beyond the theater as possible.

When deep-field stagings alternate with close-ups, the resulting reverberations emanate from the appearance of near and far-off surfaces within the film text itself. This is an organizing editing procedure in *A Place in the Sun*, where the extreme close-ups that present George and Angela's faces as pure surface are juxtaposed against the film's dominent depth stagings.[21] At their first dance, after their first embrace, they run from the stationary camera, resume their dance in the recesses of the frame, are seen soon after in an empty ballroom, still dancing, on a floor covered with balloons that serve to gauge distance. At the climax of the sequence they are caught in close-up. Throughout the film, proximity to George and Angela is opposed to the equally persistent refusal of proximity. For George, depth is loss. The film's ultimate depth is that of the Loon Lake disaster with its long shots that show the rowboat floating on the shadowy water. George's feelings reverberate between the terrible depths that threaten to engulf him and the "gorgeous" close-up life with Angela. The film repeatedly shifts between an excessively deep, abysslike field, and close-ups so extreme that the lens seems to devour the performers' faces. This emphatic system of visual/emotional hyperbole is characteristic of the films of George Stevens, where space is often meant to be perceived in measures of extravagant breadth and depth—the graveyard in *Shane*, in foreground on a high hill and ultimately dwarfed by the valley; the house and the prairie in *Giant*. In this, Stevens is much closer to Welles's athletic stretching of distance than to Wyler's patiently extended rooms. Indeed, Wyler, who rarely uses deep space in the service of neo-expressionism, is charry of close-ups that create disorienting tensions between close and far. In *Best Years*, apart from a few close-ups of Homer's face, we persistently see faces attached to necks, shoulders, and bodies; actors seated on chairs, at tables.

Depth and Roundness
The most obvious relationship between depth and affect is in the figuring of satisfying roundness, of entities that maintain a sense of roundness despite their projection on the flat screen. The illusion of depth and the illusions of cinematic fictions allow us to disengage from that flatness the performers, the objects, the whole of nature

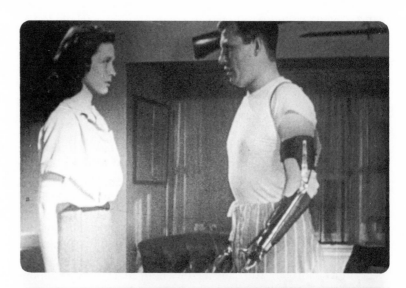

itself that our eyes seem to grasp. Witnesses to the rapprochements between on-screen enactors in spatial depth, we are caught in their embrace; we are eager to share in the affect they share, displayed in a spatial depth that sustains the fullness of their aspects. In *Best Years* there is a movement toward the two embraces that occur near the end of the film: that of Homer and Wilma and that of Fred and Peggy. During the elaborately staged homecoming of Homer, who is unable to return the embrace of Wilma on the front lawn, and at the reunion of Al and Milly in their front hall, Wyler posits the value of the embrace in a deep space that accommodates depth of character and feeling. The remainder of the film adds the depth of narra-

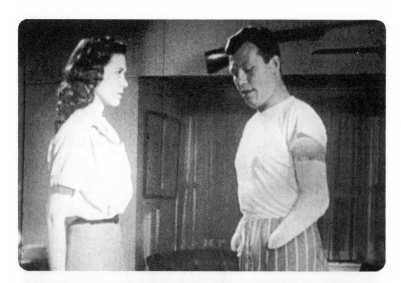

tive and time. Homer finally allows Wilma to share the intimacy of his "lack," to witness the procedures involved in removing his artificial forearms and his hooks before going to bed. This culminates as the "full" man returns the embrace with what is left of his arms. Homer has regained his fullness through the fullness of the text's visual and narrative disclosures. Fred will do the same, passing through a similar traumatic revelation in the airplane graveyard before embracing Peggy, thereby crowning the deep field of Homer and Wilma's wedding, and summing the embraces, incomplete and complete, that punctuate the film.

The camera hugs with arms it does not have, and the value of its

embrace is something like Homer's, an embrace that transcends lack, an embrace that passes from the tangible to the visual. During the final sequence of *Best Years* our eyes reach toward Homer's hooks. These objects are crucially involved in a wedding ceremony that is sanctioned by the anxious eyes of the onlookers within and outside the film. Our eyes make sense of three couples central to the fiction, captured in the camera-created depth of the living room and arranged in a pattern that establishes the primacy of vision. The camera, hovering somewhere above Fred's shoulder, allows us to see everything at once, to pull to ourselves an experience that goes beyond the spread of our arms, that makes us understand to what degree eyes are, as they must be, superior to arms in the intangible

medium of cinema. This summing shot of *Best Years*, just prior to the embrace of Fred and Peggy, is the big clinch between eye, lens, and field. It securely places feeling in cinematic depth. Homer appropriates reality and manifests his feelings with artificial hands and then with stumps of arms; the camera, in accounting for depth, hugs that which is in its two-dimensional field. Homer's hug is no more incomplete, no more "extreme" a version of embrace than any other on film, so vibrant with flatness and depth in its pictures of embrace.

Moving with the Camera

I have been examining the connections between camera presence and human presence in the deployment strategies of deep-field stagings. The dual embrace that rescues screen phenomena from their flat surface is yet fuller when the camera extends itself into the field, roaming through that which it photographs. The camera's entrance into the filmic field implies a refusal of its detached vantage point and the invulnerability of that detachment. Its movement spatializes and displays commitment. Our viewing activity readily yields to the demands of the fiction when the camera plots the lure of spatial depth.

Those demands are insistent in the films of Max Ophuls and Vincente Minnelli, where tracking shots and crane shots are analogies for desire. The choreography of the crane connects our view of Emma (Minnelli, *Madame Bovary*) on the dance floor to the vertiginous sexual desire she experiences during the waltz. Perusing the walls of her room and her memorabilia, a slowly tracking camera is suggestive of her eyes, those of the novelist Flaubert (whose voice we hear in a narrative overvoice), and, of course, of our own rhythm of scrutiny. Although camera movement that benefits from the smooth tracking of the dolly or from the miraculous "movie" levitation of the crane is not synchronous with human movement, its dynamics often constitute a version of human involvement in the deep cinematic field. With its intimations of subjectivity, the moving camera has a strong relationship to the narrational elements of a film, and when the film is indeed narrated by its protagonist, we are tempted to confuse the camera's movements and those of the character.[22] Yet, with the exception of Robert Montgomery's exercise in exclusively first person camera-eye narration, *Lady in the Lake*, the moving camera fluctuates between identification with the in-frame perceiver and with sympathetic, concerned observers: the director, the cameraman, the committed reader.

Ophuls's *Letter from an Unknown Woman* demonstrates this sympathetic transfer of vision from character to lens. Like Lisa, the protagonist, the camera gracefully steals upon data. It slithers up

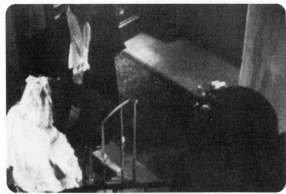

and down the front and back stairways; it slides along with her in front of the glass partition in her apartment as she follows the sound of Stefan Brand's music. Parallel to her desire to see Stefan and to the continuity of the musical code that she loves, the camera follows her everywhere, through the streets and houses of this studio-wrought Vienna. The camera becomes Lisa as she explores Stefan's apartment, fondling the objects with her eyes and her hands.[23] The character's obsessive vision is related to the camera's obsessive reproduction of the visible. Lisa *must* see Stefan and the environment he inhabits. To do that, she will move anywhere and will find vantage points that are meant for cameras, not for people.[24]

The function of such vantage points in the joining of camera movement, sight, and emotion is dramatized by the frequently cited sequence in which Lisa waits near Stefan's front door, only to see him return home with another woman.[25] She is perched on a little stairway just above the entrance to his apartment, the camera is perched above her. Its radically high angle commands her act of observation in the area observed, the stairway that she has climbed, that she hopes will lead Stefan to her, that in fact she will descend alone after her terrible disappointment. Stefan was meant to fill the space with his trajectory, as Lisa filled it herself and now fills with her desire. Here a slight adjustment of the camera's position is sufficient to contain the movement of Lisa's feelings, from her anticipation to her disillusion. This movement, a kind of visual shrug, will be recalled ironically years later when it is Lisa who accompanies Stefan up that curving flight of stairs.

Yet the camera is not Lisa; its identity with her eyes and her point of view is intermittent. The dance duet figure is a useful analogy for understanding this fluctuation of viewpoint between the moving camera and the in-frame perceiver. In the duet, one dancer reflects the pattern of the other in a variety of ways—in a precise aping or mirroring, in rhythmic and gestural counterpoint, in a kind of action/reaction complementarity. The dancers' harmony conveys doubleness, separateness, and unity at the same time. The two dancers (and why not think of the cinema's most cherishable dancing couple, Astaire and Rogers?) generate movements from each other. Partnership admits sharing and separateness, unity and individuality. The moving camera in Ophuls both mirrors Lisa's eyes and views Lisa's eyes with sympathy. We hover between lens and eyes, between movements of identification that engage us in the protagonist's desire to live the fiction and the capacity of the camera to shape the fiction with its own arabesques. Lisa and lens are linked but distinct; if an object comes too close to its image in a mirror, it will be engulfed in its reflection. It will be lost.

There is also a suggestion of mirrorness in the camera's response to the motion of in-frame enactment and the spatial configurations conducive to that motion. Why indeed does the camera track, or move at all, if not to keep up with, to anticipate, or to recall explicit and implicit movement in the frame? In *Letter from an Unknown Woman* the camera tracks to suggest the stairway. A stairway is meant to be walked on; the graceful track of the camera, its ascent or descent in relationship to the stairway, asserts the shape of the stairway and the passage of the characters upon it.[26] Fred and Ginger exchange their movements through a transfer we call graceful, a transfer extended to the curved stairways, the strategically placed furniture, the little bridges, the vivid black and white of the walls and the floors that match the clothes and the spirits of these dancers. The decor and the dancers are limned by the camera, a third member of the dance figure, harmonious with and distinct from the visible performers.

This distinction between camera and object, between camera movement and the movement of sight, tolerates a flux between our desire for the dancers imaged on the screen and their desire for each other that animates the fiction and the dance. The mirrorlike nexus of identity and separateness offers us a privileged point of suspension between our actual distance from the screen and the fiction of our closeness described by the movement of the camera. Complementary to that which is within the frame yet always outside the frame, the camera then is a vehicle for our own movement in and out of the fiction. As it "conveys" the characters in the frame to us and also conveys what they see, it conveys us somewhere out of our seats, dogging its trajectories. We swivel, rise, and fall with the slow grace of its efforts to *make* motion of sight. These movements are among the cinema's most powerful generators of viewer complicity.

The tracking of the camera urges us to prolong the movements so emphatically traced, just as the sounding of musical tones urges us to hear sets of overtones. The identificatory powers of movement and sound are deployed at the beginning of Alain Resnais's *Last Year at Marienbad*. There the camera is the eye of the narrator, and tries to double his voice as he searches the endless corridors that seem to hold his identity and the fiction of his love. But despite its first person point of view, this sequence contains a descrepancy that admits of fluctuation within and without the film. The camera movements, unlike human walking rhythms, and the voice-over in which the voice and music consistently crescendo and decrescendo, serve both to suggest and to be distinct from body rhythm and from verbal (human) articulation. We therefore shift in our relationship to the camera and microphone as (1) surrogates for the human presence and (2) pure apparatus. In the same way we are caught between Lisa observer and Lisa observed. When the camera detaches itself from Lisa's point of view and sees her seeing, it has not necessarily become "objective." It has found a mode for inscribing her eyes in their own subjectivity; its movements come to be associated with the spirit of her sight; it includes her eyes, her face, and her body in the decor that is so much a part of her presence.

The fluctuations of the moving camera tend to make us lose some of our bearings and find others. We pass in and out of the fiction through Lisa's desire to see, Ophuls's desire to make a film, and our desire to see that film. It is finally the doubleness of this movement that gives us access to Lisa the intensely emotional protagonist, the protagonist whose emotion is produced primarily through sight, and Lisa the fiction-maker, who in making fiction celebrates her emotion. The unknown woman, in the creation of her fantasy lover, retains her feelings as well as her anonymity. At one point Lisa says she is preparing herself for Stefan, preparing herself as an author does, learning about him, his music, his tradition, his decor, which then, through her desire, and the work of her eyes and imagination, are turned into a narrative of words and images.

The particular quality of that narrative is derived from the "fictional" depth the camera imparts to phenomena through its sublimatory, metaphorical procedures. Lisa, in her fiction, sublimates passion for Stefan into love for his music.[27] She fondles his piano, and that touch is meant to inspire him to compose again. After their waltz Stefan continues the music on the piano, framing Lisa's face with his arms and hands. Lisa (here a figure for music

itself) fears she will lose her muselike quality if Stefan comes to *know* her as he does other women. The priority of Lisa's vantage and the clarity of her sight must be maintained to bring the fiction to fruition. And as we have so often heard, screen performers must never *know* the camera, fully acknowledge it, if they are to remain bound by their fictions.

In a sublimation of the cinematic process itself, Lisa's passion is satisfiied one night when, still unknown, she is picked up by Stefan, taken to dinner and then to the Prater. There, in an amusement-park attraction, Lisa and the emotion-filled movements of this film resonate in the flatness of painted vistas behind the lovers' stationary carriage. Lisa describes to Stefan the workings of her imagination; the mechanical, illusionistic scene-changing procedures (the

Venetian panorama rolls to its conclusion, the Swiss one replaces it
when an old man operates a set of levers and gears) are meticulously
revealed. Lisa is utterly aware of the value of illusion and fantasy in
the depth of her fiction, as moving to her as the artifices of depth are
to us when we go to the movies.

5   Voice and Space

The inscription of a word is a gesture of eternalization; the voicing of a word is a gesture of relinquishment. Sound vanishes once it has been emitted. It cannot be stopped and scrutinized unless it is thoroughly denatured by transformation into a sign system (alphabet writing, phonetic symbols) that has none of the essence of utterance. Signs lose the presence-bearing quality of sound, the uniqueness of individual speech. Walter Ong states:

> *Sound is more real or existential than other sense objects, despite the fact than it is also more evanescent.* Sound itself is related to present actuality rather than to past or future. It must emanate from a source, here and now, discernibly active, with the result that involvement with sound is involvement with the present, with here-and-now existence and activity.[1]

From this status of presence Ong argues for sound's priority among the meaning-producing systems. "The greater reality of words and sound is seen also in the further paradox that sound conveys meaning more powerfully and accurately than sight. If words are written, they are on the whole far more likely to be misunderstood than spoken words are."[2] Sound endows verbality with a depth and a resonance that surpasses the sign-value of the word. The vocalized sign is filled with presence, its meaning thereby thickened.

Jacques Derrida posits this privilege of presence upon the detachment of voice from worldly form. Although Derrida considers "spoken" voice rather than reproduced voice, I would argue that, perceptually, we can and do respond to each in the same way. To our hearing, they are equally uninscribed. A reproduced voice seems to be as present, as much a function of the present, as closely connected with or generative of sound waves as the voice that is actually emitted in the present. Derrida, in pursuit of the voice's time, the hereness of its nature, examines "the absolute proximity" between the acts of uttering speech and hearing speech. "The ideality of the object . . . can only be expressed in an element whose phenomenality does not have worldly form. *The name of this ele-*

ment is the voice. The voice is heard. Phonic signs . . . are heard . . . by the subject who proffers them in absolute proximity of their present."[3] While words are being uttered, they are also absolutely part of (belong to) the enunciator, who needs nothing, no medium other than the air we breathe, to convey them. The conveyance and the conveyed, the signifier and the signified are therefore contiguous. "The 'apparent transcendence' of the voice thus results from the fact that the signified, which is always ideal by essence . . . is immediately present in the act of expression." The connection between the vocalized signifier and the signified is a mode of transparency, not a *connection*, since in this formulation there is no space between the two elements. Meaning *is* the sound of the voice. "This immediate presence results from the fact that the phenomenologic 'body' of the signifier seems to fade away at the very moment it is produced; it seems already to belong to the element of ideality. It phenomenologically reduces itself, transforming the worldly opacity of its body into pure diaphaneity."[4] It is, and then disappears.

The notion of diaphaneity suggests that there is an unlocatable adjacency between word and meaning, a passagelike adjacency from here to there, through a duration that manages to hold presence and identity in the flow of fictional and filmic time. We may think we capture voice on a tape or a record that then reproduces it as often as we want, but is it a true capture when the retransmission is yet another relinquishment, the necessary "letting go" through progressive time that allows us to perceive voice? The mechanisms of the sound projector convey (1) the image, stopped twenty-four times per second and held in an aperture through which passes the light that projects it onto the screen in an *illusion* of continuous movement, and (2) the continuous flow of the sound track over the sound head, a flow that creates *not* an illusion of sound but sound itself. In order for us to hear mechanically reproduced words in a lifelike manner, the flow of sound from the machine must correspond to the flow of sound in life. Stopping and playing back the words always reinitiates the flow that carries away the words. "This effacement of the sensible body and its exteriority is *for consciousness* the very form of the immediate presence of the signifier."[5] Sound then guarantees immediacy and presence in the system of absence that is cinema. Images that constantly remind us of the distance in time and space between their making and their viewing are charged, through voice, with the presence both that uttered words require for their transmission and that they lend to our viewing of the art.[6]

Reverberations

The word committed to a progressive present for its emission and perception also has a discernible duration. Its time has a beginning and an end. The time of speech, from the briefest whispers to the fully voiced declamations of the stage performer and the singer's sustained syllables, depends on the reverberation of sound waves through time and space. A word is not inscribed in space unless it is written, but reverberation does produce a suspensionlike spatial effect particularly apparent when the reverberation is prolonged by the acoustics of a cave, a gorge, a large hall, a church, the Alpine landscapes favored by yodelers, or the electronic magnifications accomplished by microphone and loudspeaker. Reverberation tends to thicken the presence of vocal utterance, to create at least the impression that the perceiver has some fleeting grasp on its ungraspable essence. As its reverberation increases, a word takes on the appearance of an object in space.

The connections between reverberation and our perception of space are favored by the experience of cinema. At the movies, through the viewer's awareness of both the imaged space on screen and the space of the auditorium, the reverberant word's suggestion of depth (augmented by the loudspeaker for sound reproduction and the audition of a large audience) is related to what is manifestly deep, the space between the viewer and the screen, and the space that stretches behind the screen in the image's fiction of three-dimensionality. Although, as Ong asserts, speech "leaves no discernible direct effect in space,'" it often informs and is informed by space when it emanates from our illusions and our experience of reality. There is so much space to fill in an auditorium that even when the literal reverberation of a word's sounding is minimal, as in whispered dialogue, the disproportion between the apparent size of the sound and the spatial field that sustains it creates the impression of reverberation. A new category of space is conjoined to voice in the extreme close-up of a mouth emitting a whisper or even a shout. The prolonged high notes of Jeanette MacDonald and Nelson Eddy are objectified by the close-ups of the gigantic open mouths that become icons of vocality, images that are then modulated into the

stasis of their kiss. (The song, seen in close-up, becomes the kiss configuration, on oral, spatial metaphor for the love they have just voiced.)

The reverberatory quality of the screen image seems to imply a factor of observance in audition. Where indeed does the space of the screen leave off and the reverberation of the sound begin if not somewhere in the "diaphaneity" of signified and signifier described by Derrida? This model of aural-spatial nexus suggests how meaning in the talkies oscillates between sound and image and between screen and viewer. These oscillations convey both data and perceiver in their animating flux; sounded images, no less fleeting for their emphatic resonance, convey the diaphanous adjacency of presence and loss.

The very notion of locus is challenged by the cinema's dynamics of flux. Outside the movie theater our voices resonate in the air and are reflected by surfaces that locate us in our environments and account for our presence. Our voices, emanations from ourselves, make additional identifying links through the conventional modes of aural communcation. But at the movies the voices that *appear* to emanate from the screen do not do so at all. They are emitted by loudspeakers that may or may not be placed behind the screen, and are in no way part of the image of the speaking character. Sound and image in the movie house are linked by our perception, not by their common origin. We witness a fiction of communication. The sound is not on the screen but in the hall.

The distinction between the true point of sound origin and the apparent point of sound origin in talkies allows us to locate speech in space as visual activity that is then sustained by the extrascreen, out-of-screen aural activity. Speech is sounded in the space we occupy; the screen contains the image; words and sounds are caught between these separate domains and catch us in a fluctuating play of word and image. It is the unifying space of the movie theater and the duration of the screening that cause the projected, amplified image and the reproduced, amplified sound to be perceived as one rather than separate. The very hall in which the film is projected, and whose depth is a medium for the reverberation of sound, sets the viewer in a relationship to the image and sound that is informed with the thickness of intervening space, space modified by aural and visual activity passing between projector and screen, between sound head and amplifier, and including the spectator in their dynamics.

Speaking Out

A viewer expects characters to speak in sound films, and that expectation is a strong element of affectivity in talkies whose protagonists are mute (*The Spiral Staircase*, *The Miracle Worker*, *The*

Heart Is a Lonely Hunter) or for whom speech is problematic (*The Bride of Frankenstein*, the Tarzan series, Chaplin's first talkies).[8] Peter Brooks gives muteness a privileged position in his melodramaturgy. Accounting for different kinds of drama in terms of "their corresponding sense deprivations," he designates muteness as being appropriate for melodrama "since melodrama is about expression," the particular fullness of expression that accommodates the fullness of meaning, the "pure moral and psychological integers" that are the genre's concern.[9] This fullness, requiring a reading of texts oversaturated with codes, is exhibited in Jean Negulesco's *Johnny Belinda* when the deaf-mute Belinda (Jane Wyman) signs the Lord's Prayer over her dead father while the doctor (Lew Ayres) speaks the words. The magnified image filled with gestural and oral discourse fills us with the movies' silent and "talked" voices. Here, muteness and speech, in their emphatic juxtaposition, test each other's expressive power, their adequacy to articulate feelings for which most discourse is inadequate. Stanley Cavell describes the effect achieved when the wordless integrity of mime is breached by excesses of feeling in Marcel Carné's *Children of Paradise*, a sound film about theatrical registers ranging from tragedy to pantomime. "The speaking of the word in those times and at those places collects to itself the fantasies it expresses and shatters them against the reality it shatters."[10]

These plays of muteness exploit the virtuality of sound in a medium some of whose basic visual conventions emanate from speech and audition. The shot/countershot pattern of classic decoupage insistently propels locution from interlocutor to interlocutor. Meaning in sound films is often conveyed through the imaging of aural configurations: "talking" faces, conversational two-shots, shouting mobs, political forums, on-screen representations of theatrical performances. (I do not mean to suggest that silent films are less reverberant than sound films. Many viewers tend to forget that silent films were not really silent at all, and that the human presence of the piano player, or that of other agents, musical and narrational, during the projection of films prior to the talkies provided aural mediation and reverberation for the screen image.) Signs of audition are repeatedly pictured on film: telephones, telephone lines, radios, microphones, mass meetings, responsive audiences. These are signs of the power of sound and of sound being powered.

A voice must be powered so that it will be heard.[11] The relationship between power and voice is exemplified by the singing voice that fills a vast auditorium, projecting the individual performer through space to thousands of auditors. The voices of opera singers project presence through power, presence that deeply moves audiences, filling them with sound and feeling. Pleasure is often derived from perceiving what appears to be the effortless emission of a tone that simultaneously fills one's head and the yawning space of the theater. The voice of the "little" soprano resonates through the Metropolitan Opera House, passing over a hundred-piece orchestra; the sturdy-lunged and chested heroic tenor holds a high note in what seems as much an athletic feat as an artistic one.

The enthusiasm for voice is demonstrated near the conclusion of W. S. Van Dyke's *San Francisco*. Mary's (Jeanette MacDonald's) operatic voice lends itself to ragtime and other popular music styles, and inspires the in-film audience to join her in a joyous rendition of

the film's title song. This is topped moments later by the spectacularly staged earthquake. At the film's climax, Blackie (Clark Gable) searches the ruined city for Mary. He witnesses scenes of despair, of happy reunion, of grief. When he finds her out of danger, singing hymns to console the disaster victims, he sinks to his knees in a prayer of thanks, his face streaming with tears. Others join their voices to Mary's, filling the sound track and filling the frame, marching ahead toward a new city rising from the ruins, made to rise from the ruins through the power of movie editing and of voice.

In the present era, whose popular music is a function of electronic amplification, the decibel level generated by the Rolling Stones and other groups in arenas and ball parks incites audiences to hysterical manifestations of approval. The affect of this phenomenon is repeatedly displayed in "performance" films (*Gimme Shelter*, *The Last Waltz*) and dramatized in *The Rose*, where the star singer (Bette Midler) is finally destroyed by the sound of her own voice. The frenzy of life she expresses in her songs accumulates in the screams of her public, and its repercussions overwhelm her in their violence. The megaphones of Greek tragedians, Jeanette MacDonald's high notes, and the loudspeakers of Mick Jagger, Janis Joplin, and Bette Midler increase an audience's hunger for the enthusiasm "carried" by the magnified voice.

The importance of powered sound among the codes of cinema has become a prime industrial consideration. Audiences are now dolbyized and sensurrounded; an enormous percentage of a film's production budget is allocated to the sound track. It is not too farfetched to suggest that the movie industry is putting its money where its mouth is because that is what the public wants to hear. But even without modern sound technology, film has employed fictional and visual magnifying systems to create a sense of rich vocal resonance. The opening of *How Green Was My Valley*, with its narrative voice-over, establishes a temporal echo that is almost immediately visualized in the hero's first recollection, that of his voice, as a little boy, echoing in answer to his sister's, reverberating across the once green valley. In this film about family links, the first is made when names are powered by lungs and throats, filling the space with identity and presence. These echoes are internalized by the film's fictional ploys, and literally so when Hew, searching for his father in the caved-in mine, "reaches" the trapped man through his echoing voice. In a medium whose primary means of expression is visual, voice serves when eyes fail.

Voices in Close-up

Magnification turns the mechanics of sound emission, of speech, into a highly visual act of expression. How then does this expressive medium preserve the ontological interiority of speech? If, as Ong asserts, "sound . . . reveals the interior without the necessity of physical invasion," and "to discover such things by sight we should have to open what we examine, making the inside an outside, destroying its interiority as such,"[12] does not the visualization of sound imperil its essential interiority? In fact, the levels and planes of depth that I have been attempting to locate in the processes of cinematic production and reception do provide for areas that can be characterized as interior to other areas, that provide the viewer's perception a dynamics that can be described as penetration, going toward the interior core of the mise-en-scène, the performer, the word. It is as if there were an interior within the expressed sound, behind the screen. The screen, in its utter superficiality, provides a jumping-off point, a readily identifiable locus of flatness that hovers above the various depths of which it is the illusory representation. We then perceive states of inwardness between the flat image on the flat screen and a wide range of utterance, vocality, reverberation.

In Elia Kazan's *A Tree Grows in Brooklyn*, Francie (Peggy Ann Garner), the mediator, generates the fiction through her coming of age, her ever-more urgent literary vocation, and her increasing ability to sort out the echoes of the said and the unsaid. The way we assimilate the film is posited on the paradox of a narrator whose own relationship to speech is problematic. Her mother, a hard-nosed pragmatist, says, "Francie, why don't you say what you mean?"; her father lends an ear to the girl's whispered effusion, "My cup runneth over." Caught between her imprecisions and her clichés, Francie identifies a rhetorical crisis in which sentiment is challenged by vocal expression.

In this demonstrative medium, any effort to hide has the countereffect of disclosure, and this holds for speech as well as for action. Whatever a character's subterfuges, the cinema's power of exposure trumpets intimacy. Both the excessively sweet voice of fantasy and "soul," and the excessively hard one of necessity and money are tested in the stagings of *A Tree Grows in Brooklyn*. Francie's father, Johnny (James Dunn), is an alcoholic, often unemployed singing waiter who habitually announces his arrival home with his voice resounding through the tenement staircase; the fam-

ily's meager living is earned by Francie's hardworking mother, Katie (Dorothy McGuire), who scrubs that staircase. A moment of happy remembrance and hope that unites the couple on a window sill is shattered when the crescendo of the pipe-dreamer's fabrications snaps the pragmatist back to harsh reality. "Stop it—stop talking." The railroad flat, with its partitions and tight little compartments, becomes then a site for disunion. Later, the distance between Johnnie and Katie in yet a smaller flat is vocalized when he, angry at her cold response to the death of a neighbor's child, defiantly sits at their piano and sings "Annie Laurie" while she angrily nails the family's tin-can bank to the floor.

After Johnny's sacrificial death Francie comes to disapprove of her mother's money-grubbing, critical ways. But in the pain preceding the birth of Johnny's posthumous child, it is Katie's voice that

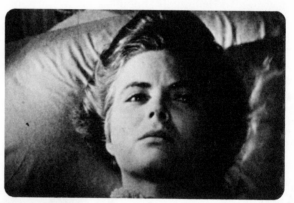

makes remarkable sense out of the film's rather pat distinctions. A series of shots brings the mother and daughter closer together in the darkened bedroom while Francie reads the story she has written about Johnny. Here, the casting of Dorothy McGuire is fully exploited. Her characteristic softness of voice and manner, subverted through the body of the film, is released by the pain of labor and her grief and loneliness. Katie, established in close-ups and in compositions that emphasize her stiffness of body and mind, her distance from a dreamy husband and an expansively loving sister (Joan Blondell), is now altered by the scrutiny of a daughter who sees her as she has never seen her before and by a camera that captures the intimacy of a bedside confession. The audience, previously denied the fey charm and lilting voice of the star of *Claudia*, is finally rewarded with McGuire's immediately identifiable aural persona, a softness of utterance that is the sum of the other soft voices previously heard in the film, and that now relates the pain of confession to the pain of repression and need.

The relationship between the star's aural personality and the locus of confession is demonstrated near the climax of Richard Boleslawski's *The Garden of Allah*. Charles Boyer, identifiable for the richness of his voice, plays a man who has left a Trappist monastery and has broken his vow of silence. He finally confesses his secret to his wife (Marlene Dietrich) in the limitless expanse of desert sand and desert sky. Given the particular fictions of *A Tree Grows in Brooklyn* (family drama) and *The Garden of Allah* ("transcendental" romance), it is not remarkable that their respective confessions take place in a bedroom and on a sand dune. Yet it is significant that we should be privy to their enactments in a medium that extracts intimacy from both loci and from the mere fact that they are spoken by these particular performers.

The particularity of cinema voices, powered by the presence of the performer, the microphone, and the loudspeaker, is further magnified by a stylistics of display. In close-up, Garbo's sigh and Garland's tremulous high note exploit the medium's visual and aural power through the ironic disproportion between the intimacy of utterance and the expanse of revelation. This disproportion is heightened in telephone scenes, where voice is simultaneously directed to the single, private ear of the receiver and to the collective, public ear of the audience. Cinema has an affinity for the telephone and its figurations of intimate discourse. From the rat-tat-tat newspaper yarns to the opening sequence of Edmund Goulding's *Grand Hotel*, where the narrative is literally plugged into a gigantic switchboard, the telephone conveys words from mouth to ear, apparently bypassing the reverberation of ambient space. Garbo in *Grand Hotel* (she transforms the receiver into a surrogate lover), Luise Rainer in *The Great Ziegfeld* (the scene won her an

Oscar), Anna Magnani in *La voce umana* (for almost the whole of the film the actress is on the phone, an object that becomes all the fiction and all her life), Liza Minnelli in *The Sterile Cuckoo* (the actress's hysteria is generated by the uninterrupted trajectory of phone call and shot), Bette Midler in *The Rose* (the singer whose voice is habitually transmitted to thousands of screaming fans in the vast expanses of arenas is pathetically isolated in a phone booth, in front of a vast, empty football stadium) exploit the double standard of telephone scrutiny in cinema. The spectator has access to the face denied the listener at the other end of the line. Capra, with great virtuosity, uses a single telephone receiver to force two characters to express the depth of their feelings for each other. In *It's a Wonderful Life*, George and Mary (Donna Reed), who have just argued, violently embrace when the receiver they have been sharing brings them into the proximity they have been avoiding during the sequence. Here, and in more conventional situations, the receiver elicits secret utterance. We share in the secrets of this surrogate for the microphone, this object that concentrates the performer's presence in voice. The concentration is further projected in visual close-up onto the screen—a close-up that is a visual analogy for the aural close-up produced by the phone and microphone.

Roland Barthes, in his hedonics of art, declares:

> it suffices that the cinema capture the sound of speech *close up* . . . and make us hear in their materiality, their sensuality, the breath, the gutturals, the fleshiness of the lips, a whole presence of the human muzzle . . . to succeed in shifting the signified a great distance and in throwing, so to speak, the anonymous body of the actor into my ear: it granulates, it crackles, it caresses, it grates, it cuts, it comes: that is bliss.[13]

Basing his argument on Julia Kristeva's formulation of *geno-song*,[14] "the space where significations germinate 'from within the language and in its very materiality' . . . that apex (or that depth) of production where the melody really works at the language,"[15] Barthes locates pleasure in perceiving "the *grain* of the voice," a vocal physicality, the precise placing of the voice in the emitting body, "the language lined with flesh."[16] The close-up makes it difficult, perhaps fruitless, to distinguish between the iconographic value of the star's face and that of the star's voice, or to argue that performers become stars because their vocal and physical aspects match. The cinematic apparatus matches them for us. Yet the vocal/aural entity, the star's immediately identifiable personality, is as much dependent on the phonogenic "grain of the voice" as it is on the photogenic configuration of body and face. In the first years of talking film, the microphone was merciless to stage actors unable to rid themselves of the projective technique, the excessively refined

diction, the pearl-shaped tones (satirized in the voice lesson sequences of *Singin' in the Rain*) necessary to make oneself heard in
large theaters. In her second talkie, *Romance*, Garbo pitches her
voice to the close-up ear of the microphone while her co-star, Gavin
Gordon, does all he can to reach the last row of a hypothetical
second balcony. At the movies, we are often closer to the speaker
than are the other in-frame performers.

The apparatus of sound reproduction allows the screen performer to expose the particularities of voice at its source of emission, what Barthes calls "the human muzzle," that vulnerable and
highly expressive area of the face adjacent to the eyes. Resonance
becomes as palpable and luminous as the gleam in the eye. The
stage actor, relying on the acoustics of the theater, breath support,
enunciation, and pitch, exteriorizes voice over great distances. This
factor counts less in films, where a speech defect (Kay Francis), a
foreign accent (Dietrich, Garbo), a vocal tic (James Stewart) can,
and often has, constituted a performer's memorable vocal personality. And what nuances those personalities impart to our experience
of film: Irene Dunne's quasi-sung heroine of *Back Street* (1932), a
model of evenness and control; Margaret Sullavan's version (1941)
of the same role, high-strung, a bit neurotic, her voice always on the
verge of breaking; Mae West's baritonal vamp; Marilyn Monroe,
whose breathiness puts words right in the listener's ear; the depth of
Charles Boyer's accented basso cantante, a range adequate to his
desire to tell the deepest secrets to the woman he loves; the staccato
rhythm of Jimmy Cagney's speech-punctuated gait.[17]

Voice and Narrativity

The relationship between voice and the oral tradition of fiction
has been widely discussed in recent narrative criticism, where it is
traced to the sagas and the *chansons de geste*.[18] The voice of the bard
validated fiction; it served to establish a life-bearing presence in the
fictional system. It was always *here*, reverberant as is sound in the
movie theater, and it brought fictions *here* from *there*, from sources
that were elsewhere temporally and often spatially. Today too our
belief in fiction is promoted by the presence of the speaker's voice.

The presence of visualized sound is operant even in silent films,
where the mere picturing of speaker and audience is enough to
suggest much of what we *ought* to hear and to inspire in us the belief
that silent speech can be heard. Lars Hansen moves his congrega-
tions in Stiller's *The Saga of Gösta Berling* and Seastrom's *The
Scarlet Letter*; Brigitte Helm incites to prayer and to riot as the true
and false Maria in Lang's *Metropolis*. The modes of vocalization
that naturally manifest themselves in all talkies convey the "sound"
of voice in "silent" films through gesticulation and audience expectation. But whether silent or sounded, both apparent and actual

115

vocalizations animate the fictions of cinema through their visual/aural resonance. The presence of voice, whether seen or heard, helps power much of cinema's narrative thrust. Our ability to follow a narrative line and to make sense of a story is not primarily a visual process, but a verbal one. Verbality is made resonant by images that the words string together in a narrative.

Vocal persuasion is contiguous to storytelling in the work of Frank Capra, where the single speaker who engages the belief of a single auditor and eventually of an audience is a recurrent figure, where the fiction's obsessive enactments of persuasion serve as models for the spectator's belief in fiction. The director's concern with the status of the democratic man in the democratic community is echoed by the agent that produces echo—the sounded voice. Ong states that "voice has a kind of primacy in the formation of true communities of men, groups of individuals constituted by shared awareness. A common language is essential for a real community to form."[19] In the characteristic Capra narrative, the hero—Mr. Deeds, Mr. Smith, John Doe—speaks in order to be heeded by the diffuse body of listeners that becomes a community when it understands the hero's language and truly hears his voice. The community imaged on film and the audience in the movie theater are held in the thrall of vocal/fictional persuasion and of fictions ranging from the American Dream to the films of Frank Capra.

The parameters of cinematic space defined by the persuasive narrativity of voice are projected by an early Capra film, *The Miracle Woman* (1931). Florence, the protagonist (Barbara Stanwyck), reads the sermon prepared by her father, a text that she interrupts with the announcement that he died in her arms five minutes before. She goes on to harangue the heartless congregation that, unable to silence her, walks out of the church in protest. One man stays and applauds her ability to "move" her audience, a talent that will be put to the service of a highly emotive and lucrative faith-healing act. Florence becomes a fiction of miracle, a fiction that instills belief in her listeners. Her voice tests credulity in a variety of contexts: the blind hero (a composer) is prevented from committing suicide when he hears her voice over the radio; she complains to her accomplice that her circuslike act will fail if she perceives the planted "cures" in the audience to be fakes; her voice is visualized in the cut-out letters of the alphabet with which she writes to the blind man. When Florence decides to speak the truth to her congregation, her accomplice tries to silence her by turning off the lights, causing a fire to break out in her tabernacle. Florence's voice then refills the space, transforms it, and calms the panicking crowd. In the darkness of the blind hero, in the hypocritical response of the first congregation, and in the various levels of belief to which she inspires her followers, Florence's voice defines its areas of aural and fictional resonance and engages us in the integrity of those definitions.

The sound of Stanwyck's voice is endowed with similar power in other films she made for Capra: a voice that transcends the words it utters to involve the warlord General Yen (Nils Asther) in the myth of Christian charity ("When you ask me like that I forget I am General Yen"), a voice, mimicking that of the director himself, that elicits from John Doe the required expression of anger for a press photograph. It is Walter Huston's voice, in *American Madness*, that quells a riot and restores order to the precisely delimited space of the bank. Claudette Colbert, the "poor little rich girl," finds her identity, her voice, and true love when she sings with "just plain folks" on a democratic bus ride in *It Happened One Night*. Mr. Deeds (Gary Cooper), the rhymster, remains silent at his sanity hearing. When finally he yields to the constant urgings that he speak to identify himself, his voice makes sense out of the courtroom and the community it presumably validates. *Meet John Doe* is the story of a man created by words, "a typical American who can keep his mouth shut." John's reticence at giving voice to words that are not his is intensified by the vocal persona of Gary Cooper, the prototypical "strong, silent" type of American films in the thirties (a persona no less operant for its failure to take into account Cooper's verbal expertise in the repartee of comedies such as *Design for Living*, *Desire*, and *Bluebeard's Eighth Wife*). In *Meet John Doe* it is the response of the studio audience that spurs him to eloquence during his first radio speech. The sound of that voice is intercut with shots of the writer (Barbara Stanwyck), who overflows with feeling at hearing her words (the words she drew from her dead father's diary) uttered with such sincerity. This spatial figure of voice and audition enacted in the confines of the radio studio is both amplified and shattered when John Doe, at last about to speak the truth to his credulous admirers (much like the Miracle Woman), is silenced when the wires to his microphone are cut. His single, unamplified voice is lost in the sea of umbrellas that fills the rain-drenched ball park. At the film's conclusion the power of voice is restored; the writer voices her own words, whose fervor prevents John's suicide. In their evocation of the original preacher/persuader/miracle man, Jesus, they are words that assert the basis of their own fictive power, the power of belief.

In Capra's films the political, social, and ethical systems that identify the protagonists are clearly spatialized by the voices that resonate within them, from the Miracle Woman's fake tabernacle to John Doe's ball park. The presidential candidate (Spencer Tracy) proclaims his political dishonesty and his love for his wife (Katharine Hepburn) over nationwide television (*State of the*

Union). George Bailey, the hero of *It's a Wonderful Life* (a film that begins, quite literally, with voices in space),[20] is made partially deaf, as a boy, when he speaks a "painful" truth; as a grown man he tries in vain to speak his life to his mother (Beulah Bondi), wife, and friends when they refuse to acknowledge that he has lived. At the conclusion of *It's a Wonderful Life* the quintessential American living room seems to be packed with the whole population of the quintessential American town. Centrifugal to the community at large, the tight enclosure radiates from the hero whose presence is both singular and plural and whose voice is the voice that sums those of "the man on the street." That individual voice, the primary locus, animates and makes resonant the space of the film and the other figures in the film. When George Bailey runs through his town, exulting over the recovery of his "wonderful life," he consecrates the streets and houses that are then resumed, crammed into, made to explode inside the living room, the ultimate home for the hero of family and community. Hero and community are voiced through the singing of the Christmas carols and "Auld Lang Syne."[21]

Much of our response to this particular sequence is elicited by Capra's invitations to us, the film audience, to "join in," just as the townspeople join their voices to celebrate George's presence. That is indeed what he is celebrating—the recovery of his presence after having been made to experience a fiction of his own absence, his deidentification to those he knows and loves. Everyone in the Bailey living room gives George money and voice, pays admission as it were, confers value on being there as witness to George's life, as we have paid our way into the theater and paid attention to the film. Even the skeptical sheriff and the man from the auditor's office (officials of the society that seems to threaten George) are moved to add their money and voices to the contributions and the songs, as we join in with our pleasure at watching the film.

Pathos and the Democratic Voice

For Capra, watching a film is inflected by hearing its specific voices. Stanwyck, Arthur, Cooper, Colman, Edward Arnold, Eugene Pallette, and Walter Brennan locate Capra's films in vocal melody as much as they do in images. And *Mr. Smith Goes to Washington*, where the production of fiction is so often calibrated by *how* the hero's voice is produced, is exemplary of Capra's ethos of vocality.

The problematic nature of Smith's utterance is established when we see him, at a political banquet, seated next to a microphone, a pompous windbag of a governor, and a United States senator renowned for eloquence. Two audiences, the spectators of the film and those within it, wait to hear Smith's first words in a configuration clearly redolent of verbality. This configuration contains a visual sign of reticence, the emotional and inarticulate persona of Jimmy Stewart, and an aural sign of empty bombast, Guy Kibbee's speechifying. In *Mr. Smith*, a celebration of the democratic process (the choice of the comon man, Mr. Smith, to speak for the common men in their most important forum), there is a crisis of speech. There is a corrective to the flow of words implied by the very existence of the forum as well as by the medium of this particular sound film. In a democracy all citizens have a right to be heard. From the debate of the town meeting to the voter's symbolic voice at the polls, the democratic individual is supposed to be accounted for and counted. The vocal democratic process that the banquet emblemizes is subverted by the caricature of the stooge's political rhetoric; the cinematic sound track is challenged by the hero's face. His inarticulateness is a function of his sincerity, his emotion at being called to embody the democratic ideal, to serve as junior senator beside his idol, the Silver Knight, who, along with Smith's martyred father, was champion of the people.

Here, at the film's outset, speech is to be perceived as both false to the democracy it ostensibly represents and inadequate to the hero's discourse. Politicians do not speak with honest voices. Mr. Smith's speech will prove to be neither false nor inadequate. As the mass audience attends the film *Mr. Smith Goes to Washington* and is made privy to its qualities of private and public discourse, so the in-film listeners will later be forced to hear Smith's voice, a sound paragon for sincerity, for political and emotional truth. The sound of his voice will force them, and us, to share in its resonance, a resonance that is a function of the chamber that produces it and that creates a sympathetic response in all its auditors.

When Smith gets up to express his feelings at the banquet, to dispel the Governor's facile bombast, and to break his own silence, he suggests how precious speech can be in film. The subsequent occasions of his speech will be invested with a virtuality of silence. His utterance, weighted with difficulties, stammerings, awkwardness, is produced by an unreliable vocal apparatus given to gulps and abrupt changes of register and dynamic level. Capra will exploit the aural/visual disparity between tall Jimmy Stewart (whose middle-American accent is distant from the stage actor's diction and whose mode of delivery seems to be informed with the real possibility that delivery will be impossible) and short Claude Rains (whose English origin and precise pronunciation are meant to suggest that his conventionally senatorial voice is used to commanding instant attention). The ultimate juxtaposition of two such distinct voices and accents, a movie voice and what appears to be a stage voice, is accomplished in the neoclassical interior of the Senate Chamber, where the appropriateness of the latter, Rains's, is taken for

119

granted. Stewart's will subsequently appropriate the chamber, making it responsive to his unconventional inflections. It is Smith who upholds the standard of true, hard-won eloquence in the film and in doing so challenges the notion that the democratic right to be heard makes it easy to speak. The quality of Smith's speech will also test the microphone and the sound track, ever-ready to capture and retransmit whatever babble they pick up. Capra reminds us repeatedly that the movies fought hard to speak, that sound makes cinematic space resound when its privilege is asserted. When Smith finally speaks at the banquet, we wonder that he is able to speak at all, that he can achieve articulation in spite of his reticence, embarrassment, the depth of his own feelings, and the context of falsity. When the democratic hero, who has the right to speak and be heard, makes speech so crucial, it becomes a source of affect to viewers of a sound film about democracy.

It is the sound of the speaker's voice that unites people in space. The area in which the speaker's voice resounds becomes a spatial integrity animated by the speaker's presence and filled with auditors attendant upon and attentive to sound. *Mr. Smith*, and other films that exploit this political space of aural presence, ought to be distinguished from those narrative films, I suppose most narrative films, where utterance is of a private, intimate nature. The audience that witnesses the film *Mr. Smith* is provided with a set of surrogate audiences within the film itself, groups at public occasions that indicate the political aspects of audition. The Senate Chamber becomes an extension of the movie screen, its gallery an analogy for our angles of spectatorship. We relish our privileged and unnoticed entry to the boudoirs of the silver screen; we belong in the crowds, the courtrooms, and the other configurations that invite our legitimate witnessing. We are supposed to hear what happens in a democratic forum. and it is upon that expectation that Capra generates much of the film's meaning and its affect. If indeed the democratic system and the dramatic locus depend upon the presence of voice, and if that voice is in jeopardy, both the political and the theatrical conventions are in jeopardy. And so is our place within those systems, as individuals in a democracy, as witnesses to its theatrical models and members of the collective that is an audience.

Mr. Smith survives his first crisis of speech at the banquet and accepts the gift offered by his Boy Rangers, the group that has secured his appointment (Governor Hopper's sons convince "Pop" that Smith is "the Greatest American we got"), boys whose childish idealism he inspires, who read his publication *Boy Stuff*, and who will struggle to allow his speech to be heard and read during the film's final minutes. Here, Smith's speech is elicited by what he perceives as the faith of the boys and that of the father figure,

Senator Paine. A good ranger, a pal, a misty-eyed hero-worshiper, he manages to express his gratitude and humility. With a promise of tears, while everyone sings "Auld Lang Syne," he also establishes a low level of pathetic intensity (boys, fathers, patriotism) appropriate to the film's opening and the dimensions of the banquet. This is a point of departure for a crescendo of feeling and an amplification of dramatic context that accommodates an amplification of voice.

The inscription of democratic words in space is almost immediately accomplished on Smith's arrival in Washington. Framed in the door of Union Station, the sight of the Capitol dome, a symbol that summarizes all the words he will write in his bill and the focal point of the forum in which his voice will make those words resound, is enough to inspire Smith to detach himself from the political hacks and henchmen, and take off on a tour of the city's monuments, a pilgrimage for the democratic idealist who is also an average, wide-eyed tourist. (The Capitol dome appears ironically during the banquet sequence in a flowered effigy behind the dais that unites the Governor's rhetorical hypocrisy and Smith's utterance of sincerity.) The sight-seeing montage features several representations of graphic inscription—a picture of the signing of the Declaration of Independence, of Jefferson's hand holding a quill, a reenactment of John Hancock affixing his signature. This culminates at the Lincoln Memorial with shots of Lincoln's words, literally carved in stone, and then of a young boy (always the voice of truth in this film) reading the words aloud, hesitantly, but with conviction. The strains of "Red River Valley" bring to mind John Ford, for whom it was an emotional signature tune. The ultimate measure of the Ford hero is an expanse that surpasses the compass of voice, the horizon stretching far beyond the frame, the nature-made monuments of the director's favorite valley. Capra's heroes must be heard, but the great words they utter are hard to say. Such words require enclosures that favor resonance, that now resound in the presence of a man-made monument, a statue of a distinctly American speaker. They are voiced in this memorial space by a boy, presounding Smith's brand of eloquence. They are also qualified by the sentimenal conventions associated with the Lincoln legend, the death of the martyr to emancipation, and the young boy/old man relationship. (An elderly black man stands behind at a distance that in 1939 denoted respect and seems shocking today in its offensive humility.) Smith is sensitive to the images and words. His eyes avidly read them and respond to the eyes of the Lincoln statue that, as he will soon say, are "lookin' straight at you while you're coming up those steps." The words of Lincoln, inscribed on the walls of a spatial entity devoted to his spiritual presence, read by us and by the in-frame perceivers, and voiced by the boy, are made the focus of visibly moved representatives of the ostensibly free democracy he

121

championed and for which he died. This is a model for the emotional value of the words Smith himself will voice in the Senate beneath the dome.

Soon after, when the dome is captured in the rear window of an automobile, its inspiration has an immediate effect on Smith; Saunders (Jean Arthur), the cynical aide bored by the sights of official Washington, refuses to look. Soon after, searching for the words to frame his bill establishing the boys' camp, Smith looks out the window of his office. The refrained image of the dome links (1) the office, a space reserved for politicking and wheeling-dealing, (2) the Capitol, the space in which Smith will fully identify himself as the democratic man, and (3) the evocation of the camp that is to be a

training ground for democracy (a singularly male version of democracy in this film). Smith's voice, so often hesitant and out of control, takes on assurance and finally wins its audience, Saunders, the representative of the most jaded among us. He speaks of seeing the light after coming out of a dark tunnel (a line later echoed by Saunders), and that light is caught in a close-up of Saunders whose luminosity is expressive of sympathy. The motif of space as text (the dome, the camp, the Lincoln Memorial) acquires meaning and elicits an emotional response through its voicing. Space becomes the right words. As Smith says, "Liberty is too precious to be buried in books." At a loss for words, he had asked Saunders, "How do you say it?" When he sees the dome, he immediately knows how to say it. Subsequently, he will find yet greater inspiration in the chamber symbolized by that dome.

Smith's first demonstration of senatorial public speaking takes the form of an initiation that suggests several ranges of discourse, and the relationship between various speakers and the forum. Smith is ushered to his place by a page boy who passes on, to the former editor of *Boy Stuff*, a version of parliamentary decorum that is a mixture of ageless practicality and youthful idealism. The Silver Knight, in the avuncular, resonant tones of Claude Rains, establishes the priority of that decorum, formally presenting and requesting acknowledgment of Smith to the assembled body. The distance on the floor of the Senate between the desk of the fledgling appointee, his senior colleague, and the chair marks the primary area of verbal resonance. Speakers take the floor, address the chair, are addressed by each other, thereby filling the rectangle with voices that emanate from various vantage points and pass through readily perceptible distances. The Senate is thereby fully voiced, its space endowed with speech, reserved for speech, in fact a function of speech. That space, organized visually during the exchange between Smith and the page boy—the rising semicircular tiers of desks, the still higher podium of the President of the Senate, the public gallery—is emblematic of the amphitheater, in its forensic and theatrical functions. Both are served here, the first by the film's dramatic pretext, the second by the theatricality of the medium. Throughout this sequence Smith speaks with the voice of the novice, professing his ignorance of the forum's rules. His voice responds submissively to the institutional sound of the Senate Chamber, the voicing of its rituals, the discourse of its habitual status. After the oath he is told, "You can talk all you want to now," but it will take more meaningful rituals to endow him with the power made possible by that permission. The hero has not yet found the words that will redefine this space and make it resound with the voice of his own authority.

Smith's two subsequent appearances on the floor of the Senate mark the beginning of the transformation of his verbal power. First, armed with words that mix idealism and legislative decorum, the result of his collaboration with Saunders, the professional wordster, he rises to introduce his bill and immediately provokes laughter with the unruly fortissimo of his "Mr. President." After then speaking too softly, he delivers the text in a shaking voice, with shaking hands, elicits the laughter of floor and gallery, then cheers and applause for his ingenuousness and sincerity. "The young senator will make a good orator when his voice stops changing," says the President. The next time, out of ignorance of parliamentary rules, he yields his voice to Senator Paine. Not yet having found "his" voice, he is silenced by the man who is his paragon for speech. At this point, because Smith's voice has been denied its personal resonance, it is Paine who commands the public's ear. The senators rush back to the floor to hear the vituperation. When Smith tries to interrupt, he is roundly booed. The on-screen auditors conspire with the rules of the Senate to deny Smith's right to speak.

Smith's truth unheard, he stops at the Lincoln Memorial before returning home in disgrace; Lincoln's words are carved in stone and near-forgotten. A shot of the Lincoln statue relinks the dead hero and one who is figuratively dying. In the shadow of the colonnade Smith sits on his valise and breaks into sobs. (Smith's eyes filled with tears at the send-off banquet. This is Jimmy Stewart, not Gary Cooper or even Henry Fonda. Stewart portrays the hysterical, vulnerable American hero again for Capra in *It's a Wonderful Life* and for Hitchcock in *Vertigo*.) He exhibits his emotion often during the film. Inflamed with anger, he pursues the slanderous news-papermen. And it is this manic energy and this emotional prompt-ness that will animate his filibuster; its effectiveness is a function of emotional release rather than political or oratorical know-how. Sobbing, silhouetted against the marble of the Lincoln Memorial, seated like the statue of the hero whose legend is informed with compassion, he establishes his credentials to speak with the voice of compassion. It is in this position, expressive of his vulnerability and his heroic, emotional capacity, that he is discovered by Saunders. And the resulting two-shot of their silhouettes, sharply detached from the marble background and defining columns, is the point of departure toward speech that will be heard. To rescue the democra-tic ear, the words carved in stone (about which Smith complains) must be voiced in a space that favors their resonance. In the pre-vious Lincoln Memorial sequence a young boy gave life to Lincoln's words and his statue. Here, Saunders, moved by Smith, the weep-ing boy (she previously told him, "Don't stay around here making people feel sorry for you"), and moved by his incarnation of the Lincoln myth, proposes to give him back his voice, or, more accurately, permit him to call on all his voices. If she can be moved to tears and to love, so can the whole democratic nation.

On his previous appearances in the forum Smith was identified as a buffoon, a naïf, and a grafter. He submitted to the rules and the judgment of the political body that now his voice will redefine. He has passed through false soundings of his presence to the filibuster, a supreme verbal act that is parallel to living itself, that equates talking and existence. As long as he keeps talking he "can hold this floor a little short of doomsday." The initiation of the filibuster realigns the vocal coordinates of the Senate Chamber in a way that challenges the conventional patterns so clearly established during the previous sequences (the page boy's guided tour, the oath-taking ceremony, the triumph of the rules that results in Smith's silencing). Now Smith enters laden with words (in the form of books and papers) and resoundingly responds to the roll call, just when his absence has been taken for granted. The gallery, previously indicated as ingenuous (the Boy Rangers) and ironic (the press corps), is embodied by Saunders, the source of knowledge and political savvy, and infused with love for Smith and his cause. The habitual relationship between auditor (someone in the gallery) and the speaker on the floor is immediately transformed into a model that accommodates discourse apt for the democratic system (clear communication between constituency and spokesman) and romantic comedy (a film genre that informs much of *Mr. Smith* and in which various means of communication are pretexts for speaking about love). This transformation is also operated on the Senate Chamber as sounded space. Its quality as resonating chamber will be newly qualified by the voice of the hero, a voice in contact with and strengthened by the fullness of the chamber, a voice that animates the chamber and is animated by its level of audition. On signal from Saunders, Smith jumps to his feet, shouts, "Mr. President," and succeeds in being recognized, through his voice, by the presiding officer, just as his voice is about to be silenced. From the gallery, Saunders shouts, "Let him speak," demonstrating that the true authority for his speech comes from these privileged heights, this area suggestive of the democracy he represents and the audience for which he performs. The President gavels order but bows to this collective expression and "recognizes Senator—Smith." And so do we. The hero has earned his right to speak.

The spatial integrity of the chamber and the integrity of its rules supply the dynamics of most of the remainder of the film. Smith indeed has the floor. His eyes, no longer clouded by hero-worship and ignorance, newly measure the forum, the distances between himself, his colleagues, the chair, and the gallery. This comprehensive glance is a call for eye contact with his listeners. His eyes are met with understanding by the President and Saunders, surrogates for the increasingly wider audience he will reach with his voice through the course of his filibuster. The ways in which he will be heard and seen inflect the fiction and enact modes of sympathetic attention not unrelated to how the film is to be viewed.

Soon after the start of the filibuster the Silver Knight manages to incite his colleagues to walk out in protest to Smith's alleged dishonesty and disrespect. (I am struck by one small irony here—the second senator to renounce Smith is played by H. B. Warner, an actor who never really shook off his impersonation of Jesus in De Mille's *King of Kings*.) The absence of the other senators exposes Smith's voice as it traverses the familiar distance between the speaker and the podium, made unfamiliar by the emptiness of the forum. All that gaping space, vacated by misinformed, misled senators, becomes a vast field, relieved of formal discourse. It is as if the air had been cleared, permitting new resonance, new communication between Smith, the grown-up Boy Ranger whose voice still has a tendency to break, a sign of his boyhood/manhood, and the laconic President of the Senate, who has heard it all, but hears something like his own youth in the ironic intimacy engineered by the film, an intimacy that traverses the breadth of the Senate Chamber and is on view to the gallery and to us. Smith and the President are about to prove that Boy Rangers can grow into democratic political men, and find their true voices by losing them.

The President, as portrayed by the amiable, bemused Harry Carey, is another common-man figure, sympathetic to Smith in every sense of the word. That sympathy redefines the oath administered earlier in the film and the initial recognition offered by the President in his official capacity. Now he judges Smith's voice by the sincerity of its tone and by the high price paid for its articulation. Through the rest of the film the President's smile is a persistent sign of sympathy and his not-so-reluctant approval of Smith's gallant defiance of the very body over whose decorum he is charged to preside. This smile is conferred at the moment Smith is most desperate, when he reads the disapproving telegrams and letters. Its warmth includes the President in the fervent communication between Smith and Saunders, who, unable to speak directly from floor to gallery, are linked by a set of signals, glances, word-mouthings, codes of pseudovocal visibility. (At the early banquet scene there is a significant prefiguration of the emotional value of mouthing words that cannot be fully voiced when Smith's mother [Beulah Bondi] and Senator Paine reacknowledge their relationship to each other during Smith's evocation of his martyred father.) The space is therefore not only filled with the sound of voice; the voices of Smith and Saunders, with which we are abundantly familiar, are seen as well, openly displayed, on view to the parliamentarian who cannot

authorize their sounding but who cannot resist expressing his sympathy for theirs.

The sympathetic transmission of Smith's voice by the press to the nation at large and to his home state is frustrated by the power of boss Taylor (Edward Arnold). But Saunders, again the purveyor of the word, this time Smith's word (a sign that he has learned to speak for himself), dictates the news to Smith's mother, who passes it on for publication in *Boy Stuff*. The phone juxtaposes the conspiratorial Taylor, distorting Smith's message, and the conversation between Saunders and Mrs. Smith in which the women's affectionate recognition of each other qualifies and amplifies the words that are

127

resounding in the Senate Chamber. But even reliable extensions of Smith's voice—girl friend, mother, and idolizing, energetic boys— are blocked by Taylor's aggressive silencing tactics (recalling similar methods in *The Miracle Woman* and anticipating the wire cutting in *Meet John Doe*). Grown men beat up small boys and run their truck off the road. The big voice and the small voice are sharply distinguished at an anti-Smith rally during which the hero's only supporter, a boy, is carried off by Taylor's goons.

The degree of pain inflicted on the boys is, of course, transferred back to Smith, increasing the pathos produced by his speech. The pain it costs him to stand and make himself heard during the filibuster is a measure of pathetic sound. The mediators of that sound, Saunders, Smith's mother, and the boys, in their effort to prolong its reverberation are also made conscious of the percussive effects of such reverberation. But if the larger audience is denied Smith (and, in fact, the boys' voices are ineffectual except as pathetic ploys), he is able to find the proper resonance in the Senate Chamber. First, the gallery cedes and its enthusiastic applause qualifies a shot of the completely unresponsive senators. Smith is working to be heard, to fill this space with his voice in tones of anger, supplication, reason. Standing in the aisle, framed by ranks of turned backs, his words unheeded, he whistles to provoke a reaction. Just when his voice seems to fail, Saunders sends him written instructions to read the Constitution and a confession of her love. A long pause. He looks at her, she at him. The silence that can prove fatal to Smith is broken by his declaration, "I feel fine." The

combination of purely visual eye language, the written word, the language of love, and the language of patriotism somehow conspires to revive this dying voice.

At the climax everyone within earshot pays attention to Smith. The previously averted heads of the senators now turn to him. He has managed to become the aural focus of all levels of the chamber, and all eyes now connect each level to the source of its sound in the densest representation of the repeated motif of on-screen scrutiny and audition in the film. Gallery, podium, and floor listen with a raptness that echoes the pattern of sympathetic audition. H. V. Kaltenborn says to his radio listeners, "All official Washington is here to be in on the kill." The kill is a form of sacrificial suicide, a spending of oneself through words, a draining of voice in an ever-more-raucous whisper. Such a voice, so emptied of conventional resonance, both figurative and literal, and so disproportionate to the size of the resonating chamber, makes everyone that more avid to hear. The audience hangs on Smith's every word because every word might be his last. The space has tested dynamic levels ranging

from full-throated fortissimo to near-inaudible pianissimo; degrees of attention indicated by empty desks, turned backs, and sleeping senators, to shots that show the chamber filled to bursting with listeners desperate to know what Smith is saying.

Smith's voice, made precious as it fills the chamber and the film, becomes increasingly pathetic as it fulfills these functions with ever greater difficulty. The space that has been made so resonant now accommodates Smith's silence and the stunned silence of his listeners as he looks at the mountains of telegrams protesting his filibuster, words that are "Taylor-made" lies. Saunders cries, "Stop, Jeff, stop." The President sheepishly smiles. Everyone is connected through pity for Smith's presumably lost cause. "Lost cause" is the phrase that Smith throws back at his opponent, Paine. A low-angle shot from behind the seated Paine supplies Smith with the back-

ground of the gallery that now believes in him. His rasping whisper, *fully heard*, commands the sympathetic approval of gallery and floor and finally provokes Paine's aborted suicide and confession of malfeasance.

The final images of the film are filled with a euphoric chaos of voices echoing the hero's triumph, doubly resumed in Saunders's scream of "Yahoo" and the President's smile. The "Yahoo" and the smile, conclusive proofs that Smith has captured his audience, reflect the approval of the on-screen perceivers through the specific quality of their sympathy. A shout from the gallery and a smile from the co-opted chair form a model of response to the emphatic assertion of Smith's voice, its heroic power to transcend conventional audition. "Every word that boy said is the truth," shouts the defeated Silver Knight. The boy said the truth, but boys must be pathetic before men will listen to them. When pathos accords them full visual attention and amplifies their voices, they can command respect. And the quality of this attention and amplification is a function of the democratic audience, whose relationship to the speaker is one of ostensible equality. The scheme of democratic representation is served by the fiction's premises—the power of the machine to distort the democratic process, the indication of the right man by the children's voices (Governor Hopper's boys), the subversion of that man's intentions by the various systems of power through which he must pass to be heard, eventually, as the democratic hero, whose voice is the sympathetic reverberation of the democratic myth. He has rescued the words from their stone inscription and, through their progressively crucial voicings, makes them sound as if his and everyone else's lives depended on them.

6 The Stages of Feeling

Cinematography accounts for "nature as it is" to a greater degree than do other media that inscribe art. We read written fictions only and always as "language" (even when that language is at the service of narrative forms on which the reality-effect is imposed—the journal novel, the first-person novel, the epistolary novel). Each element of a painting is meant to be expressive and to convey meaning; each element is *inside* the work of art and has an artistic status. We expect written fiction and paintings to be expressive because they are clearly *not* what they represent. They are designed to elicit readership. Fiction film, on the other hand, is congenial to configurations, objects, and categories of events that demand neither literacy nor interpretation. Many of the elements in the film frame can be perceived much as they are in life and are not necessarily related to the particular narrative scheme to which they belong. This factor of intermittent readership (negative/positive) is present in the most naive viewing of a film, but also in quite sophisticated ones; the amount of data we receive from the film image and the flux of film images tolerate intermittent readership. In film, the fiction-effect and the reality-effect are almost contiguous, sometimes identical, and therefore the loss of a sense of unreality, of representationality, is the rule rather than the exception.

When, then, the artifice of the medium is made apparent, when it is even forced upon us through dramatic or technical strategies, we become aware of passing from the viewing of a field that is so close to life as to almost be life, to one that appears to be fully expressive. These fields are made to coexist and to be perceived at the same time. Cinema engineers such rapid passages between the fiction-effect and the reality-effect that at times we hold both in our minds and eyes.

Real Performers

If all art is ultimately about itself, self-reflexive art draws the viewer's attention to that fact.[1] Art is made its own subject when its fictional pretexts refer to its modes of creation, of execution, of performance. "Show biz" configurations in films function the way trompe l'oeil techniques, virtuosic lighting, and other blatant devices of perspective do in painting. It has been argued that these displays of technique and artifice make it difficult to respond affectively to art since they create distance between the fiction and the viewer. Can the illusions of art and performance survive their self-analysis, their *mise-en-abîme*? Can we be lost in the illusion if we witness it from backstage? What is affecting about a movie's movieness, the performance of a performer? The oscillation between the reality-effect and the fiction-effect in film becomes a source of affect when we see *how* performers express their feelings in the service of their performance and as a reflection of their lives. The fiction-effect then comes to be identified by the specific expressive activities of performance. The self-reflexive film makes us more alert to the passage between the two effects than do other sorts of narratives, where the fiction-effect is carefully hidden. Indeed, what has been described as the classic Hollywood style is meant to hide the fiction-effect altogether. But when the characters and the fictions themselves pass from one status to the other—the actor in the dressing room and then performing a role within a role in a play/film within a film—we become conscious of a high level of fictivity.

Because of its all-encompassing trueness of representation, cinema redefines the junctures and the distinctions between fictivity and verisimilitude. Early in James Whale's version of *Show Boat* a naive viewer of the show boat's melodrama, unfamiliar with the illusions of fiction, shoots at the on-stage villain. A moment later he is entertained and distracted, along with the other spectators, by Captain Andy (Charles Winninger), the impresario who acts the rest of the play himself, assuming all the roles in a tour de force. The on-screen audience is as delighted by Captain Andy's version, in which the workings of the melodrama are fully exposed, as it was by the more conventional performace so noisily interrupted.[2] The film's principal characters, Magnolia (Irene Dunne) and Gaylord (Allan Jones), relate to each other within the narrative, sing their feelings, play them out in the melodramas performed on the show boat, and at the film's conclusion recognize each other in a full theatrical/filmic configuration that contains all these passages. Reunited after a separation of many years at their daughter's opening night, they sing together from the audience. Through the spatial alteration of the performance/audience nexus, the film tests the painful closeness between what we are meant to perceive as reality and as fiction. Reality and fiction are confused during Joe's (Paul Robeson's) rendition of "Ol' Man River," where the almost 360 degree turn of the camera establishes a locus that holds both the studio set and location shots of the river. The intercuts of blacks

133

toting barges, lifting bales, getting drunk, and landing in jail belong
to the stylistics of cinema, the voice of Robeson to the stylistics of
music; and the two expressivities merge in the reality of Robeson's
presence. When Julie (Helen Morgan) sings "Bill," the performance, purported to be a rehearsal in a nightclub, is transformed into
something so moving that the charwomen, bartenders, and showgirls stop what they are doing and become an audience. They are
moved by Julie's rendition of lovesickness as well as by her obvious
affliction with the same disease. A moment later Julie hears Magnolia sing, with a soulfulness expressive of her loss of Gaylord, "Can't
Help Lovin' Dat Man of Mine." This pattern of private emotion
made public culminates when Magnolia, having replaced Julie (who
sacrifices her job to her old friend), tries to sing "After the Ball" to a
raucous New Year's Eve audience. No one listens to her faltering
voice until Captain Andy, who happens to be in the audience,
instills her with his confidence and fatherly love, tells her to smile

and to project. The whole nightclub becomes part of the song that re-creates the expressive dynamics of the preceding fiction, the relationships between the characters, the lifelikeness of the narrative, and the manner of Magnolia's performance. Everyone, of course, sings and dances to this degree of urging.

Self-reflexive films oblige us to reexamine our response to reality and to art, perhaps to discard the too facile categorizations we make, and to grant to art its "real" status. The audience is disoriented by the elisions of fiction and life effected by Robeson and Joe, Helen Morgan and Julie. Where does the performance end and reality begin? The film that makes a fiction of performance tests the

medium's approximation of verisimilitude against fictivity; our affect becomes a function of our reading activity, our ability to see performance as performance. Art is *at least* as moving as life when its expressivity is perceived to be contiguous to that which moves us in life.

This contiguity is displayed in a wide range of fictions, from the "stagings" of everyday life (*Stella Dallas*, for example)[3] to the theatrical narratives of *Children of Paradise, A Double Life,* and *All about Eve,* reflections on cinema and photography such as *Funny Face* and *Pretty Baby,* and the movies' own inside stories, *Sunset Boulevard, A Star Is Born,* and *The Bad and the Beautiful.* The recent Soviet film, Nikita Mikhalkov's *A Slave of Love* (1978), recounts the trials of a group of filmmakers in Yalta during the Russian Revolution. Juxtaposing their childish characters and the frivolity of the film they are shooting against the harsh historical reality around them, *A Slave of Love* exposes many cinematic modes: the documentary, the fiction film, the silent film, the talkie, the black and white film, the color film. Life is "played" in front of the camera by the movie star heroine of *A Slave of Love,* who is literally trapped in a tracking shot, pursued by cavalry as she rides, alone, on a trolley; by Norma Desmond in the final, halated close-up of *Sunset Boulevard*; by the quasi-amateur theatricals of *Sylvia Scarlett,* by the travesties of Dietrich (*Morocco*) and Garbo (*Queen Christina*); by the screen-effect at the conclusion of *Stella Dallas*; by the passage from high fashion, still photography to the moving camera in *Funny Face,* where Fred Astaire's acting lessons turn Audrey Hepburn into a mobile "Winged Victory" in the Louvre. Photographer and model later dance a love duet that transcends the stillness of photography with the graceful camera movements characteristic of Stanley Donen films. Cinematic self-reflexivity is generated by these explicit fictional pretexts and by the properties of the medium I treated in the preceding chapters (framing, display,

136

etc.). This mesh of references engages the viewer in the art's quest for a movement toward its interior, toward its intrinsic nature.

On Stage

One of the most obvious manifestations of self-reflexivity in the movies is the specifically camera-eye view of show biz. In Busby Berkeley production numbers, for example, the lens has the privilege of seeing that to which the theater audience has no access; through its constantly variable vantage the camera seems to create patterns from the mere capacity for shift. Another device, the play within a play, or the play/film within a film, recalls the baroque conventions of sixteenth- and early seventeenth-century theater. These strategies tend to turn things inside out, backward-forward, upside down, to thrust upon fiction and viewer a radical spatial disorientation that parallels the modal disorientation. In Cukor's *A Double Life* the performance of *Othello* and the performer Tony are seen onstage, from the wings, and from the audience's point of view, continuously shifting one into the other, alternately distinguished and superimposed through the camera's ubiquity. In Robert Z. Leonard's *Ziegfeld Girl* the showgirls walking up and down flights of stairs are seen from angles that challenge our ability to know where we are, and indeed where they are in relation to the proscenium that is presumably delimiting their movements. These challenges to spectatorship are also challenges to performance.

Sometimes the proscenium itself, emblematic of theatricality, fixed or movable, defines the "cinematic." The opening sequences of Olivier's *Henry V*, with their reconstruction of the Globe Theatre and Elizabethan stage conventions, provide a point of departure toward the more obviously filmic spectacle of the battle scenes.[4] Near the beginning of Resnais's *Last Year at Marienbad* a highly stylized performance of Ibsen's *Romersholm*, its statuelike actors in front of an emphatically two-dimensional backdrop of a park, serves as prelude to the stretching out, through a vast repertoire of cinematic devices, of the relationship of the film's protagonists, A (Delphine Seyrig), M (Sacha Pitoëff), and X (Giorgio Albertazzi). It can be argued that the energetic deployment of technique in *Last Year at Marienbad* serves to authenticate feeling. A fiction of affect (did A love X last year at Marienbad? will she leave M?) is tested against various cinematographic modes; the flatness of the Ibsen episode and the flatness of the hotel's silhouette in the film's final shot are linked through incessant trackings that take full account of space and through dissolves and cuts that make time into a circle. The film juxtaposes Robbe-Grillet's disquisition on narrativity, the puzzle of what? when? where? and Resnais's love of the medium, of objects, and of characters. Resnais's manipulation of the medium in

137

the optical ploys of flatness and depth—the exaggerated perspective and the blatantly cinematic editing (with which we have become familiar through *Hiroshima mon amour, Stavisky,* and *Providence*)—makes the activity of filmmaking parallel to X's technique of seduction. The strategies (storytelling, photographic evidence) he uses to draw the woman to her feelings are the same as those of any film that draw the viewer into its fiction.

The woman in *Last Year at Marienbad*, so clearly subservient to manner in her high fashion costumes and Garboesque poses, more a rhetorical figure than a conventional character, is a sister to the Ziegfeld girl, the woman walking up and down a flight of stairs because a "creative" man has put her there, and because other men have bought tickets to see her, to stare at her, to identify her through their gaze. The woman in film, particularly in elaborate musical production numbers, often functions as a trope for this specular activity.[5] When a showgirl walks in what we immediately identify as a space peculiar only to cinema, she forces us to recognize artifice and the objectification of the performer. The showgirl does not seem to be breathing. Her being is a function of her walk, a walk that is supposed to display sexuality but that is dissociated

from sexual walking. She is near-expressionless, as expressionless as Resnais's Ibsen performers and his A. The showgirl is a walking image, nearly devoured by an absurd costume that is not a dress, that is difficult to wear, that makes her top-heavy and/or bottom-heavy, that weighs her down and must be carried up. The woman is lost in the metaphoric value of a costume shot through with stars, awash with subaqueous vegetation. The "American Woman" is "glorified" through fictions that deny essential aspects of her womanness. (A man is not often desexualized in production numbers. Even in mass configurations he is obviously a man.)

In the Warners musicals that bear his stamp, Busby Berkeley (the director of the Ziegfeld-style parades in *Ziegfeld Girl*) often anatomizes women for metaphorical purposes obvious to the most naive viewer. In the kaleidoscope of arms, legs, faces, eyes, meaning shifts from the woman as surface to woman as love, as death. The movies make us see the map of the city in the inverted face of Wini Shaw, the ultimate victim of that city in "Lullaby of Broadway" (*Gold Diggers of 1935*). But if the mannerist camera objectifies and metaphorizes the woman, it also catches her human presence. Wini Shaw *is* a vibrant singer; Resnais's A *is* Delphine Seyrig. The Ziegfeld girl, when seen from the multiplicity of angles in the purview of the camera, is also liberated from the purely approving gaze or the leering eyes of men. She is revealed to have eyes of her own, a life of her own. Cinema does this to image. Its surface generates depth, activity, space. We perceive its images as superficial and then locate those images amidst various spatial, temporal, and narrative planes. The very modalities of cinema that relieve objects and performers of their referentiality, their burden of representation, give them an aura of roundness as they reverberate in the space between the act of performance and that which is being performed.

In *Ziegfeld Girl* the play of flatness and depth is further displayed by the distinctions made between the three protagonists. We immediately perceive Hedy Lamarr and Lana Turner as showgirl types who obviously know how to walk up and down stairs. In many films Lamarr and Turner function primarily as specular objects, bearers of figure and face. We are told that Mr. Ziegfeld got into an elevator, saw "Red" (Turner), the operator, and decided on the spot that she should be in the Follies. "Beautiful" (Lamarr) just happens to be standing on the stage of the theater, is seen, and is signed as well. It is enough to see these women to turn them into showgirls, into images that walk. Susan (Judy Garland) has to perform actively, to exhibit a performing talent that is not exclusively related to her appearance. At the film's conclusion she is the only surviving performer of the three, singing, dancing, and also revered as image, perched atop a spiral column (a crafty insert from

The Great Ziegfeld, released five years previously, in 1936). The film puts her through a series of tests that validate her talent; she becomes an object without losing her status as active performer. (This double nature resonates in Garland's life. Her biographers have commented on the singer's terrible feelings of glamourlessness at that glamour-filled studio, MGM. In *Ziegfeld Girl* Susan is told, "You're not a showgirl.")

Involved Audiences

Ziegfeld Girl reminds us that as filmgoers we are ideal spectators, something we never are in the theater. Cinema's displacements of point of view give us great knowledge and an acute vision that are often figured in reaction shots. The validation of on-screen performance by the approving glance of an on-screen viewer, a frequent device of cinematic self-reflexivity, becomes a sign of affect when that viewer also has a specifically personal relationship with the performer/image. The first production number of *Ziegfeld Girl* features reaction shots of Beautiful's disappointed husband (Philip Dorn), Red's enthusiastic brother (Jackie Cooper), slightly nervous boyfriend (James Stewart), and prospective lover (Ian Keith), and Susan's proud father (Charles Winninger). In Cukor's *A Star Is Born* it is through Norman's (James Mason's) viewing, intercut with Esther's (Judy Garland's) rendition of "The Man That Got Away," that we come to know about her talent and about why he falls in love with a women who possesses such talent. Norman's point of view is brought to bear upon Esther as a look of love, coming closer and closer to her through the doors and shadows of the near-deserted nightclub as her voice comes closer to him and to us, and as the staging gives her free access to the instrumentalists while it allows her to make all of that space her own. We are more privileged than Norman, the only spectator on screen, since we see his enactment of spectatorship as well. The transfer between the image of his raptness and the camera's point of view favors the full resonance of the space around the performer. There is, of course, a risk in picturing the complete satisfaction of such spectatorship, the risk that the performance viewed by the movie audience will not be appreciated to the degree the fiction demands. Indeed, we are often disappointed by the nonmusical "numbers" performed in films. The dramatic recitations of Katharine Hepburn in *Morning Glory*, Bette Davis in *Dangerous*, Barbara Stanwyck in *All I Desire*, and Ronald Colman's first rendition of *Othello* in *A Double Life* are unconvincing proofs of the acting ability demonstrated elsewhere in these films. Yet even at the beginning of *A Star Is Born* we readily identify the talent of the performer, Esther/Judy, exhibited in its accustomed movie space, doing what it was always meant to do.

The spectacle within the fiction is meant to elicit sight, as does the picturing of the reaction to it. This reflects back upon our own activity, or activities, shown in the inserts during the first production number in *Ziegfeld Girl*, activities that include satisfaction, pride, wounded pride, and a leering appraisal of the soon-to-be-bought object/woman. The magnification of the viewing process obviously increases our sense of the woman as the viewed object. The three star faces in *Ziegfeld Girl* suggest something of the range of the viewed, from Hedy Lamarr's near-death mask, a figure of stasis (her smile is intrusive to the utter calm of the mask), to Lana Turner, whose American beauty face actively acknowledges and provokes the admiration of men's eyes, to Judy Garland, whose face is, at this point in her career, a field of constant energy, "pep." To draw our gaze, Hedy simply *is*, Lana *shows*, Judy *performs*. The film's narrative structure will pivot on the malleability and responsiveness of the Turner character, and use the other two stars as

polar versions of the performer type. We perceive the woman/ object between motion and immobility. It is there that she exposes her own feelings, makes us conscious of spectatorship, and invites our passage through various stages of involvement and detachment from the work of art. Self-reflexive art clearly locates us as spectators and engages us in the work of the art.[6] Where are we when we see films from backstage, and at whom are we looking when we look at Ronald Colman playing Tony playing Othello playing a character in *A Double Life*, or Lana Turner, aware of her need to be seen and desired by men as a movie star, as a Ziegfeld girl, as a character within the fiction of the film? We are many places at once, looking at the object prismatically, applying particularly cinematic perspectives, long and short, close up and far away, in and out, that connect the manner of our seeing to our thoughts and feelings about what we see, when what we are meant to do, precisely, is to see.

In *Ziegfeld Girl*, among the spectatorial relationships to the showgirl, that of the father is most insistently inscribed. The father is the "author" of the fiction, the generator of the spectacle. He is the authority for what is transpiring before our eyes and the ultimate judge of his own creation. When the creation takes on a life of its own, he becomes anguished, disapproving, and he threatens to withdraw his gaze, his love. Ziegfeld, the godlike father of the Ziegfeld girls, never appears in the film, but is provided with mediators, high priests who pass on his wisdom and do his bidding. He is the one for whom the girls perform and for whom they must "behave." Susan's father (played by Charles Winninger, the father/ impresario of *Show Boat*) provides a locus of enactment for the Ziegfeld father configuration. He trains his daughter, constantly expresses his authority and experience (is seen performing with her near the film's beginning as a contemporary, sexual partner), stands in the wings offering encouragement and advice, and threatens rejection if she ignores that advice.

The affective power of this parental authority, eye, gaze almost destroys the daughter's talent. Pop forces Susan to sing a ridiculously "upbeat" rendition of "I'm Always Chasing Rainbows" during an audition. When she betrays his authority, performing the song slowly for the Ziegfeld surrogates, the camera shows her fluctuating relationship to her crestfallen father, seated hunched over at the piano, his back turned to her. She touches his shoulder, drawing strength from his presence, but sings for other men, men who are willing to buy her talent. By dividing the father figure between Pop and the absent Ziegfeld, the film gives the performing act a wide resonance, suggesting that one can care about the performance in very different ways. Its cost is high. A loving hand is placed on the shoulder of the disapproving spectator whose presence validates the performance; it is this spectator who most wants the performance to take place and who fears that when it takes place it will deidentify him. This sequence holds closely together the creation of the performance (what Pop has trained Susan to do) and the loss of a daughter, a loss sounded and seen in the sad song performed for Ziegfeld's men and his girls, charged with the emotion Susan is feeling for her father. And what are the Ziegfeld girls thinking as they watch Susan perform with a talent that we are all meant to esteem more highly than theirs? (Lana Turner, the sweater girl, is told in this film *not* to sing.) The depth of Susan's talent reflects negatively on their superficiality. All they have to do is walk; Susan must prove herself by singing her way to the top of that enormous white pillar. In doing so, she forces us to gauge the distance between her heartfelt singing and the anonymous brunette, balancing half a tree on her head. Our gaze scans the distance between Susan and the showgirl, and then reflects back on itself with some sense of complicity in the ploys that extract performance from acts of emotional display and of self-objectification. If a performer is very lucky, she gets to sing for her supper.

Dressing Room Mirrors

So many self-reflexive films are posited on the false perspective created optically by the cinema, its illusion of depth in two-dimensionality. The cinema captures a theatrical action that transpires on a sound stage or a location; the screen can then be construed as a mirror of the action that takes place in front of the lens. Self-reflexivity doubles the situation of that which is doubled in a mirror. The fiction that represents another fiction doubles its processes, prolongs its echoes, catches performances in a multitude of reflections that increases the affective value of the reflected elements. When this dynamics of reproduction is inscribed in the fiction itself (performers looking into mirrors, seen in mirrors, etc.), the medium's mirrorlike capture is extended to even greater, more "artificial" depths. The reflection of feeling in the faithful, impassive mirror blurs conventional boundaries between what we call reality and what we call art. Film fictions that test this art/reality juncture in terms of narrativity and fictivity suggest that a staged, mirrored action can be identical to reality, can in fact be the only reality. Self-reflexive modes, in the blatancy of their artifice, achieve this disorientation through slippage from one status to the other.

In *A Star Is Born*, following their onstage meeting, Norman sees Esther kneeling in front of a mirror, putting on makeup. He takes her lipstick and inscribes their names on the wall of the theater, an inscription that moves her at the film's end, after Norman's death. Mirrors capture the ludicrous efforts of the studio makeup artists

143

who tranform Esther's face into a caricature of glamour; the re-transformed, "natural" Esther appears in Norman's dressing room mirror. (The persona of the natural Judy Garland is exploited in Charles Walters's *Easter Parade* when Fred Astaire comically and unsuccessfully attempts to make her resemble his former dancing partner, svelte, sophisticated, long-legged Ann Miller.) The screen itself is mirrored when Norman, on a drunken spree, inadvertently slaps Esther (now renamed Vicki Lester) during the Oscar ceremony. This complex gesture of theatrical display is witnessed by the shocked in-frame spectators and the implied TV viewers receiving the image shown on the giant screen included in the frame. Later, Esther/Vicki sits in her dressing room, in front of a makeup mirror, in her hayseed costume, mascara streaming down her face. As she cries in despair over her self-destructive husband, she "mirrors" Judy Garland's own life in a film that also ironizes, with its constant references to "going on with the show," the actress's intermittent ability to perform. The mirrors of the film's final sequences at the beach house and the shots of Norman's suicide superimpose the planes in which Norman and Esther appear, and turn their relationship into an optical illusion, albeit a valuable one, as is a film.[7]

When the mirror captures the slippage between the fiction-effect and the reality-effect, it jolts our belief in representation. In Cukor's *Sylvia Scarlett* the slippage within the narrative, from the true identity of the characters to their con-game disguises, their playful disguises, and their theatrical disguises is subsumed in Sylvia's (Katharine Hepburn's) travesty of sexual identity, an oscillation that keeps theater and life in such close proximity that "representation" becomes difficult to locate. Travesty and playacting are ways to the fullest expression of the truth, the most expressive self. Sylvia must pass through her impersonations of Sylvester and of Pierrot in order to grow up. When Maudie (Dennie Moore) paints a moustache on the youth Sylvester, who then "boyishly" averts her face from a kiss, Sylvia is both recognized and not recognized. For Sylvia, decor becomes nature. She looks at a design on wallpaper, exclaims "the sea!", inspires her tawdry companions to shake off their tired impersonations as they joyously dance and sing, "I'd Love to Be beside the Seaside." In the house of the painter, Michael (Brian Ahearn), a house that is like a stage (one of its walls is as imaginary as "the fourth wall"), Sylvia's male/female oscillations echo her previous impersonations. When Michael finally accepts her double, masked-unmasked identity, she is able to feel and we are able to feel. Play becomes life and emotion.

The specifically theatrical elements of Hepburn's persona, the extremes of diction, her readily indentifiable "actressy" mannerisms, serve most of her work in the thirties, before she assumes the "modern" woman roles of the films with Tracy. In John Cromwell's

Spitfire she plays a hillbilly who, despite traces of a Connecticut Yankee accent, moves her community with the fervor of her prayer. That same fervor animates her Jo in *Little Women*. And are we so terribly surprised to see her attired as a firefly in Dorothy Arzner's *Christopher Strong*? She wears the garb of allegory with a naturalness appropriate to fiction, not to life. For such an actress, good artifice is truth and feeling.

This is precisely what Hepburn demonstrates in Gregory La Cava's *Stage Door*. She plays the matter-of-fact Terry, who learns her art by discovering her deep feelings after the suicide of another aspiring young actress. The denizens of the theatrical boarding

house (Ginger Rogers and Ann Miller), in the audience to sabotage Terry's opening night, express, with torrents of tears, their approval of her and her art. Terry and her calla lilies show the way life has fed art, and how both are nourished by the activity of cinema that so closely connects the life of the performer to spectatorship in and of film. This activity is a motif in the work of George Cukor. We see it in the extravagant theatrics of *The Royal Family of Broadway* (1931), the movieland referentiality of *What Price Hollywood?* (1932) (a source for *A Star Is Born* in versions by William Wellman [1937] and Cukor himself [1954]), reconstructions of ninteenth-century performing practices in *Zaza* (1939) and *Heller in Pink Tights* (1959), and the musical jokes inserted in the *Rashomon*-like structure of *Les Girls* (1957). But what is ultimately moving about the films of Cukor is the intensity with which the medium exposes acting and performance, as the fiction's explicit pretext (*A Double Life*, 1953) or as captured in a "simple" three-shot of Spencer Tracy, Teresa Wright, and Jean Simmons seated at a table (*The Actress*, 1953). A bottle of catsup at the center of the frame is charged with Tracy's energy and concentration as he *plays* a father reluctant to allow his daughter to go on the stage.

A Double Life (coscripted by Ruth Gordon, the budding actress played by Jean Simmons in *The Actress*) is perhaps Cukor's most systematic exploration of the onstage/on-film tension. Here, the mirror motif sustains the actor's confusions of life and performance as well as the film's title. We first see Tony (Ronald Colman) standing in front of his own portrait, then near a bust of himself. When Tony considers playing Othello, he contemplates his own face in a dark mirror, illuminated by a flashing sign. A moment later he sees his costumed, made-up reflection in the window of a travel agency advertising Venice. And at the apartment of Pat (Shelley Winters), the waitress he picks up, he tries on one of the woman's earrings and looks in her mirror, prefiguring the mirror of the stage that is her bedroom and the murder he will commit there, when he is overcome by Othello's jealousy. At the end of *A Double Life* Tony plays the Othello of his life (compounded of his failed marriage and his guilt over murdering Pat) before the eyes of the audience in the theater, his fellow actors, and the police who have come to arrest him.

This performance rings with the doubleness of Ronald Colman, the movie actor nearing the end of his long career as star in the silents and the talkies. The movie referentiality of Ronald Colman's voice becomes apparent near the beginning of the film when Tony evokes the stages of his career, from carefree apprentice to leading man and finally to committed, accomplished actor.[8] Colman, one of the few great stars of the silents who retained the full aura of his stardom in the talkies on the basis, in part, of his memorable, polished voice, says, "I had to teach myself to talk." (Colman's persona is similarly utilized in *Random Harvest*. During the first part of the film the character he plays has a speech impediment. The same sort of paradox is developed visually in Cukor's *A Woman's Face*, 1941, where Joan Crawford's pristine countenance, the perfect MGM skin stretched taut by those famous cheekbones, is marred by a livid scar.) A man of the movies if there ever was one, Colman tests himself against the stage and its prestige. Tony's first performance of *Othello* is that of a hammy tragedian who moves both the in-screen audience and us when he *stops* talking and smothers Desdemona with a kiss, a bit of gestural business. At the end of the film his rendition of Shakespeare is relieved of its "great literature" level of elocution because fictional time and action have intervened and have accrued upon Shakespeare's words, tying them more intimately to *A Double Life* than to *Othello*. We finally see Colman's acting as a function of film rather than as a film of a movie actor having a go at Shakespeare. The distance between Colman's first and last performance of the role measures the gulf between stage and screen. He dies in the wings, half his makeup removed. As *A Double Life* shifts through its various registers, it satisfies us by finding the right audience—the camera and us.

One of the ways "theatrical" films such as *A Double Life* remind us that movies are *not* plays is through their deployment of the medium's capacity for replay. If a film can be projected and reprojected, a scene can be replayed; in *A Double Life* the onstage drama and the offstage drama are in a fluctuating pattern of play and replay. The sound sometimes functions contrapuntally to the image track, trapping Tony aurally in an obsessive reenactment of the murder, no matter where he is. The medium favors plays of doubleness and replication in simultaneous visualizations and sonorizations of past and present: Maxim de Winter (Laurence Olivier) and his wife (Joan Fontaine) in the projection beam of home movies shot at a happier time (Hitchcock, *Rebecca*); Norma Desmond (Gloria Swanson) lighted in the *present* images of Billy Wilder's *Sunset Boulevard* (1950) by the past images of Erich Von Stroheim's *Queen Kelly* (1928); the star (Hildegarde Knef, Marthe Keller) made nearly eternal through cosmetic replication in Wilder's *Fedora* (1978). Tony's emotions will be charged, to a pathological degree, by haunting replications. A slightly askew replay has the power to incite him to murder. Life in the theater is excessive, it is emotional—it is life. Just before Tony's last performance, he leans back on Desdemona's bed in physical and emotional exhaustion and confesses that he has nothing left. His ex-wife/leading lady (Signe Hasso) takes him in her arms to comfort the actor who literally lives and dies for his art.

Tony's death binds us to art-making at the point where we are able to evaluate its cost to the makers. Sylvia Scarlett's sexual desire is repressed in disguise; Vicki Lester's tears run through her makeup; Baptiste (Jean-Louis Barrault) is called out of his Pierrot act by his love for Garance (*Children of Paradise*); director Ken Russell expresses his feelings about art in the fantasies of ecstasy and self-destruction of other artists (Tchaikovsky, Lizst, Mahler, and the cast of *The Boy Friend*). The rupture of the reality-effect in each of these instances proves the power of the medium; each breach is repeatedly mended by the enclosing film, its inexorably unfolding strip, and the unblemished mirror of the screen.

Ironic Sentiment/Sentimental Irony

As *A Double Life* forces us to see Tony on stage and screen, in and out of fiction simultaneously, it forces us to read the film as a function of ironic modes. These modes range from the patent doubleness of the title to the in-text stage/life juxtapositions, with their intricate spatial discordancies, the conventional dramatic ironies sustained by our knowledge of the characters, and the extrafictional reverberations of stage, screen, acting, and Ronald Colman. These ironic transfers come to a stop in the film's final shot, where the stage curtains part for the actor who is not there. The irony of this image is so obvious that it ceases to function ironically; it is deadly serious in its figuring of absence through the superimposition of stage and screen. Locating the nonironic term of many ironic readings, Wayne Booth describes the relationship between grace and irony that is a mark of the self-reflexive fictions I have been evoking:

Where then do we stop in our search for ironic pleasures? Where the work "tells" us to, wherever it offers us other riches that might be destroyed by irony. . . . it takes something beyond cleverness to resist going too far: the measured tempo of the experienced reader, eager for quick reversals and exhilarating turns, but always aware of the demands both of the partner and of the disciplined forms of the dance.[9]

The "graceful" workings of these ironic readings tell us something about the status of irony in the cinematographic image. The final image of *A Double Life*, in its doubleness, demonstrates that images *show* something in addition to and other than what they *show*, and that irony is another form of space within the film text that invites the viewer's activity. Irony creates a distance to be traversed, from the oblique referent (humor, parody, satire, skepticism, travesty, decorativeness) to the open expression of feeling. In these sentimental films the traversals from irony to sincerity lead also to belief that the expression of feeling is superior to the "quick reversals and exhilarating turns" that precede it.

The contiguity of irony and sentiment in *Desire* (1936) invites auteurist analysis. Directed by Frank Borzage, whose temperament seems uncongenial to insistent irony, it was supervised by Ernst Lubitsch, a director whose celebrated "touch" was a decidedly ironic one. During the first section the kinds of visual humor we immediately identify as the work of Lubitsch are used to set up the relationship between Madeleine (Marlene Dietrich) and Tom (Gary Cooper) that will dominate the second half of the film, where the testing of authentic feeling is reminiscent of Borzage's romantic ethos. At the outset, the "play" of automobiles, a black one and a white one, accompanies the black and white costumes that Madeleine wears during her sublimely assured con game. (Lubitsch exploits the black/white of movies and costumes when a wardrobe and even a cat are transformed with the rapidity of cinematic editing to signal that his "Widow" has decided to become "Merry.") This conceit is integrated into the comic courtship of an American car designer and a European femme fatale, a courtship posited on flat tires and stuck horns. Tom's lovely non sequitur sums it up: "You stole my car and I'm insane about you." It also reminds us of Von Sternberg's ironization of Dietrich and Cooper in *Morocco*, where the characters' romance is one of cultural disparities; it is captured in the film's last image, a visual pun on glamour in the movies, of the cabaret singer, in high heels, pulling a goat, following her American foreign legionnaire through the desert sands.

But non sequiturs and visual puns are not the way Borzage hears and sees true love. In *Desire*, when the protagonists reach their

destination and fall in love, the film shifts register. Madeleine is forced to measure her true feelings and make the "moral" decision to tell Tom that she is a jewel thief. A high angle shot of a very tall leading man kissing a much shorter leading lady (imagine this configuration in a film of Lubitsch!) makes the embrace an analogy for desperate passion. The same strategy dominates much of the staging in Borzage's *A Farewell to Arms* where the radically angled shots hold the embrace of tall Cooper and petite Helen Hayes. The Lubitsch mode and the Borzage mode are consecutive in *Desire*, mutually qualifying in anticipation and retrospection, suggesting that the film can be seen as an example of either ironic sentiment or sentimental irony; the priority of adjective or noun is happily obscured. What emerges from this double reading of *Desire* is that Borzage's sentiment survives Lubitsch's irony and that Lubitsch's irony is informed with Borzage's sentiment. Most of Lubitsch's films are love stories, and their modes, their obliquity, and the brittleness of their textures lead us toward the same full expression of feeling that we encounter in the films of Borzage, films saturated with sentiment. For Lubitsch, feeling achieves its highest intensity of expression through badinage and comic-opera brio, in a labyrinth of situations, in jokes about love and the movies themselves. He makes *silent* films of texts that would seem to depend nearly exclusively on voice—an Oscar Wilde play (*Lady Windermere's Fan*, 1925) and a Sigmund Romberg operetta (*The Student Prince in Old Heidelberg*, 1927). He extracts sentiment from smirks, winks, and double entendres. The Angel (in the film with that title, 1937) and conjugal love materialize in a *maison de passe*.

Rather than examine the varieties of invention that sustain Lubitsch's sentimental irony throughout his long career, a task whose scope far surpasses the measure of this chapter, I would like to suggest its deployment in his version of *The Merry Widow* (1934), a film that demonstrates both the director's and the medium's affinity for the Mittel-European ethos of operetta (*The Love Parade*, 1929; *Monte Carlo*, 1930; *The Smiling Lieutenant*, 1931; *One Hour with You*, 1932; even the posthumous *That Lady in Ermine*, 1948, finished by Otto Preminger). In *The Merry Widow* the ironic transfers between speech, song, and dance, between image and meaning, and the alternance between figurations of singular and plural, bring Danilo (Maurice Chevalier) and Sonia (Jeanette MacDonald) to an affirmation of love. Widowhood, money, Don Juanism, and farce define the sexual politics of lovers who are forever being thrust together and driven apart by private and public waltzes.[10] Can Danilo dance with one woman and then walk with her through life? He and Sonia find out only after the waltz has been examined through a spectacle of mirrors where the single couple is distinguished from and lost in an infinite series of couples. The

obliquity of irony, its tortuous conventions, and its exhaustingly doubled meanings involve Sonia and Danilo in a wide range of humor—the "Girls, girls, girls" of the opening sequence are intermingled with cows in the main street; the tenor in the duet with the lovesick widow turns out to be the comic Sterling Holloway, who sings in (but is probably dubbed, himself) for the singer Maurice Chevalier in this musical film; champagne is served in jail; a priest performs the wedding ceremony through a slit in the cell door. All this leads to the voicing of those difficult words, "I love you." The comic, subversive ploys make precious that voicing and its visualization.

At the center of the film the ironic links are worked out in purely

spatial terms when Danilo, who loves *all* the girls at Maxim's, lures Sonia, who is disguised as a Maxim's girl, to a private dining room. Their distance and rapprochement (he refuses serious commitment, she thinks of nothing else) is perceived in the magnetic attraction of the waltz, its musical strains urging her to dance, pulling him to her, uniting them in an embrace. She is forced to acknowledge her feelings by the rhythm that has literally commanded her to dance and has brought her into one man's arms. For him, the dance and the embrace of this one woman should be followed by the dances and embraces of Frou Frou, Jou Jou, and all the other pretty girls. Lubitsch tantalizes the viewers with the intimacy of the two-shot that caps this sequence, a two-shot that signifies closeness in opposing ways to each of the partners. But the waltz is a whirling pattern, and Sonia and Danilo will return twice more to each other's arms after passing through greater spatial and verbal tests, surviving the ironies of a ballroom so filled with couples that *the couple* is lost and of a prison cell endowed with the amenities of comic opera, to dance a last waltz that modulates to a mating walk and an embrace.

Sad Ironies

Among the filmmakers most frequently indentified by an ironic stance vis-à-vis sentimental configurations, Douglas Sirk has been characterized as near-Brechtian for the supposed distance his often parodic posture creates between the viewer and the obviously sentimental fictions of his most celebrated films, *Magnificent Obsession* (1954), *All That Heaven Allows* (1955), and *Imitation of Life* (1959).[11] Sirk's methods invite a process of textual deconstruction distinct from the *positive* ironic readings generated by the films I have discussed in this chapter. Can the effect of irony serve the sentiment it is presumably deconstructing? Sirk's is not the irony of complicity between filmmaker, viewer, and fiction that is the mark of Lubitsch. Sonia and Danilo are in on the game, along with Lubitsch and with us. This full pattern of complicity is inoperant when the fictions and the characters persistently "know" less about what is being done to them than we do.[12] In Sirk's *Imitation of Life* the conventions of sentimental expression are disengaged from a fiction of coherence by the knowledge we must have in order to read the film.[13]

The first film version of Fannie Hurst's *Imitation of Life*, directed by John Stahl (1934), demonstrates the sufficiency of the sentimental scenario in cinema and offers a useful point of comparison for the kind of reading that is dictated by Sirk's interventions. Stahl's version exemplifies the near-invisible stylistics of many thirties films. The film's most insistent elements are the clarity of its enactments and the straightforwardness of its stagings and its attitudes about the emotional centers of the film, motherhood and race. Meant to be perceived as a model of clarity, the persona of the film's star, Claudette Colbert, is informed with self-possession, intelligence, tact, and wit. These are the qualities of Bea, the character, who has an unerring sense of where things are, who people are, and who she herself is. The film's title bears no reference to her, but rather to Peola (Fredi Washington), the young black woman who tries to pass for white, the daughter of Bea's black maid, Delilah (Louise Beavers). Bea's resourcefulness, ambition, taste, and understanding are successfully exhibited throughout the film in situations that affirm the values she shares with the white, middle-class audience for which the film was intended. Whatever irony there is in this film is so blatant that it does not require the slightest bit of obliquity in order to be read. (Commenting on little Peola's high intelligence, Delilah says, "We all starts out that way. We don' get dumb 'til later on.") The unruffled succession of master shots and close-ups, of action-reaction shots, the *obviously* codified decor, and the sentimental configurations of mother love and death conspire to reflect negatively on the imitative life of the black woman who does not know her place. Peola refuses to do what is expected of her; everything else in the film illustrates the comfort of the expected.

Sirk's *Imitation of Life* is a film about race in the late fifties, in an America that has loudly articulated but certainly not resolved the issue of civil rights. What is a viewer to make of a scene in which a black woman embarrasses her white benefactress with a takeoff of a shuffling darky? In terms of the fiction, Mary Jane (Susan Kohner, a white actress) offends her "good" black mother, Annie (Juanita Moore), but her refusal of the "servant" role and her caricature of traditional race relationships elicits a reading ironic to the in-film reaction of the righteously indignant white woman, Lora (Lana Turner). Yet the ironic reading, the one sanctioned by a society that no longer laughs at Stepin Fetchit, does not completely destroy the sentimental one sustained by the presumed victim of the caricature, the black mother who suffers nobly throughout the film.

For Sirk, the issue of motherhood is just as clouded as that of race. The black and white of motherhood are exposed in clichés of excessive love and excessive egotism; selfless love from a generous heart, love bought with money; the all-too-present mother, the eternally absent one; the nurturing ideal, the sex object. Mother has difficulty surviving these clichés as well as the inflections of the clichés. The good black mother neglects her own child and dotes on the white child in her care. ("I like taking care of pretty things.") The bad white mother supports the two fatherless families. Yet it is through the bald opposition of negligence and sublimity that the film becomes ironic to motherhood itself. Juanita Moore, the embodiment of a mother's soul, with trembling voice and moist eyes, and Lana Turner, whose inadequate soul is worn as plainly as her highly publicized wardrobe and jewelry (thirty-four costumes!), are displayed in two-shots and in shot/countershot rhythms that threaten mother love itself in their dialectic antagonisms. In Stahl's *Imitation of Life* Claudette Colbert and Louise Beavers enact complementary versions of the good mother. Sirk provides us with a set of discordancies, of subversions of our expectations of mother love fictions.

The black mother who loses her daughter and dies of a broken heart seems to be the film's emotional center, but she is challenged for that distinction by the actress/star/bad mother whose victimization engages the viewer in tensions no less provocative than the racial ones. We perceive Lana Turner to be as inauthentic as the "jewels" that cascade behind the credits. The vitality of the Ziegfeld girl has been codified, reduced to movie star posturing, "dated," sewn into costumes that are aggressively sexual and often unflattering. If she has forgotten that Ziegfeld girls should not age, she is brutally reminded by a producer who tells her, "You're no longer a chicken." Much of the characterization is made to resonate against our extrafictional knowledge of Lana Turner, a knowledge not of film buffs but of the vast moviegoing public. Lana and Lora share more than their heavily rhymed names. We first see the "sweater girl" anxiously looking for her daughter, leaning over a railing and almost out of her bodice. And it is in this pose that she is caught by the photographer who says, "My camera could easily have a love affair with you." The same audience cannot fail to link the in-film rivalry between daughter and mother for the same man with the recent scandal in Turner's life (lightly fictionalized in the novel and film, *Where Love Has Gone*)—Turner's lover stabbed to death by her daughter in the actress's bedroom.

Lana, the clotheshorse movie star, plays a great actress, thereby reviving persistent doubts about the acting ability of Hollywood stars in general, and in particular a star like Turner whose career was built upon her appearance. This is not the first time her abilities have been ironized. Even in *Ziegfeld Girl* she plays "merely" a showgirl. In Minnelli's *The Bad and the Beautiful*, in the role of a movie star, her screen test is supposed to show the inadequacy of her acting. In spite of this she is engaged by a producer who is struck by her "star quality." When she is giving what is meant to be a great performance in the film within the film (a pastiche of *The Scarlet Empress* and *Queen Christina*, in which the presences of Dietrich and Garbo hover over poor Lana), the camera sweeps back over the visibly moved people on the set and up to a light operator whose tear-filled eyes are ironic for those of us, so many of us, who remember a similar camera movement in *Citizen Kane*, from Susan Alexander's pathetic opera stage to her critics in the flies. But even without such a memory, viewers of *The Bad and the Beautiful* must have difficulty in sorting out Turner's good acting from what is explicitly labeled as bad acting. Even her big scene of hysteria (she loses control of herself while driving a car) is a movie-created effect of editing and lighting. In *Imitation of Life* her acting is constantly and explicitly undercut. The neglected daughter (Sandra Dee) responds to the star's histrionics with "Oh, Mama, stop acting. Please don't play the martyr."[14] The absurd mise-en-scène of her stage triumphs, in front of crudely painted backdrops, is ironic to any notion of what Broadway plays are supposed to look like.

The film's climax, Annie's grandiose funeral, receives a spectacular staging with music, white horses, and a rapt audience, befitting Hollywood's notions of spectacle as well as those of the black woman lying in the flower-strewn coffin. Annie's soulfulness reaches its apogee in the gospel singing of Mahalia Jackson, the voice of black soul acceptable to white America in 1959. Sirk repeatedly intercuts Jackson's singing, whose expressionism is so thick it is often difficult to distinguish musical sound from weeping and wailing, and the grieving blonds, Lana Turner and Sandra Dee. Somewhere between these comfortable black and white codes lurk disruptive feelings that finally burst forth when Sarah Jane runs to the hearse and pours her sorrow over her mother's casket. Ever conscious of appearances, Lora intervenes to restore order in an

155

imitation of decorous bereavement. Feeling lies between Lora and Sarah Jane, in the play of ironies and ambiguities, not on the surface of the images. The surface belongs to the cascading jewels, the "glamorous" ethos of producer Ross Hunter, the industry that sold Lana Tuner as a sweater girl and as an imitation of a great actress, the moviegoers who bought her, and the society that identified black and white in terms of caricatures and all-too-easily-read fictions.

Imitation of Life is not an easily read fiction. Its obsessively ironic slant tunes us to a disillusionment so great that it inspires compassion for performers and characters. Forced to deconstruct the fiction, we are left floating in the irresolution of the film's pseudo-happy ending. Sirk himself said, "In *Imitation of Life*, you don't believe the happy end, and you're not supposed to."[15] The comic-inspirational mode the director uses for the endings of *Magnificent Obsession* and *All That Heaven Allows*,[16] with their heavily conclusive, posterish iconography (a painted backdrop of a desert, a deer grazing in the forest), would be inappropriate for a fiction as torn within itself as is *Imitation of Life*. Its profusion of ironies leads us not to some stable value, but rather to the value of the ironic processes and their multiple, unresolved readings. The nonvalues of bad/good, black/white, mother/actress/woman are ironic muddles that catch the muddles of an industry and a society, muddles intolerant of even a patently false resolution. The elements that constitute the muddles remain distinct as they submit to the cruelties of irony. Lora is "five years too late" in starting her career. Lana's career started more than twenty years before, and she too is too late. Civil rights are centuries too late. And another mordant irony is reserved for Hollywood itself, feeding on itself in remakes like *Imitation of Life*, trying to hang on to its illusory beauty with the cosmetics of wide screen and Eastmancolor, but as over-the-hill as the film's star. Sirk's irony draws us to this kind of knowledge, to sympathy for blacks in a white society and for stars in Hollywood.

We are even brought to feel sympathy for the "Hollywood" film of the late fifties, a product of the studio system's decadence.

The final ironies are reserved for the director himself, who is played out in the ambivalences of this, his final, film. Sirk's meticulous art found solutions for the obligatory becolored, CinemaScopic manners of the fifties; irreparably faded, their stagings made senseless in the amputated 16 millimeter prints we most often see, his films make us wonder if cinematic art is indeed more durable than the transient beauty of a movie star.

7   Seeing It Through

Unlike prose and theater, cinema is strictly timed. Its verisimilitudinous fictions submit to and are enhanced by the regular stop-start of the film's passage through the gate of the projector. Cinema's tense is relentlessly present. Yet film narratives tamper with that present in their retrospections, auguries, and fantasies. Editing and trick photography alter existential time, modify its inexorably ticking clock. Film images of flashback and flash-forward are always *present*, but they create fictions of radical temporal disengagement and rupture—the grown-up narrator of *I Remember Mama* seated next to her image as a young girl, captured in a mirror; the separation of image and voice track in *How Green Was My Valley* and *Letter from an Unknown Woman*; Emily's (Martha Scott's) ghost confronting her former self in Sam Wood's *Our Town*. Beginnings and ends are juxtaposed, defiant of time's passage. Rae (Margaret Sullavan) dies in front of Walter's (Charles Boyer's) photograph at the end of Robert Stevenson's *Back Street*, imagining what would have happened had the lovers met at the steamboat landing so many years

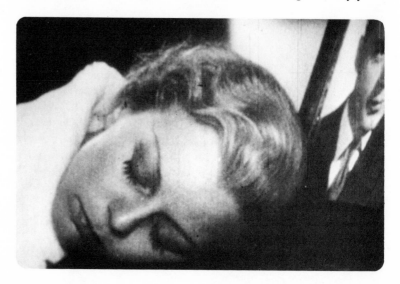

before; at the end of *How Green Was My Valley* the miracle of faith expressed by Mrs. Morgan becomes a movie miracle of sight that draws from disaster and loss images of how things were at the beginning, when the family was one and full of life. The impression of eternity conveyed by these images survives the medium's flow, is perhaps even created by the medium's flow from beginning to end and back again.[1]

Film invites us to respond to both its seemingly eternal status and its ineluctable fleetingness. Infinitely repeatable, continuous in its unfolding, discontinuous in its syntax, its temporalities catch us in modes of forward, reverse, and stop. The conventional length of a film, the narrative structure of the fiction, the duration of shots, and the rhythm of their intercutting govern the spectator's cinematic time sense. They create visual and emotional expectations that are related to the progressive, unwinding aspects of the medium and to our knowledge of its ultimate depletion. Stephen Heath asserts that, "in the intermittence of its images," film narrative generates "a model of closure" and that narrative economy is "a relation of transformation between two homogeneities ('beginning' and 'end') in which the second is the replacement of the first, a reinvestment of its elements."[2] Along with sound recordings and tapes, the cinematic apparatus shows its progress from beginning to end in the unwinding and winding of its reels, in the transfer of itself from the to be seen to the seen. Stanley Cavell pursues the analogies of clocks and reels:

> The roundness of clocks is convenient, but it naturally misleads us about something clocks tell, because its hands repossess their old positions every day and every night. The reels on a projector,

like the bulbs of an hourglass, repeat something else: that as the past fills up, the future thins; and that the end, already there against the axle, when the time comes for its running, seems to pick up speed.[3]

To view film *as it is* we must let it go, let it deplete, let the presence of its images recede into the past.

The necessary disappearance of the viewed produces both pleasure and anguish. The latter is evoked by Sartre in *Les mots*. "What a malaise . . . when the lights went on, I was distraught with love for these characters and they had disappeared, carrying away their world."[4] What we come to hold dear is taken away; as we enjoy we lose. Even our reenjoyment is suffused with the inevitability of loss. If part of our pleasure is posited on knowing that we can see a film again (a reseeing that is never the same as the first viewing), it is a fugitive pleasure, marked with the comfort of temporal boundaries and foreshadowed by the nonpleasurable state that is to follow. But we sometimes love the ends of fictions that loom ahead of us precisely because the promise of loss brings the promise of a new pleasure.[5] Frank Kermode explains the temporalities of fiction in terms that harmonize these conflicting apprehensions:

> In the middest, we look for a fullness of time, for beginning, middle and end in concord. For concord or consonance really is the root of the matter, even in a world which thinks it can only be a fiction. . . . We achieve our secular concords of past and present and future, modifying the past and allowing for the future without falsifying our own moment of crisis. We need, and provide, fictions of concord to make our peace with time.[6]

Concords, from the simplest of rhyme schemes to the complexities of Proust's epiphanies, remind us that conclusions are not final when they precede new beginnings. This dynamics of reiterability is similarly conveyed by the apparatus of cinema and the specifics of film reception.

Viewers have high expectations of the endings of narrative films. Puzzles are solved, identities revealed, meetings finally come to pass, deaths are died. Some of the films I have referred to in this book use climax as a kind of lode toward which everything points. They are organized as a series of frustrations and conflicts aimed at a final eruption of feeling, quite overwhelming in comparison to what has preceded.[7] The vignettes of the governess's life in *The Blue Veil* are subsumed in the last moments of the film when her former charges, now grown, are grouped around her in homage to her loving spirit. The identity of the amnesiac hero in *Random Harvest*, that is just beyond his reach through the film's considerable length, bursts upon him and us in the last shots and the face of his now-remembered wife. The same pattern holds for Jody (Olivia de

Havilland) in *To Each His Own*, when she is finally recognized by her son (John Lund). So great is the viewer's expectation of ending

in "recognition" fictions that the in-fiction acknowledgment of identity can be withheld, as it is in Irving Pichel's *Tomorrow Is Forever*. John (Orson Welles) never admits to Elizabeth (Claudette Colbert) that he is indeed her husband, thought to have been killed in the war twenty-five years previously. What Elizabeth suspects at the film's climax, the audience knows, and audience recognition is the one that ultimately counts. These fictions deploy an abundance of narrative information, most of it of low emotional intensity, that fills up the duration with deferrals of the satisfactory climax.

Family saga films on the other hand (*How Green Was My Valley, A Tree Grows in Brooklyn, I Remember Mama,* etc.) have little narrative complexity but sustain high emotional intensity. Here incident matters less than the definition of character through patiently chosen details. Emotion-filled moments are found in everyday events, each one a climax. Their accumulation is the fiction of a life, not necessarily a plot we enjoy for its complications. Time itself is emotion-laden, as is the hero (Robert Donat) of Sam Wood's *Goodbye, Mr. Chips,* a figure of time. Aging throughout the film, he stands at the threshold of Brookfield school to hear the hellos and goodbyes of the passing generations.

But whether in films that constantly engage our emotions or in those in which our intermittent feelings are merely preliminary to their final, cathartic exercise, the highly charged climax is something viewers of sentimental fictions have been primed to expect. We often locate the sense of a film in its climax and thereby comprehend, in the most literal way, the limits of the fiction and the extent of its conclusion—George (*A Place in the Sun*) marching to his execution, his close-up kiss of Angela superimposed over his face; Mr. Smith's Senate Chamber ringing with the voices his own utterance released; Red, the dying Ziegfeld girl, swaying down a

staircase (not onstage, but in an empty lobby) in a delirium of grace, filled with the knowledge that although no one is there, everyone is looking.

Cutting

The formality and the rituals of a film's conclusion are marked by the words "The End," the passage from the darkened viewing room, whose only light emanates from the screen, to the darkening of the screen, its loss of light, often the closing of curtains, and our return to an ambience in which we ourselves and the environment are lighted. Some of these conditions are analogous to the way we witness the end of a play enacted by live performers: the closed curtain, the transfer of light from viewed to the viewer. Yet, in its modes of access to reality, film duration and climax must be distinguished from the theatrical model. The constant alteration of viewpoint in film makes the viewing field a place of limits that are forceful in the rapidity of their fluctuation and constant resetting. Space is here and gone on film as it cannot be in the comfort of our playhouses, where the stage and the audience remain locked in an unchanging relationship.

One of cinema's limits, the cut, is a particularly insistent sign of ending. The cut deprives us of some aspect of the viewed. Generated by the essential organization of cinematic images, the cut establishes a link as it *ends* one shot and *begins* the next. Even a naive viewer of a film, unable to define what a shot is, has no difficulty in reading a given shot as distinct from the succeeding one. Many films from the so-called Hollywood era of classical editing try to create a texture of near-invisible junctures between shots, but many others, with their elaborate wipes, dissolves, roll-overs, fan-effects, fades, call upon those junctures to mark endings, repeated and insistent endings that weight the viewer with the pall of conclusion from the outset and that lead inexorably to the last fade-out.

Through the cut the cinematic image becomes temporal. It acquires a beginning and an ending that, in contradistinction to how we perceive an image in books or museums, or how we make images out of our life experience, identify a duration beyond our control. During the normal projection of a film an image appears on the screen and has a specific, measurable, finite duration dissimilar to the durational aspects of other pictorial forms of successivity. Cartoons and scrolls depend on our movement; cinematic images are cut from our perception, from the time in which we exist. Whether the cut is a radical, brutal one or is effected more gently in the form of a fade, a wipe, or a dissolve, it takes the image away from viewing. The devices of cinematic punctuation increase our sense of the image's creation and its destruction, its materialization and subsequent dematerialization.

Movies are often images of people, images that terminate people. The lifelikeness the medium gives to these images is made crucial because of the menace of limited duration. What seem to be moving, breathing, feeling creatures appear and disappear with distressing frequency. The close-up, a privileged shot in cinematic stylistics until the fifties, comes to have a durational value. Unlike the "still" portrait, it cannot persist. It grants us unique yet fleeting proximity to a performer's face, so often a face we are meant to perceive as a paragon of beauty and the sole locus of meaning. The end of a movie portrait, the end of a film, and the end of a life coincide in the last shot of Edmund Goulding's *Dark Victory*, the close-up of Judith Traherne (Bette Davis) going out of focus and fading as the heroine dies. Yet, even without such expressionistic gestures, the span of the close-up conveys the sight of ending when it extends itself beyond conventional limits. With its promise of possession and its all-too-imminent playing out, the close-up's impression of increased purview holds viewers in a thrall of knowledge and a state of anxiety. We are polarized by such purview and such deprival at the end of *Queen Christina*, with its "terminable" close-up of Garbo; at the end of *Brief Encounter*, where after having contemplated close-ups of Laura through most of the film's duration we discover yet another expression, one adequate for the end of an affair and a film, and so terminal that even her rather insensitive husband can see what it means; at the end of *Make Way for Tomorrow*, when the old woman, who has kept up a brave appearance all through the film, shows us, just before she turns away from the camera, what it will be like to die alone.

Cinema and its views of ending move; we are stationary. Even our knowledge of the images' repeatability cedes before our experience of their ungraspability. They cannot be stopped unless they cease being moving pictures. They must be denatured to be stopped. We test our sense of possession and loss in this system of movement, in this artifice that is a model for depletion and whose continuity is marked by its cutting into bits and pieces. Do we possess and lose with greater intensity at the movies than we do in our life experience? It is possible to consider the image we see on the screen more "ours" than the presence of a loved one, of a being independent of the fictions of duration and cinematic space. Our companions in life relate to us through many degrees of connection and detachment, but always live a life of their own. Stage performers live for us while they are acting and then go off in the wings to smoke a cigarette and continue their lives until their next entrance (like the Queen of the Night in Ingmar Bergman's *The Magic Flute*). The movie star is projected toward us with concentration and singular purpose, as an integral and discrete image meant only for us. The very accessibility of the image (emphasized by its magnification) is tried by the series of endings and deprivals to which it is prey. We have it greatly but ever so briefly. What does it mean to see the *end* of that which is there only for us? This is the emotional charge the cinematic image bears in its termination. The fiction of presence cannot be greater; the sense of ending is commensurately great.

The durations and tropes of film narrative exploit this movement toward closure. It is the time it takes Helen Morgan to sing "Bill," a recapitulation of lost love, or Paul Robeson to sing "Ol' Man River," where lyrics and camera movement express the vast cycle of life. It is the time it takes to read a letter from an unknown woman, or for Fred and Ginger to dance in and out of each other's arms. In *Make Way for Tomorrow* a watch is *not* looked at, thereby marking the cruciality of the few hours that remain to Lucy and Bart. This duration is ended ironically when, during the old couple's last waltz, the bandleader *begins* the radio transmission of his dance music with a reference to the time they have not wanted to acknowledge. These and so many other characters of sentimental fictions are menaced by closure and cut from each other and from us in enactments of farewell: Ma and Tom Joad separated by the space of the dance floor that so recently linked them, and then by the shadows engulfing Ma and the horizon transfiguring Tom; the train pulling the old husband away from his wife in *Make Way for Tomorrow*. Cinematic space, so highly valued in the integrity of its inscription, wrenches us with it voids, with its absences—the Morgan dinner table in *How Green Was My Valley*, the lifeboat in Richard Sale's *Abandon Ship!* at first filled to bursting with the survivors of a sea disaster, the only place *for* life in the film and then progressively less full as the officer in charge (Tyrone Power) is forced to throw overboard those who are unlikely to survive: a child's parents, an old opera singer, a seasick playwright.

These fictional and spatial configurations and these rhythmic durations expressive of emotional time derive meaning from the viewer's perception of ending and of loss in the widest sense, and the acknowledgment that art is indeed life in its existential unfolding. All films begin and end, and many incorporate a consciousness of limited duration in their structures. We all know what The End means. Frank Kermode describes it as a figure for death.[8] Peter Brooks, in his analysis of Freud's *Beyond the Pleasure Principle*, comes to the same conclusion.[9] Film, with its cuts and its extinguishings, does not let us forget it for long.

Meeting/Parting

David Lean's *Brief Encounter* resonates with conclusion: its pattern of beginnings and endings extends the film's central locus, the refreshment room of a depot, into the narrative's increasingly anguished enactments of arrivals and departures. A text that celebrates the value of the frame as threshold, *Brief Encounter* relates the frame to what is, in fact, a junction, a place of passage, tracks, platforms, and passageways, and an even more circumscribed place of passage within—the refreshment room. The arrivals and departures that mark the film's significant encounters also mark painfully brief meetings with signs of filmic duration, signs as forceful as the bourgeois conventions that define and ultimately separate the protagonists. The desperate meetings between trains, the time and space of the "waiting room," the metaphoric timetable of train platforms and station passageways demonstrate that time is strictly measured and that time is running out.

At the beginning of the film a duple pattern is established when a train cuts the frame diagonally before the credits, and another, traveling in the opposite direction, does the same at their conclusion. Later, Laura comes to realize the seriousness of her rela-

tionship to Alec in the time it takes her to walk up and back on the platform, in and out of pools of light, negative and positive space whose polarity is analogous to her situation. The shot is given a precise 1–2 rhythm by the principal forward and back unit of movement that holds within it the sub-units of light and dark. This figure is emphasized when Laura returns to the spot on the platform from whence she began, stops, and a train rushes by marking, cutting, ending, giving discrete space and time to her thinking and feeling. The duration of the lovers' first kiss, in a lurid underpass, is the duration of the express train going through the station. The kiss, like their relationship, is as *dramatic* as the passage of a train through a station—emptiness, immobility overwhelmed by an excess of activity, followed by emptiness and immobility. Throughout the film we become painfully sensitive to these desperate durations, short and long. Laura, after refusing to go to Alec's friend's apartment, jumps off the train as it begins to pull out of the station. Then, in one of the film's most elaborate shots, her entry to the building and passage through its halls and stairs to the door of the apartment is ironically protracted as the camera refuses to let her out of its sight. The end of each sequence brings the lovers nearer the end of the film of their encounter, an ending that we witness at the film's beginning and again at its conclusion: the intrusion upon the lovers' last moments together by the chattering Dolly Messiter. The replay, seen from a different angle, is invested with the density of all the previous fiction. And then, not unexpectedly, during her suicide attempt Laura measures her life by the passage of the express train.

To the pattern of limits, of endings, of precise measure that pervades *Brief Encounter* must be added the viewer's response to the film's status as sentimental melodrama, a response elicited by excess, by measure surpassed. Suffused with feelings, the viewer's body is summed in eyes that overflow with tears. This intermittent loss of control is, of course, related to the film's sexual content, the

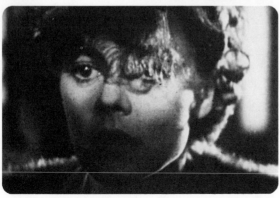

area of the fiction in which the characters seem to repress their feeling and which therefore accounts for so much of the intensity. The lovers' apparent exertion of control is sustained by the fiction's conventions of control, expressed in its classical structure, its limited loci, its modulated Thursdays of encounter (1. chance meeting, 2. exploration, 3. courtship, 4. romance, 5. guilt, 6. renunciation), and in the propriety of its diction. These rules of coherence are regularly punctuated by Rachmaninoff themes, trains, and teacups.

It is regularity that sets off the film's irregular pulse of sexuality, most insistent during the couple's second "date." Alec has missed the appointed meeting and Laura is sitting in the familiar refreshment room, waiting for her train home, wondering if Alec has

decided the whole business is not worth the trouble. Alec then runs in, and because of the noise of the station and the crescendo of the music on the sound track we do not hear his explanation. Laura urges him to hurry to catch his train; she runs with him down the ramp, through the underground passageway, up the other ramp, all to thundering Rachmaninoff. When, as his train is pulling out, Alec exacts a promise for a meeting the following week, Laura's assent is filled with an excitement and a loss of restraint that are the culmination of the quiet waiting in the station and the frenetic run through a course we and they have repeatedly measured. The camera, complicitous in that run, has also posited Celia Johnson's face and eyes as the emotional locus of the film. It now shows that face flushed to overflowing in this briefest of the film's encounters, in eyes that mirror unbridled excitement when there is no time for words or thought. The station is filled to excess with the woman's desire. The visual and musical crescendos lead us to this peak, the highest in a film of increasingly tense durations, where the lovers' meetings are measured in minutes and seconds, in the ever-shortening span of shots and time and space they share between trains. They catch us in the film's thresholds, lingering for brief, long moments against the flow toward ending.

The weight and thickness of the film's codes (voice-over narration, music, the obvious patterns of time and space) are, to some degree, in ironic disproportion to the lives of the protagonists and the banality of their dilemma, to their patently insignificant bourgeois situation, played out in little houses and an unexceptional railroad depot. But the portentous codes are subsumed into the seriousness of the film by enactment that brooks no irony, by the decorum and the voices of the stars, by the wide eyes of Celia Johnson. The film's style, one of upmost measure, allows us then to measure the fiction's insignificance with such precision that the resulting clarity becomes a factor of importance. This clash of proportions is operant in Laura's tiny sitting room, with its overstuffed furniture, her placid, dependable husband who manages to fit "romance," "delirium," and "Baluchistan" into his crossword puzzle, and the radio that brings the decadent, overripe romanticism of Rachmaninoff into the couple's after-dinner comfort. The resulting disproportions contribute to the amplificatory productions of cinema and are quite rightly overwhelming to us, as they are to Laura. The precise measure of the film's brief encounters is exposed on a huge screen that painfully inflates miniature lives and a miniature fiction, choking us up in the clash between bourgeois continuities and the glamorous finalities of fiction and of film.

In a textual afterlife, *Brief Encounter* is comico-tearfully replayed more than twenty-five years later in Melvin Frank's *A Touch of Class*; the adulterous Steve (George Segal) and Vicki (Glenda Jackson) watch, weep, and identify with the anguish of Alec and Laura on a television screen in their Soho hideaway. But in *Brief Encounter* Laura, the romantic heroine, is the spectator of her own movie romance. Each Thursday she goes to the movies, looking for the distraction and the excitement that her humdrum life does not offer. Laura and Alec spend their first afternoon together at the movies. The film announced during the coming attractions is a "stupendous, colossal, gigantic, epoch-making" jungle adventure entitled *Flames of Passion*, a film ironic both to the style and scope of *Brief Encounter*, and to itself: what appears to be a version of *King Kong* and *Jungle Princess* is drawn, its credits tell us, from a novel called *A Gentle Summer*! The romantic transgression of Alec and Laura becomes a movie transgression a week later when they leave before the end of *Flames of Passion* under the disapproving eye of the usherette. Their own movie is passionate enough, whether it is a played out in the grimy depot or on the screenlike window of Laura's train compartment, in romantic images projected from her eyes. The lovers' brief encounter is like ours with the screened fiction: intermittent, with its own rituals and conventions, its escape from the everyday, its music, its fantasy-fulfillment, its finitude, its replays, its transformations, even its rude awakening at the end. Vivid, intense, *brief*, it satisfies us as well as Alec and Laura. During their final meeting Laura says, "I want to die—if only I could die." Alec answers, "If you died you'd forget me—I want to be remembered." Laura is forced to agree. "Yes, I know—I do too." At the end of a movie we have it both ways.

Notes

Chapter One

1. The dates of films will appear in the index unless necessary to the sense of my argument.

2. W. K. Wimsatt, Jr., *The Verbal Icon: Studies in the Meaning of Poetry* (Lexington: University Press of Kentucky, 1954), p. 21.

3. Susan R. Suleiman and Inge Crosman, eds., *The Reader in the Text: Essays on Audience and Interpretation* (Princeton: Princeton Univeristy Press, 1980), provide an excellent bibliography for reader-oriented criticism.

4. Stanley E. Fish, "Literature in the Reader: Affective Stylistics," in *Self-Consuming Artifacts: The Experience of Seventeenth-Century Literature* (Berkeley: University of California Press, 1972), p. 390.

5. Stanley Cavell, *The World Viewed: Reflections on the Ontology of Film*, enlarged ed. (Cambridge, Massachusetts, and London: Harvard Univeristy Press, 1979), pp. 14–15.

6. Beginning in 1978, a series of articles has appeared under the rubric "Guilty Pleasures" in *Film Comment* in which various critics discuss the "bad" films they love most.

7. Susan Sontag, *Against Interpretation and Other Essays* (New York: Farrar, Straus & Giroux, 1966), p. 177.

8. Sontag, p. 179.

9. Nick Browne, "Narrative Point of View: The Rhetoric of *Au hasard, Balthazar*," *Film Quarterly* 31 (Fall 1977): 19–31.

10. Jean Mitry, *Esthétique et psychologie du cinéma. I. Les structures* (Paris: Editions Universitaires, 1963), p. 147. (This and all subsequent translations from cited foreign language editions are mine.) Edgar Morin is just as insistent on the function of affect in the production of cinematic meaning. "We must conceive of affective participation as cinema's *genetic stage and structural foundation*." *Le cinéma ou l'homme imaginaire* (Paris: Editions Gonthier, 1958), p. 91.

11. Hugo Münsterberg, *The Film: A Psychological Study, The Silent Photoplay in 1916* (1916; reprint. New York: Dover, 1970), p. 53.

12. Mitry, p. 179. Jean-Pierre Meunier, in *Les structures de l'expérience filmique: L'identification filmique* (Louvain: Librairie Universitaire, 1969), examines this in terms both of the notion of intersubjectivity developed by Hesnard and of the phenomenology of Merleau-Ponty and Sartre. Although he distinguishes between a viewer's sense of "being with" and

"being like" the fictional character, he attaches the cinematic experience firmly to categories of lifelike recognition and resemblance.

13. Mitry, p. 188.

14. Münsterberg, pp. 51–52.

15. Christian Metz, "The Imaginary Signifier," trans. Ben Brewster, *Screen* 16 (Summer 1975): 58.

16. Metz, "Imaginary Signifier," p. 15.

17. Thierry Kuntzel, "A Note upon the Filmic Apparatus," *Quarterly Review of Film Studies* 1 (1976): 266–71.

18. Metz, "Imaginary Signifier," p. 47.

19. Christian Metz, "The Fiction Film and Its Spectator," trans. Alfred Guzzetti, *New Literary History* 8 (August 1976): 98.

20. Martha Wolfenstein and Nathan Leites, in what was probably the first book-length analysis of cinema within a Freudian discourse, *Movies: A Psychological Study* (Glencoe, Illinois: Free Press, 1950), examine film fictions almost exclusively in terms of the viewer's fantasy configurations and projections.

21. Morin, p. 81.

22. Metz, "Fiction Film," p. 79.

23. Metz, "Fiction Film," p. 102.

24. Wolfgang Iser, *The Implied Reader: Patterns of Communication in Prose Fiction from Bunyan to Beckett* (Baltimore: John Hopkins University Press, 1974), p. 279.

25. Wolfgang Iser, *The Act of Reading: A Theory of Aesthetic Response* (Baltimore: Johns Hopkins Univesity Press, 1978), pp. 128–29. Stanley Fish in "Interpreting the *Variorum*," *Critical Inquiry* 2 (Spring 1976): 474, also emphasizes the temporal experience of the text in his description of reading as interpretation.

26. Iser, *Act of Reading*, p. 116.

27. Claudine Eizykman, *La jouissance-cinéma* (Paris: 10/18, 1976), pp. 7–8.

28. Eizykman, p. 13.

29. Thomas Elsaesser, in his rich and allusive "Tales of Sound and Fury: Observations on the Family Melodrama," *Monogram*, vol. 4 (1972), makes extensive use of the musical analogy. "Considered as an expressive code, melodrama might therefore be described as a particular form of dramatic mise-en-scène, characterized by a dynamic use of spatial and muscial categories, as opposed to intellectual or literary ones" (p. 6). And later, "The aesthetic qualities of this type of cinema depend on the ways 'melos' is given to 'drama' by means of lighting, montage, visual rhythm, decor, style of acting, music—that is, on the ways the mise-en-scène translates character into action" (p. 8).

30. Robert Scholes, "Narration and Narrativity in Film," *Quarterly Review of Film Studies* 1 (1976): 290.

31. O. Mannoni, *Clefs pour l'imaginaire ou l'autre scène* (Paris: Editions du Seuil, 1969), p. 12.

32. Mannoni, pp. 163–64.

33. Peter Brooks, *The Melodramatic Imagination: Balzac, Henry James, Melodrama, and the Modes of Excess* (New Haven: Yale University Press, 1976), p. 41.

34. Brooks, p. 4.

35. Robert Heilman redefines melodrama in somewhat different terms. He extends the genre to a wide range of "serious" fictions that can be characterized as belonging to "the realm of disaster." Another distinguishing feature of melodrama is its deployment of "undivided" characters. "Melodrama, in sum, includes the whole realm of conflicts undergone by characters who are presented as undivided or at least without divisions of such magnitude that they must be at the dramatic center: hence melodrama includes a range of actions that extends from disaster to success, from defeat to victory, and a range of effects from the strongest conviction of frustration and failure that serious art can dramatize, to the most frivolous assurance of triumph that a mass-circulation writer can confect." *Tragedy and Melodrama: Versions of Experience* (Seattle: University of Washington Press, 1968), p. 86.

36. See below, pp. 76–78.

37. Frank McConnell bravely rescues "sentimental" in his ingenious coupling of romantic art and film. "The naive perceptions of a child—or, for Schiller, of the childhood of poetry and culture, the archaic masterpieces—are forever closed to us, readers and viewers of a later day. Sentimental art, the art of the romantic imagination, recognizes both the necessity of recapturing those naive perceptions for the sake of a fully human, fully conscious life and the impossibility of recapturing that life without the aid of the sophistication, the intelligence, and the techniques of artifice which separate it from us so irrevocably." *The Spoken Seen: Film and the Romantic Imagination* (Baltimore: Johns Hopkins University Press, 1975), pp. 40–41.

38. Raymond Bellour, "Le blocage symbolique," *Communications*, no. 23 (1975), pp. 235–350.

39. Fish, "Interpreting the *Variorum*," pp. 473–85.

40. Frank Kermode, *The Sense of an Ending: Studies in the Theory of Fiction* (New York: Oxford University Press, 1967), p. 70.

41. Morin, p. 39.

42. David Thomson states, "In Borzage's best work, passion, visual eroticism, and fidelity to the ideal of love produce imagery so psychically material as to make story lines only pretexts." *America in the Dark: Hollywood and the Gift of Unreality* (New York: William Morrow, 1977), p. 213. While in Borzage's films "the ideal of love" certainly emanates from style and enactment, it is also shaped by the idealizing fictivity of the "story lines," elements too lightly dismissed by Thomson.

43. Philip Rosen, in "Difference and Displacement in *Seventh Heaven*," *Screen* 18 (Summer 1977): 99, assesses the value of light as "signifier for all of the insubstantialities of the film," insubstantialities resumed in the film's miraculous conclusion.

Chapter Two

1. Jean-Louis Baudry, "Ideological Effects of the Basic Cinematographic Apparatus," *Film Quarterly* 27 (Winter 1974–75): 42.

2. Stephen Heath, "On Screen, in Frame: Film and Ideology," *Quarterly Review of Film Studies* 1 (1976): 260.

3. *Las meninas* is a favored example of these processes. Michel Foucault

devotes the first chapter of *Les mots et les choses* (Paris: Gallimard, 1966) to an analysis of this painting and its modes of representation. Jean-Pierre Oudart uses it as the point of departure for his discussion of the relationship between painting and cinema, the suture effect (see below, p. 56) and the reality effect, in "L'effet de réel," *Cahiers du cinéma*, no. 228 (March/April 1971), pp. 19–26.

4. Lawrence Gowing, in *Vermeer* (New York: Harper & Row, 1970), writes of the framing devices in Vermeer and their emotional power. In describing the *Dresden Letter Reader*, he says, "We gather from her and the immutable terms of her confinement an impression of the forces that move yet stay the painter, and discover a tension of feeling that is in essence poetic" (p. 35). And later, commenting on the general aspect of representation in Vermeer, "The possibility of an art in which issues of immediacy and withdrawal, nearness and distance, play such a part certainly hardly existed before his age" (p. 62).

5. The affective appeal of Vermeer and of his concentrative framings is referred to throughout Proust's *Remembrance of Things Past*. Sacrificing the more familiar tea-soaked madeleine as the privileged event in the search for lost time, Harold Pinter, in his screenplay for Proust's novel, *A la recherche du temps perdu: The Proust Screenplay* (New York: Grove Press, 1977), repeats a shot of a yellow frame that, at the end, is revealed to be a detail from Vermeer's *View of Delft*. Claude Goretta's *The Lacemaker* concludes with a shot and a textual reference to Vermeer's painting of the same name. Claude Chabrol's *Violette* closes with a further gesture of intertextuality, a shot of the protagonist (played by Isabelle Huppert, the heroine of *The Lacemaker*), patiently embroidering.

6. Gaston Bachelard, *La poétique de l'espace* (Paris: Presses Universitaires de France, 1958), p. 191.

7. Mitry, pp. 175–76.

8. Noël Burch, *Theory of Film Practice* (New York: Praeger, 1973), p. 29.

9. Pascal Bonitzer, *Le regard et la voix: Essais sur le cinéma* (Paris: 10/18, 1976), p. 15.

10. Sigmund Freud, *Beyond the Pleasure Principle*, trans. and ed. James Strachey (New York: Liveright, 1961), pp. 10–11.

11. Jacques Lacan, *The Language of the Self: The Function of Language in Psychoanalysis*, trans. and ed. Anthony Wilden (Baltimore: Johns Hopkins Press, 1968), p. 83.

12. Mannoni, p. 169.

13. Sigmund Freud, "Psychopathic Characters on the Stage" (1905), *The Standard Edition of the Complete Psychological Works of Sigmund Freud*, vol. 7 (London: Hogarth Press, 1953), p. 305.

14. Jacques-Alain Miller, "La suture (éléments de la logique du signifiant)," trans. Jacqueline Rose, *Screen* 18 (Winter 1977/78):25.

15. Jean-Pierre Oudart, "Cinema and Suture," trans. Kari Hanet, *Screen* 18 (Winter 1977/78):36.

16. The centrality of shot/countershot in Oudart's formulation in forcefully attacked by William Rothman, "Against 'The System of Suture,'" *Film Quarterly* 29 (Fall 1975): 45–50, and Barry Salt, "Film Style and Technology in the Forties," *Film Quarterly* 31 (Fall 1977): 46–56.

17. Stephen Heath, "Notes on Suture," *Screen* 18 (Winter 1977/78): 63–64.

18. The automatic nature of cinema is examined for quite different purposes by Walter Benjamin, "The Work of Art in the Age of Mechanical Reproduction," *Illuminations*, ed. Hannah Arendt (New York: Harcourt Brace, 1968), and Stanley Cavell, *World Viewed*.

19. For a discussion of the notion of value in photography, see Susan Sontag, *On Photography* (New York: Farrar, Straus & Giroux, 1977).

20. Daniel Dayan, in "The Tutor-Code of Classical Cinema," *Film Quarterly*, vol. 28 (Fall 1974), resuming Oudart's formulations, states that representation is, in effect, "the signifier of the presence of a subject who is looking at it," and that "the spectator's imaginary can only coincide with the painting's built-in subjectivity. The receptive freedom of the spectator is reduced to the minimum—he has to accept or reject the painting as a whole" (p. 27). Without having to subscribe to all the terms of the suture formulation one can appreciate the importance of this figuration of the subject in the subject's rejection of sentimental art, particularly if the "taste" of the subject is incompatible with the particular subjectivity of sentimental codes.

21. See above, p. 23.

22. Jeanette MacDonald specialized in these spectral serenades, where speech and song seem to bridge life and death—*Bitter Sweet* (1940), *Smilin' Through* (1941), and a comic variant, *I Married an Angel* (1942).

23. Ford directed an earlier version of this basic scenario, *Judge Priest* (1934). It contains many of his characteristic strategies of affect: the judge looks through a window and sees past images of himself and his young wife, talks with her "spirit," and after an intricate play between his reflection and his shadow on the frame of a tintype continues his conversation with her framed image, and finally her tombstone. The graveside soliloquy is obsessive in Ford. *My Darling Clementine* (1946) and *She Wore a Yellow Ribbon* (1949) immediately spring to mind. *Judge Priest* ends triumphantly (unlike *The Sun Shines Bright*) after a courtroom scene prophetic of *Young Mr. Lincoln* (1939), but without the intimations of loss inscribed in the conclusion of that film. *Young Mr. Lincoln* is a particularly rich text to submit to analysis for sentimental characteristics. The resonance of the hero-to-be-martyred, suggested throughout the film, is overwhelming in the last image, where Lincoln (Henry Fonda) strides out of the frame as a storm bursts. I will resist the temptation to comment more fully on a film that has already stimulated so much critical discourse. See editors of *Cahiers du cinéma*, "John Ford's *Young Mr. Lincoln*," in Gerald Mast and Marshall Cohen, eds., *Film Theory and Criticism*, 2d ed. (New York: Oxford University Press, 1979); and Richard Abel, "Paradigmatic Structures in *Young Mr. Lincoln*," and J. A. Place, "*Young Mr. Lincoln*, 1939," both in *Wide Angle* 2, no. 4: 20–26, 28–35. In the same issue of *Wide Angle* Peter Lehman examines the echoes of off-screen space in relation to Ford's *The Man Who Shot Liberty Valance*, "An Absence Which Becomes a Legendary Presence: John Ford's Structured Use of Off-Screen Space," pp. 36–42.

24. Brooks, *Melodramatic Imagination*, pp. 41–42.

25. Leo Braudy, in *The World in a Frame: What We See in Films* (Garden City: Anchor-Doubleday, 1977), explores a wide range of visual "significa-

tions" through his distinctions between open and closed systems, based on the relationships between contextual meaning, decorative style, framing, and directorial personality. See in particular pp. 44–103. He also develops the notion of genre as "The Conventions of Connection," and discusses Ford's generic patterns, pp. 128–32.

26. Leo Braudy, pp. 143–47, examines other aspects of this partnership, specifically in reference to *Shall We Dance?*

27. Gaston Bachelard, in his "poetics of space," gives the home (the "happy space" [*espace heureux*]) a privileged position. "It concentrates being at the center of protecting limits" (p. 17). The enclosure configuration that is home is formative, resonant in dreams, fantasy, the realm of the imaginary. "The house is one of the greatest forces of integration for man's thoughts, memories and dreams" (p. 26). It is a persistent model for that which is deepest in us. "The house, even more than the landscape, is a state of mind. Even reproduced in its exterior aspect, it speaks intimacy" (p. 77).

28. William Luhr and Peter Lehman, in *Authorship and Narrative in the Cinema: Issues in Contemporary Aesthetics and Criticism* (New York: G. P. Putnam's Sons, 1977), are quite condescending to the affect produced by popular cinema. They attempt to rescue Ford from what might be construed as his bent toward sentiment by stressing the director's interest in myth and history. "One critic remarked that John Ford lost his home a long time ago and has been searching for it ever since. The family and home (and their antithesis, the homeless wanderer) have been overemphasized in Ford criticism. While these situations occur repeatedly, they are usually part of a much larger pattern. Films of family cohesion are a box-office staple. Its lack is generally depicted in personal terms as catastrophic, frequently in the most maudlin manner possible. But Ford's primary interest lies not in orphans or other potentially sentimentalized victims . . . it is just this repeatedly evident concern with larger forces of culture, environment, and history that prevent Ford's interest in family cohesion from being merely maudlin or sentimental" (p. 143).

29. Oudart assimilates the horizon into the suture principle. "The cinema which seemingly is without horizon, does in fact possess one, an imaginary horizon, on the other side. Thus the ambiguity of the field, at once present and absent, unreal and imaginary, can be called cinematic since it is through this duality that the cinema engenders itself. The suturing effect of any presence in the imaginary field shows how, in the cinema, the space and the signifier join their effects even while vanishing." "Cinema and Suture," p. 43.

30. The relationship between fiction, ideology, and camera movement in *Le crime de M. Lange* has been examined by André Bazin, *Jean Renoir*, ed. François Truffaut, trans. W. W. Halsey II and William H. Simon (New York: Simon & Schuster, 1973), pp. 44–46 (on p. 44 there appears a diagram of the courtyard and the camera movement); by Leo Braudy, *Jean Renoir: The World of His Films* (Garden City: Anchor-Doubleday, 1972), pp. 116–20; by Raymond Durgnat, *Jean Renoir* (Berkeley: University of California Press, 1974), pp. 108–26. A further discussion of the cyclical camera movement in *Lange* can be found in Alexander Sesonske, *Jean Renoir: The French Films, 1924–1939* (Cambridge: Harvard University Press, 1980), pp. 212–18.

31. Robert Scholes, in "Narration and Narrativity in Film," *Quarterly Review of Film Studies* 1 (1976): 284, states that narration "rests upon the presence of a narrator or narrative medium (actors, book, film, etc.) and the absence of the events narrated. These events are present as fiction but absent as realities."

32. Luhr and Lehman discuss the formal use of doorways in *The Sun Shines Bright* and other films, pp. 154–55.

33. See below, pp. 97–103.

34. Stanley Cavell's distinction between the frame of a painting and the movie screen *as* frame takes into account the fluctuating dimensions of the filmic field. "Because it is the field of a photograph, the screen has no frame; that is to say, no border. Its limits are not so much the edges of a given shape as they are the limitations, or capacity, of a container. The screen *is* a frame; the frame is the whole field of the screen—as a frame of film is the whole field of a photograph, like the frame of a loom or a house. In this sense, the screen-frame is a mold, or form. The fact that in a moving picture successive film frames are fit flush into the fixed screen frame results in a phenomenological frame that is indefinitely extendible and contractible, limited in the smallness of the object it can grasp only by the state of its technology, and in largeness only by the span of the world." *World Viewed*, pp. 24–25. Contrary to Cavell, I am not ready to discard the model of a painting's "border" and "frame" for the screen image, but I do find that his analogies of "loom," "house," "mold," and "form" inflect, with great subtlety, cinema's variable dynamics of limits.

35. Metz, "Imaginary Signifier," p. 60.

Chapter Three

1. See above, pp. 13–14.

2. Freud, "Three Essays on the Theory of Sexuality" (1905) and "Instincts and Their Vicissitudes" (1915), *Standard Edition*, vols. 7 and 14. Jacques Lacan, *The Four Fundamental Concepts of Psycho-Analysis*, ed. Jacques-Alain Miller, trans. Alan Sheridan (New York: W. W. Norton, 1978); see in particular pp. 67–104, 180–82.

3. Roland Barthes, "En sortant du cinéma," *Communcations*, no. 23 (1975), p. 105.

4. Metz, "Imaginary Signifier," p. 59.

5. Metz, "Imaginary Signifier," p. 64.

6. Roland Barthes, *The Pleasure of the Text*, trans. Richard Miller (New York: Hill & Wang, 1975), p. 10.

7. Linda Williams, "The Film Body: An Implantation of Perversions," *Ciné-Tracts*, no. 12, pp. 19–35.

8. Roland Barthes, *Image—Music—Text*, trans. Stephen Heath (New York: Hill & Wang, 1977), p. 59.

9. Barthes, *Image—Music—Text*, p. 61.

10. Oudart, "Cinema and Suture," p. 39. See above, pp. 30–31.

11. Oudart, "Cinema and Suture," p. 42.

12. Hitchcock was well aware of the priority of dimension in the screen image: "I maintained the rule of varying the size of the image in relation to its emotion importance within a given episode." François Truffaut, *Hitchcock* (New York: Simon & Schuster, 1967), p. 131.

13. The importance of this sequence to Stevens is conveyed by Patricia Bosworth, *Montgomery Clift: A Biography* (New York: Harcourt Brace Jovanovich, 1978), p. 184. She writes of Stevens that "when he edited the scene he did not use a movieola. Instead he set up two projectors and viewed the reels of Monty's close-ups and Taylor's close-ups simultaneously on a projector screen which covered an entire wall, then spliced the film in such a way that the cameras seemed to roll from Monty's face to Taylor's face."

14. See Nick Browne, "The Spectator-in-the-Text: The Rhetoric of *Stagecoach*," *Film Quarterly* 29 (Winter 1975–76): 27–37.

15. Charles Affron, *Star Acting: Gish, Garbo, Davis* (New York: E. P. Dutton, 1977), pp. 198–99.

16. The script of *Brief Encounter* has been published in *Masterworks of the British Cinema* (New York: Harper & Row, 1974).

17. In Henry King's version of *Stella Dallas* (1925), one scene in particular exploits the display/concealment nexus. Stella (Belle Bennett), after seeing Laurel off on the train she thinks is carrying her daughter out of her life for good, tries to apply mascara that her tears keep washing away.

Chapter Four

1. Baudry, "Ideological Effects," p. 45. McConnell, p. 89.

2. Boris Eikenbaum, "Problems of Film Stylistics," *Screen* 15 (Autumn 1974): 14.

3. Sergei Eisenstein, *Film Form: Essays in Film Theory*, ed. and trans. Jay Leyda (New York: Harcourt, Brace & World, 1949), p. 249.

4. Norman N. Holland, *The Dynamics of Literary Response* (New York: Oxford University Press, 1968), p. 150.

5. Eisenstein, p. 173.

6. Eisenstein, p. 166.

7. Charles Harpole, in "Ideological and Technological Determinism in Deep-Space Cinema Images," *Film Quarterly* 33 (Spring 1980): 11–21, provides a succinct history of the pervasive use of deep space. Patrick L. Ogle, in "Technological and Aesthetic Influences upon the Development of Deep Focus Cinematography in the United States," *Screen* 13 (Spring 1972): 45–72, explains deep focus in terms of the development of film stock and lighting procedures. He includes an extensive bibliography. Jean-Louis Comolli, "Caméra, perspective, profoundeur de champ," *Cahiers du cinéma*, nos. 229–32 (May–November 1971), nos. 234–35 (December 1971–February 1972), no. 241 (September–October 1972), provides an ideological analysis of the phenomenon.

8. Bonitzer, p. 9.

9. André Bazin, *Qu'est-ce que le cinéma? I. Ontologie et langage* (Paris: Editions du Cerf, 1958), pp. 149–73.

10. Bazin, *Qu'est-ce que le cinéma*, pp. 166–68.

11. Baudry, "Ideological Effects," p. 42; also see above, p. 24.

12. Bazin, *Qu'est-ce que le cinéma*, pp. 150–54.

13. Jacques Lacan, *Écrits*, trans. Alan Sheridan (New York: W. W. Norton, 1977), pp. 1–7.

14. Metz, "Imaginary Signifier," p. 53.

15. Michael Anderegg discusses this configuration and similar ones in

Sunset Boulevard and *The Shootist,* in *William Wyler* (Boston: Twayne, 1979), pp. 138–39.

16. Heath, "Notes on Suture," p. 64; also see above, p. 24.

17. Max Ophuls comments on this atemporality of description in prose fiction in an interview with Jacques Rivette and François Truffaut that appeared in *Cahiers du cinéma,* no. 72 (June 1957), and was reprinted in Paul Willemen, ed., *Ophuls,* trans, Jennifer Batchelor (London: British Film Institute, 1978), p. 28. "When Balzac talks about politics, about Napoleon etc. . . . realism plays its true role. It upsets and slows down the dramatic flow. You have to concentrate your forces to touch the heart; it's there, between that desire to touch the dramatic nerve-ends and your emotions: and it slows things down. It is its only dramatic function and it's splendid. When you dare to use it like that, you get an unbelievable control. It's like in a symphony, when you separate emotional truth from the truth of life."

18. Metz, "Imaginary Signifier," p. 58; see above, p. 54.

19. Stanley Cavell develops the notion of the lens in this sequence as "a sort of figure of speech, or synecdoche of sight, for both a gun and a camera." *World Viewed,* p. 222.

20. The last shot of *The Rules of the Game* is one of the most frequently cited images in cinema. Cavell's analysis of its cinematic and theatrical functions is particularly persuasive, in *World Viewed,* pp. 219–30.

21. See above, pp. 59–61.

22. David Bordwell, in an exposition of the connections between stylistics, narrative, and economic exigency, states that "camera movement tends to eliminate any spatial ambiguities in the image and to specify a single pro-filmic layout and a unified perceptual viewing position. Perceptually, then, camera movement can be a powerful surrogate for the active locomotion which we surrender upon settling into our cinema seat. Camera movement also tends to yield an image of continuous order and duration of narrative events. All these features—coherent space, unified viewing position, narrative continuity—were canonized by the classical narrative style of filmmaking." "Camera Movement, the Coming of Sound, and the Classical Hollywood Style," *Film: Historical-Theoretical Speculations, the 1977 Film Studies Annual, part 2* (Pleasantville, New York: Redgrave, 1977), p. 30.

23. Metz comments on the erotic quality of camera movement—its showing and then the refusal of the shown in caressing tracking shots through "veiling-unveiling procedures." "Imaginary Signifier," pp. 75–76.

24. Baudry, in "Ideological Effects," p. 43, emphasizes the power of the moving camera, arguing that it creates a camera-viewed world. "And if the eye which moves is no longer fettered by a body, by the laws of matter and time, if there are no more assignable limits to its displacement—conditions fulfilled by the possibilities of shooting and of film—the world will not only be constituted by this eye but for it."

25. See Andrew Sarris, *The American Cinema: Directors and Directions, 1929–1968* (New York: E. P. Dutton, 1968), pp. 69–72, and Michael Kerbel, "*Letter from an Unknown Woman,*" *Film Comment* 7 (Summer 1971): 61.

26. Claude Beylie, in *Max Ophuls* (Paris: Editions Seghers, 1963), pp.

98–103, discusses the director's quasi baroque use of staircases, mirrors, and curtains.

27. Paul Willemen, in "The Ophuls Text: A Thesis," in Willemen, ed., *Ophuls*, p. 73, sees in the dynamics of camera movement, with its frequent refrains, the dynamic relationship of desire and repression. "Each of these registers of text contruction inscribes simultaneously a breakthrough of excess, the transgression of a 'rigid and merciless discipline' as Karel Reisz put it, and the strategies to contain and recover, to neutralise through reinscription or repetition what the Law had to expell, to repress in order for it to come into existence. In that sense, Ophuls' cinema can be seen as the dramatisation of repression, where the repressed returns and imprints its mark on the representation, undermining and at times overwhelming that manifestation of secondary elaboration called 'a coherent scenario.'"

Chapter Five

1. Walter J. Ong, *The Presence of the Word: Some Prolegomena for Cultural and Religious History* (New Haven: Yale University Press, 1967), pp. 111–12.

2. Ong, p. 115.

3. Jacques Derrida, *Speech and Phenomena: And Other Essays on Husserl's Theory of Signs*, trans. David B. Allison (Evanston: Northwestern University Press, 1973), p. 75.

4. Derrida, p. 77.

5. Derrida, p. 77.

6. Stanley Cavell's distinction between sight and sound is based on his observation that language must account differently for the copying procedures of photographs and recordings. "The problem is that even if a photograph were a copy of an object, so to speak, it would not bear the relation to its object that a recording bears to the sound it copies. We said that the record reproduces its sound, but we cannot say that a photograph reproduces sight (or a look, or an appearance)." *World Viewed*, p. 19. Jean-Louis Baudry states, similarly, "And it is true that in cinema, as in all the other talking machines, it is not an image of sound, but the sounds themselves that we hear. The procedures of recording and of restitution may deform sounds; they are reproduced, not simulated. Illusion can only be concerned with their source of emission, not their reality." "Le dispositif: Approches métapsychologiques de l'impression de réalité," *Communications*, no. 23 (1975), p. 61.

7. Ong, p. 40.

8. Frank McConnell, pp. 57–71, examines the affectivity of momentous utterance in these and other films.

9. See Peter Brooks, *The Melodramatic Imagination*, pp. 56–57, and above, pp. 13–14.

10. Cavell, *World Viewed*, p. 152.

11. Ong, p. 112, states, "Being powered projections, spoken words themselves have an aura of power."

12. Ong, p. 118.

13. Barthes, *Pleasure of the Text*, p. 67.

14. Julia Kristeva, *Semiotike: Recherches pour une sémanalyse* (Paris: Seuil, 1969), pp. 278–89.

15. Barthes, *Image—Music—Text*, p. 182.

16. Barthes, *Pleasure of the Text*, p. 66.

17. Gerald Mast, in *Film/Cinema/Movie: A Theory of Experience* (New York: Harper & Row, 1977), pp. 206–37, is particularly sensitive to movie voices. He is one of the few critics to have paid sustained attention to sound in cinema.

18. See Robert Scholes and Robert Kellogg, *The Nature of Narrative* (London and New York: Oxford University Press, 1966), pp. 17–56 and bibliography.

19. Ong, p. 24.

20. See above, p. 13.

21. Cavell, in *World Viewed*, p. 190, writes, "The sentiment in the scene is very deep. It has been constructed as cunningly as a Keaton gag; what caps it, finally bursting the dam of tears, is the crowding of this band of goodness into this hero's house, each member testifying individually to his or her affection for him; so that the good society, the good of society at large, is pictured as this man's family (personally sponsored, what's more, by a denizen of heaven)."

Chapter Six

1. "Self-reflexive" is perhaps a cumbersome designation, but its utility is demonstrated by Susan Sontag, *Styles of Radical Will* (New York: Farrar, Straus & Giroux, 1976), p. 139, in her description of Ingmar Bergman's *Persona*. "In the ways that Bergman made his film self-reflexive, self-regarding, ultimately self-engorging, we should recognize not a private whim but the expression of a well-established tendency. For it is precisely the energy for this sort of 'formalist' concern with the nature and paradoxes of the medium itself which was unleashed when the nineteenth-century formal structures of plot and characters . . . were demoted." Sontag goes on to define self-reflexivity in terms of modernism. The designation seems equally applicable to cinematic fictions that have those "nineteenth-century formal structures of plot and characters."

2. Mannoni, p. 164, writes, "It is that something in us, something like the child that we were, and who must subsist in some form, in a certain place in the Ego, towards perhaps what Freud, after Fechner, also calls (and why this metaphor?) the *scene* of the dream, it would be this part, hidden within us, that is the place of the illusion about which we don't yet quite know what it is. It is this part of ourselves that is represented, personified by the credulous people of long ago . . . or by the bumpkin who is fooled by the illusion."

3. See above, p. 73.

4. See André Bazin, *What Is Cinema?*, ed. and trans. Hugh Gray (Berkeley: University of California Press, 1967), vol. 1, pp. 87–88, for observations on these sequences.

5. See Lucy Fischer, "The Image of Woman as Image: The Optical Politics of *Dames*," *Film Quarterly* 30 (Fall 1976): 2–11.

6. Colin MacCabe, in "Principles of Realism and Pleasure," *Screen* 17 (Autumn 1976): 16, defines the viewer's dual situation, inside and outside the fiction, in linguistic terms developed by Beneviste. He distinguishes between the *sujet de l'énoncé* and the *sujet de l'énonciation*, "the spectator

as viewer, the comforting 'I,' the fixed point, and the spectator as he or she is caught up in the play of events on the screen, as he or she 'utters,' 'enounces,' the film. Hollywood cinema is largely concerned to make these two coincide so that we can ignore what is at risk. But this coincidence can never be perfect because it is exactly in the divorce between the two that the film's existence is possible."

7. The chain of show-biz reflections is extended through time to Martin Scorsese's *New York, New York* (1977). The complete version of that film, released in 1981, features a production number, "Happy Endings," whose point of departure is a cinema audience. The usherette (Liza Minnelli) projects her desire to be a star into a screen fantasy modeled, to some extent, on the production number, "Born in a Trunk," performed by her mother, Judy Garland, in *A Star Is Born*. The usherette's fantasy is re-played as if it were "real life" near the end of the number. The climax is then performed on a gigantic mirrored set. All of this is being witnessed by yet another in-film film audience and a specific spectator, the musical star's husband (Robert De Niro). And, of course, the number reflects back on the narrative of the whole film.

8. Mannoni's remarks about the actor's doubleness (p. 305) are specifically applied to the theater, but seem as pertinent to the cinema. "We go to the theater to see acting, and spectators identify with the actor as actor at the same time they do with the character, in an original combination that is not found as such in other modes of spectacle."

9. Wayne Booth, *A Rhetoric of Irony* (Chicago: University of Chicago Press, 1974), p. 190.

10. Nancy Schwartz, in "Lubitsch's Widow: The Meaning of a Waltz," *Film Comment* 11 (March–April 1975): 13, develops the film's "metaphor of the waltz, which becomes the ultimate, perfect vision of surrogate sex, coupling without consummation."

11. Paul Willemen, in "Distanciation and Douglas Sirk," *Screen* 12 (Summer 1971): 67, accounts for distanciation in terms of stylistic disjuncture as it superimposes "on to the cinematic mode of representation (i.e. the duplication of the pre-filmic world) a rhetoric informed by the theatrical concepts and theories developed at the beginning of this century in Russia and Germany." Sirk's stylization is then used "to parody the stylistic procedures which traditionally convey an extremely smug, self-righteous and *petit bourgeois* world view paramount in the American melodrama." Willemen, in a subsequent article, "Towards an Analysis of the Sirkian System," *Screen* 13 (Winter 1972/3): 128–32, pursues Sirk's subversions of the melodramatic mode.

12. Wayne Booth, p. 73, in his discussion of parody, describes this discrepancy of knowledge. "In relying on our knowledge as insiders, parody is like most irony that is revealed through style. We can be sure of ourselves only when we have good reason to believe that the author's conception of how to write would exclude his speaker's way of writing." Laura Mulvey tries to distinguish between those moments in Sirk's films in which character and spectator share knowledge and those of ironic discrepancy, in "Notes on Sirk and Melodrama," *Movie* 25 (Winter 1977/78): 55. "Sirk allows for a certain interaction between the spectator's perception of incident, channelled through an aspect of *mise-en-scène*, and its overt

impact within the diegesis, as though the protagonists, from time to time, *read* their dramatic situation with a code similar to that used by the audience. Although this skillful device uses some aesthetic as well as narrative aspects of the film to establish points for the characters on the screen as well as for the spectator in the cinema, it cannot cover elements such as lighting or camera movement, which still act as a privileged discourse *for* the spectator." Instances in which character and spectator have parallel readings are, however, almost nonexistent in *Imitation of Life*.

13. Stephen Handzo, in "Imitations of Lifelessness: Sirk's Ironic Tear-Jerker," *Bright Lights* (Winter 1977–78), pp. 20–22, 34, gives a keen ironic reading of the film. His analysis has helped me illustrate my argument.

14. Richard Dyer, in "Lana: Four Films of Lana Turner," *Movie*, vol. 25 (Winter 1977/78), provides an excellent analysis of Turner's persona, her "sexy-ordinary" image. He also makes reference to several of the ironizations of her status as actress to which I refer. He writes of the car scene in *The Bad and the Beautiful*, "What we seem to be getting here is the moment of real reality, assured by the notion that only untrammelled, chaotic, violent emotion is authentic. All the rest is illusion. It is the supreme masterstroke to fabricate this authenticity so completely in a studio mock-up of a car and with the epitome of star artifice, Lana Turner" (p. 45). Of the line "Mother, stop acting," he comments, "The film here draws attention to Turner's posing acting style, making its use of the style to embody 'imitation' explicit" (p. 50).

15. Jon Halliday, *Sirk on Sirk* (New York: Viking, 1972), p. 132.

16. See Jean-Loup Bourget, "God Is Dead, or Through a Glass Darkly," *Bright Lights* (Winter 1977–78), pp. 23–26, 34, for an interesting analysis of melodrama in *Magnificent Obsession*.

Chapter Seven

1. Raymond Bellour, in "To Analyze, To Segment," *Quarterly Review of Film Studies* 1 (1976): 331, writes, "From beginning to end, the classic film ceaselessly repeats itself because it leads to its resolution. This is the reason why its beginning and its end often reflect each other with ultimate insistence. The film acknowledges itself as a result, by inscribing the systematic condition of its itinerary, by giving us its signature with a fine flourish, presenting the operation which built it piece by piece."

2. Heath, "On Screen, in Frame," p. 261. See Serge Daney and Jean-Pierre Oudart, "Travail, lecture, jouissance," *Cahiers du cinéma*, no. 222 (July 1970), pp. 39–50, for a discussion of the integrities of framing and duration in film. See also Barbara Hernstein Smith, *Poetic Closure: A Study of How Poems End* (Chicago: University of Chicago Press, 1968), for a thorough examination of the problem of closure.

3. Cavell, *World Viewed*, p. 75.

4. Jean-Paul Sartre, *Les mots* (Paris: Gallimard, 1964), p. 102.

5. Colin MacCabe (p. 16) inflects this modality of the image's temporal status with the threat of the "gaze of the other" on the image's integrity. "Desire is only set up by absence, by the possiblity of return to a former state." The loss of the image or even the implication of its loss is "smoothed over and it is in that smoothing that we can locate pleasure—in a plenitude which is fractured but only on condition that it will *be re-set*."

6. Kermode, pp. 58–59.

7. David Thomson, in *America in the Dark*, p. 195, characterizes sentimental fictions in terms of their projections of finality. "We lodge our affections and sympathetic support with a character who is then thwarted by the action of the film. This often centers on death and the retrospective but useless wish to have behaved differently, in a way that might have averted the loss or failure. In mythic terms, the weeping is not just a lamentation for unrequited loves but intolerance of death, aging, the passing of time, and every mistake we make."

8. Kermode, p. 7.

9. Peter Brooks, "Freud's Masterplot," *Yale French Studies*, no. 55/56, pp. 283–84.

Bibliography

Abel, Richard. "Paradigmatic Structures in *Young Mr. Lincoln*." *Wide Angle* 2, no. 4: 20–26.

Affron, Charles. *Star Acting: Gish, Garbo, Davis*. New York: E. P. Dutton, 1977.

Anderegg, Michael. *William Wyler*. Boston: Twayne, 1979.

Bachelard, Gaston. *La poétique de l'espace*. Paris: Presses Universitaires de France, 1958.

Barthes, Roland. "En sortant du cinéma." *Communications*, no. 23 (1975), pp. 104–7.

———. *Image—Music—Text*. Trans. Stephen Heath. New York: Hill & Wang, 1977.

———. *The Pleasure of the Text*. Trans. Richard Miller. New York: Hill & Wang, 1975.

Baudry, Jean-Louis. "Le dispositif: Approaches métapsychologiques de l'impression de réalité." *Communications*, no. 23 (1975), pp. 56–72.

———. "Ideological Effects of the Basic Cinematographic Apparatus." *Film Quarterly* 27 (Winter 1974–75): 39–47.

Bazin, André. *Jean Renoir*. Ed. François Truffaut. Trans. W. W. Halsey II and William H. Simon. New York: Simon & Schuster, 1973.

———. *Qu'est-ce que le cinéma? I. Ontologie et langage*. Paris: Editions du Cerf, 1958.

———. *What Is Cinema?* Ed. and trans. Hugh Gray. Berkeley: University of California Press, 1967.

Bellour, Raymond. "Le blocage symbolique." *Communications*, no. 23 (1975), pp. 235–350.

———. "To Analyze, to Segment." *Quarterly Review of Film Studies* 1 (1976): 331–63.

Benjamin, Walter. "The Work of Art in the Age of Mechanical Reproduction." In *Illuminations*. Ed. Hannah Arendt. New York: Harcourt, Brace, 1968.

Beylie, Claude. *Max Ophuls*. Paris: Editions Seghers, 1963.

Bonitzer, Pascal. *Le regard et la voix: Essais sur le cinéma*. Paris: 10/18, 1976.

Booth, Wayne. *A Rhetoric of Irony*. Chicago: University of Chicago Press, 1974.

Bordwell, David. "Camera Movement, the Coming of Sound, and the Classical Hollywood Style." *Film: Historical-Theoretical Speculations,*

Bibliography

the 1977 Film Studies Annual, part 2. Pleasantville, New York: Red-grave, 1977.

Bosworth, Patricia. *Montgomery Clift: A Biography*. New York: Harcourt Brace Jovanovich, 1978.

Bourget, Jean-Loup. "God Is Dead, or Through a Glass Darkly." *Bright Lights* (Winter 1977–78), pp. 23–26, 34.

Braudy, Leo. *Jean Renoir: The World of His Films*. Garden City: Anchor-Doubleday, 1972.

———. *The World in a Frame: What We See in Films*. Garden City: Anchor-Doubleday, 1977.

Brooks, Peter. "Freud's Masterplot." *Yale French Studies*, no. 55/56, pp. 280–300.

———. *The Melodramatic Imagination: Balzac, Henry James, Melodrama, and Modes of Excess*. New Haven: Yale University Press, 1976.

Browne, Nick. "Narrative Point of View: The Rhetoric of *Au hasard, Balthazar*." *Film Quarterly* 31 (Fall 1977): 19–31.

———. "The Spectator-in-the-Text: The Rhetoric of *Stagecoach*." *Film Quarterly* 29 (Winter 1975–76): 27–37.

Burch, Noël. *Theory of Film Practice*. New York: Praeger, 1973.

Cavell, Stanley. *The World Viewed: Reflections on the Ontology of Film*. Enlarged ed. Cambridge, Massachusetts, and London: Harvard University Press, 1979.

Comolli, Jean-Louis. "Caméra, perspective, profondeur de champ." *Cahiers du cinéma*, nos. 229–32 (May–November 1971), nos. 234–35 (December 1971–February 1972), no. 241 (September–October 1972).

Daney, Serge, and Jean-Pierre Oudart. "Travail, lecture, jouissance." *Cahiers du cinéma*, no. 222 (July 1970), pp. 39–50.

Dayan, Daniel. "The Tutor-Code of Classical Cinema." *Film Quarterly* 28 (Fall 1974): 22–31.

Derrida, Jacques. *Speech and Phenomena: And Other Essays on Husserl's Theory of Signs*. Trans. David B. Allison. Evanston: Northwestern University Press, 1973.

Durgnat, Raymond. *Jean Renoir*. Berkeley: University of California Press, 1974.

Dyer, Richard. "Lana: Four Films of Lana Turner." *Movie* 25 (Winter 1977/78): 30–52.

Editors of *Cahiers du cinéma*. "John Ford's *Young Mr. Lincoln*." In Gerald Mast and Marshall Cohen, eds., *Film Theory and Criticism*, 2d ed. New York: Oxford University Press, 1979, pp. 778–831.

Eikenbaum, Boris. "Problems of Film Stylistics." *Screen* 15 (Autumn 1974): 7–32.

Eisenstein, Sergei. *Film Form: Essays in Film Theory*. Ed. and trans. Jay Leyda. New York: Harcourt, Brace & World, 1949.

Eizykman, Claudine. *La jouissance-cinéma*. Paris: 10/18, 1976.

Elsaesser, Thomas. "Tales of Sound and Fury: Observations on the Family Melodrama." *Monogram* 4 (1972): 2–15.

Fischer, Lucy. "The Image of Woman as Image: The Optical Politics of *Dames*." *Film Quarterly* 30 (Fall 1976): 2–11.

Fish, Stanley. "Interpreting the *Variorum*." *Critical Inquiry* 2 (Spring 1976): 465–85.

———. "Literature in the Reader: Affective Stylistics." In *Self-Consuming*

Artifacts: The Experience of Seventeenth-Century Literature. Berkeley: University of California Press, 1972.

Foucault, Michel. *Les mots et les choses*. Paris: Gallimard, 1966.

Freud, Sigmund. *Beyond the Pleasure Principle*. Trans. and ed. James Strachey. New York: Liveright, 1961.

———. "Instincts and Their Vicissitudes" (1915). "Psychopathic Characters on the Stage" (1905). "Three Essays on the Theory of Sexuality" (1905). *The Standard Edition of the Complete Psychological Works of Sigmund Freud*. Vols. 7 and 14. London: Hogarth Press, 1953, 1957.

Gowing, Lawrence. *Vermeer*. New York: Harper & Row, 1970.

"Guilty Pleasures." *Film Comment,* vols. 14–18 (1978–82).

Halliday, Jon. *Sirk on Sirk*. New York: Viking, 1972.

Handzo, Stephen. "Intimations of Lifelessness: Sirk's Ironic Tear-Jerker." *Bright Lights* (Winter 1977–78), pp. 20–22, 34.

Harpole, Charles. "Ideological and Technological Determinism in Deep-Space Cinema Images." *Film Quarterly* 33 (Spring 1980): 11–21.

Heath, Stephen. "Notes on Suture." *Screen* 18 (Winter 1977/78): 48–76.

———. "On Screen, in Frame: Film and Ideology." *Quarterly Review of Film Studies* 1 (1976): 251–65.

Heilman, Robert. *Tragedy and Melodrama: Versions of Experience*. Seattle: University of Washington Press, 1968.

Holland, Norman N. *The Dynamics of Literary Response*. New York: Oxford University Press, 1968.

Iser, Wolfgang. *The Act of Reading: A Theory of Aesthetic Response*. Baltimore: Johns Hopkins University Press, 1978.

———. *The Implied Reader: Patterns of Communication in Prose Fiction from Bunyan to Beckett*. Baltimore: Johns Hopkins University Press, 1974.

Kerbel, Michael. "*Letter from an Unknown Woman*." *Film Comment* 7 (Summer 1971): 60–61.

Kermode, Frank. *The Sense of an Ending: Studies in the Theory of Fiction*. New York: Oxford University Press, 1967.

Kristeva, Julia. *Semiotike: Recherches pour une sémanalyse*. Paris: Editions du Seuil, 1969.

Kuntzel, Thierry. "A Note upon the Filmic Apparatus." *Quarterly Review of Film Studies* 1 (1976): 266–71.

Lacan, Jacques. *Écrits*. Trans. Alan Sheridan. New York: W. W. Norton, 1977.

———. *The Four Fundamental Concepts of Psycho-Analysis*. Ed. Jacques-Alain Miller. Trans. Alan Sheridan. New York: W. W. Norton, 1978.

———. *The Language of the Self: The Function of Language in Psychoanalysis*. Trans. and ed. Anthony Wilden. Baltimore: Johns Hopkins University Press, 1968.

Lehman, Peter. "An Absence Which Becomes a Legendary Presence: John Ford's Structured Use of Off-Screen Space." *Wide Angle* 2, no. 4: 36–42.

Luhr, William, and Peter Lehman. *Authorship and Narrative in the Cinema: Issues in Contemporary Aesthetics and Criticism*. New York: G. P. Putnam's Sons, 1977.

Bibliography

MacCabe, Colin. "Principles of Realism and Pleasure." *Screen* 17 (Autumn 1976): 7–27.

Mannoni, O. *Clefs pour l'imaginaire ou l'autre scène*. Paris: Editions du Seuil, 1969.

Mast, Gerald. *Film/Cinema/Movie: A Theory of Experience*. New York: Harper & Row, 1977.

Masterworks of the British Cinema. New York: Harper & Row, 1974.

McConnell, Frank. *The Spoken Seen: Film and the Romantic Imagination*. Baltimore: Johns Hopkins University Press, 1975.

Metz, Christian. "The Fiction Film and Its Spectator." Trans. Alfred Guzzetti. *New Literary History* 8 (August 1976): 75–105.

————. "The Imaginary Signifier." Trans. Ben Brewster. *Screen* 16 (Summer 1975): 14–76.

Meunier, Jean-Pierre. *Les structures de l'expérience filmique: L'identification filmique*. Louvain: Librairie Universitaire, 1969.

Miller, Jacques-Alain. "La suture (éléments de la logique du signifiant)." Trans. Jacqueline Rose. *Screen* 18 (Winter 1977/78): 24–34.

Mitry, Jean. *Esthétique et psychologie du cinéma. I. Les structures*. Paris: Editions Universitaires, 1963.

Morin, Edgar. *Le cinéma ou l'homme imaginaire*. Paris: Editions Gonthier, 1958.

Mulvey, Laura. "Notes on Sirk and Melodrama." *Movie* 25 (Winter 1977–78): 53–56.

Münsterberg, Hugo. *The Film: A Psychological Study, the Silent Photoplay in 1916*. 1916; reprinted New York: Dover, 1970.

Ogle, Patrick L. "Technological and Aesthetic Influences upon the Development of Deep Focus Cinematography in the United States." *Screen* 13 (Spring 1972): 45–72.

Ong, Walter J. *The Presence of the Word: Some Prolegomena for Cultural and Religious History*. New Haven: Yale University Press, 1967.

Ophuls, Max. Interview with Jacques Rivette and François Truffaut. *Cahiers du cinéma*, no. 72 (June 1957). In Paul Willemen, ed., *Ophuls*. Trans. Jennifer Batchelor. London: British Film Institute, 1978.

Oudart, Jean-Pierre. "Cinema and Suture." Trans. Kari Hanet. *Screen* 18 (Winter 1977/78): 35–47.

————. "L'effet de réel." *Cahiers du cinéma*, no. 228 (March–April 1971), pp. 19–26.

Pinter, Harold. *A la recherche du temps perdu: The Proust Screenplay*. New York: Grove Press, 1977.

Place, J. A. "*Young Mr. Lincoln*, 1939." *Wide Angle* 2, no. 4: 28–35.

Rosen, Philip. "Difference and Displacement in *Seventh Heaven*." *Screen* 18 (Summer 1977): 89–104.

Rothman, William. "Against 'The System of Suture.'" *Film Quarterly* 29 (Fall 1975): 45–50.

Salt, Barry. "Film Style and Technology in the Forties." *Film Quarterly* 31 (Fall 1977): 46–56.

Sarris, Andrew. *The American Cinema: Directors and Directions, 1929–1968*. New York: E. P. Dutton, 1968.

Sartre, Jean-Paul. *Les mots*. Paris: Gallimard, 1964.

Scholes, Robert. "Narration and Narrativity in Film." *Quarterly Review of Film Studies* 1 (1976): 283–96.

Scholes, Robert, and Robert Kellogg. *The Nature of Narrative*. London and New York: Oxford University Press, 1966.

Schwartz, Nancy. "Lubitsch's Widow: The Meaning of a Waltz." *Film Comment* 11 (March–April 1975): 13–17.

Sesonske, Alexander. *Jean Renoir: The French Films, 1924–1939*. Cambridge: Harvard University Press, 1980.

Smith, Barbara Hernstein. *Poetic Closure: A Study of How Poems End*. Chicago: University of Chicago Press, 1968.

Sontag, Susan. *Against Interpretation and Other Essays*. New York: Farrar, Straus & Giroux, 1966.

———. *On Photography*. New York: Farrar, Straus & Giroux, 1977.

———. *Styles of Radical Will*. New York: Farrar, Straus & Giroux, 1976.

Suleiman, Susan R., and Inge Crosman, eds. *The Reader in the Text: Essays on Audience and Interpretation*. Princeton: Princeton University Press, 1980.

Thomson, David. *America in the Dark: Hollywood and the Gift of Unreality*. New York: William Morrow, 1977.

Truffaut, François. *Hitchcock*. New York: Simon & Schuster, 1967.

Willemen, Paul. "Distanciation and Douglas Sirk." *Screen* 12 (Summer 1971): 63–67.

———. "The Ophuls Text: A Thesis." In Willemen, ed., *Ophuls*. London: British Film Institute, 1978.

———. "Towards an Analysis of the Sirkian System." *Screen* 13 (Winter 1972/73): 128–32.

Williams, Linda. "The Film Body: An Implantation of Perversions." *Ciné-Tracts*, no. 12, pp. 19–35.

Wimsatt, W. K., Jr. *The Verbal Icon: Studies in the Meaning of Poetry*. Lexington: University Press of Kentucky, 1954.

Wolfenstein, Martha, and Nathan Leites. *Movies: A Psychological Study*. Glencoe, Illinois: Free Press, 1950.

Index of Illustrations

Index of Names and Titles